Industrial Psychology

AF517384

INDUSTRIAL PSYCHOLOGY

By

Dr. Rajan Misra

M.A.(A.C.) Sociology, N.E.T., M.B.A., Ph.D.,

Director, Dr. Bhim Rao Ambedkar Polytechnic,

Agra, Uttar Pradesh

UNIVERSITY SCIENCE PRESS

(An Imprint of Laxmi Publications Pvt. Ltd.)

BANGALORE • CHENNAI • COCHIN • GUWAHATI • HYDERABAD

JALANDHAR • KOLKATA • LUCKNOW • MUMBAI • PATNA

RANCHI • NEW DELHI

Published by :

UNIVERSITY SCIENCE PRESS

(*An Imprint of Laxmi Publications Pvt. Ltd.*)
113, Golden House, Daryaganj,
New Delhi-110002

Phone : 011-43 53 25 00
Fax : 011-43 53 25 28

www.laxmipublications.com
info@laxmipublications.com

Copyright © 2011 by Laxmi Publications Pvt. Ltd. All rights reserved. No part of this publication may be reproduced, stored in a retrieval system, or transmitted in any form or by any means, electronic, mechanical, photocopying, recording or otherwise without the prior written permission of the publisher.

First Edition: 2011

OFFICES

✆ **Bangalore**	080-26 75 69 30	✆ **Chennai**	044-24 34 47 26
✆ **Cochin**	0484-237 70 04, 405 13 03	✆ **Guwahati**	0361-251 36 69, 251 38 81
✆ **Hyderabad**	040-24 65 23 33	✆ **Jalandhar**	0181-222 12 72
✆ **Kolkata**	033-22 27 43 84	✆ **Lucknow**	0522-220 99 16
✆ **Mumbai**	022-24 91 54 15, 24 92 78 69	✆ **Patna**	0612-230 00 97
✆ **Ranchi**	0651-221 47 64		

UIP–9573–135–INDUSTRIAL PSYCHOLOGY–MIS **C. 2546 /010/11**

Typeset at : Monu Printographics, Delhi

Dedicated to my

Father (Prof.) Late Shri. S.K. Misra

and my

Mother Late Smt. Savitri Misra

Contents

Unit–I

Unit–II

Preface

This book covers U.P. Technical University, Lucknow syllabi in the papers entitled Psychology in Industry or Industrial Psychology. As the book includes all the topics presented and does not include any out of the course, the students may dependent on this work for securing good marks. Each topic has been divided into sub-topics, each of which is included in one simple question. Attempt has been made to pretent the subject matter, drawn form authentic works, under as many points and sub-points as possible. Language used is lucid, simple and in small sentences so that the students may not find any difficulty in grasping the subject matter. Examples has been drawn from Indian life as far as possible for that the students may follow the applications of Industrial Psychology in the world around him.

Thus, in nut shell the author has listed to pretent a book by mastering which, one may be fully prepared answer any question under the preview of the subject.

I acknowledge the debt I owe to my friends, family members and colleagues who have helped me in various ways in the pursuit of human values. I give my special thanks to Dr. Dev Swaroop, Jt. Secretary, U.G.C., New Delhi for the guidance and support provided by him for carrying out this work of writing. Lastly, I dedicate my father, (Prof) Late Shri S.K. Misra and my mother Late Smt. Savitri Misra work for all the inspiration and courage I gathered while writing this book.

—Author

Unit I

Chapter 1 INDUSTRIAL PSYCHOLOGY AND GENERAL PSYCHOLOGY

Psychology is a positive science of behaviour, the term behaviour being interpreted most liberally, for in comprehends not only both objective and subjective forms of human behaviour, but also the behaviour of the higher animals. Human behaviour includes man's behaviour under all kinds of conditions and circumstances, normal, abnormal, social, industrial, legal, in childhood, in adolescence, in old age. Psychology studies behaviour in all these conditions, but with reference to the environment and situations.

WHAT IS GENERAL PSYCHOLOGY?

Psychology is a positive science in which facts are studied. It tries to find out causal relations in behaviour by using the methology of science. As a science, psychology finds out the principles of human behaviour and once it has established some causal relations, it makes predictions about behaviour. General psychology is the most extensive branch of psychology. Perhaps it is better called an aspect rather than a branch for it involves the study of all the general principles used in all its other branches. It studies all processes of human behaviour such as learning, memory sensation, perception, emotion, feeling and personality. It also makes a study of the origins, the well springs of human behaviour such as motivation, nervous system, the various levels of consciousness, etc. It even outlines the methodology of psychology. It differs from Industrial psychology because its explanations are more theoretical while those of Industrial psychology are more concerned with the practical application of psychological principles.

Distinction from General Psychology

From the above elucidation of General psychology it is amply clear that Industrial psychology differs from General psychology. The major differences are the followings :

1. *Difference of Nature*: As has been pointed out, Industrial psychology is a branch of practical psychology while, on the other hand, General psychology is more theoretical.
2. *Difference of Scope*: The scope of Industrial psychology is more limited and in fact different. General psychology studies, in general, human behaviour under all kinds of situations. Industrial psychology, on the other hand, studies human behaviour only in industrial and business situations.

3. *Different Points of View*: The point of view of General psychology is more theoretical but that of Industrial psychology is chiefly practical.

Relation with General Psychology

Despite the above mentioned differences between the two, there is an intimate relationship between general and industrial psychology. In Industrial psychology the psychologist makes use of those principles in an industrial situation which he has learnt from General psychology. For example, the conclusions of General psychology about such psychological processes as learning, perception, attention, memory and association, etc., are utilized under processes. The psychology of interest and attention is much used in the field of advertisement. In this manner, the industrial psychologist must have extensive knowledge of General psychology, although the opposite is not true. The general psychologist does not need knowledge of Industrial psychology.

NATURE OF INDUSTRIAL PSYCHOLOGY

It is easier to understand the nature and scope of Industrial psychology by analyzing its definition. Industrial psychology is a science, hence its nature is scientific. It employs scientific techniques to study the social aspect of human behaviour. It is a science in the same way in which general psychology and sociology are sciences. Along with the study of individual behaviour, Industrial psychology also makes a study of group dynamics. The aim of this study also is to find facts and establish causal relations between them, to derive universal laws based on these causal relations and then to apply these laws to concerned situations and solve problems of a social nature.

What is a Science?

In order to test the validity of the statement that Industrial psychology is a science, it is necessary to find out what a science is. Science is the study of a limited field. If a study is to be called scientific, then its scope must be limited and also systematic. Yet a study cannot be called science only if its subject matter possesses both these traits, for the study must also make use of the scientific method. In fact science differs from the arts and philosophy on account of its method, and its peculiar nature depends more upon the method than upon the subject matter.

Characteristics of the Scientific Method

It is, therefore, necessary to understand the scientific method if we are to understand the nature of science. In the scientific method the subject patience, courage, hard work, creative imagination and objectivity. In the absence of this scientific attitude or scientific attitude or scientific spirit no person can derive the full benefit of using the scientific method. Before starting his work, a person conducting research should make a detailed analysis of the problem which he wants to study, because if the analysis of the problem which he wants to study, because if the analysis is detailed enough the study itself becomes more facile. The scientific method is constituted by the following steps:

1. *Observation*: The first step in the scientific method is a careful and detailed observation of the subject matter, often, by the use of apparatus. The apparatus itself must be accurate and dependable.
2. *Recording*: The second step in the scientific method is the careful and systematic recording of all the observed facts. Objectivity is a necessary element in recording.
3. *Classification*: Now the recorded information has to be classified and organised. This is an important and serious step. In Karl Pearson's words: "*The classification of facts, the recognition of their sequence and relative significance is the function of science.*" Classification must be done in such a way that one can see some pattern and relationship between the scattered facts which have been observed. For this it is essential that the information is arranged on a logical and coherent basis.
4. *Generalisation*: The next important step in the scientific method is the derivation of general laws on the basis of patterns observed in the organized matter. This general law, which a arrived at, is called a scientific law.
5. *Verification*: Verification is the fifth stage because the scientific method does not conclude with the derivation of a universal law. It is necessary to test and verify the truth of this law. Validity is an essential condition of a scientific law, for without validity, the law cannot be called scientific.

Essential Elements of Science

We have now seen the elements that are necessary for any study to be classed as a science. Simply stated, a study must possess the following characteristics to be called scientific:

1. *Scientific Method*: As has been pointed out above, a study is called scientific not because the subject matter is of a particular kind but because it makes use of the scientific method.
2. *Factual*: Science is the study of facts, it searches for facts. Its subject matter is constituted by facts, not ideals.
3. *Universal*: Scientific laws have a validity which can be put to test at any time. Whenever they are tested, they are proved correct.
4. *Veridical*: Scientific laws have a validity which can be put to test at any time. Whenever they are tested, they are proved correct.
5. *Discovery of Cause-effect Relationship*: Science aims at the discovery of cause and effect relations between the various facts of the subject. Having found the cause-effect relationship, it pronounces certain universal and valid laws.
6. *Prediction*: Science can make predictions about the future on the strength of the universal laws enunciated by it, because these laws are based on cause and effect relationships between facts-relationships which always hold true. Science itself is based on faith in causality. The scientist believes that what will happen in the future can be determined on the basis of what is, because the law of causality is incontrovertible and universal.

Industrial Psychology is Scientific

We will find all the above elements in Industrial psychology, and hence we can conclude that Industrial psychology has a claim to be considered scientific.

1. *Industrial Psychology Uses the Scientific Method*: All the methods of Industrial psychology are scientific. It makes the greatest possible use of the experimental method. In the experimental method the subject of study is placed in predetermined conditions and then studied. After careful observation the industrial psychologist record all the facts observed, follows this up by a logical classification and the derivation of universal laws by generalization. It is these universal laws which make up the principles of Industrial psychology. In this way, it is obvious that Industrial psychology makes use of the scientific method. Although the other methods employed by Industrial psychology are not as scientific as the experimental method, every effort has been made to invest them with a factual and scientific character, and much success has been achieved in this direction. Industrial psychologists may have many different opinions about the value and the utility of a particular method, but all of them agree that the method of study must be scientific.
2. *Industrial Psychology is Factual*: Industrial psychology makes a factual study of behaviour, its conclusions are objective and impartial. Its conclusions about behaviour are not normative. It describes behaviour and tries to find out laws which govern it. Hence it is concerned with facts, not values.
3. *The Laws of Industrial Psychology are Universal*: The laws enunciated by Industrial psychology produce the same results everywhere, under identical conditions. These rules prove to be the same at all times and places, irrespective of the differences in character of the persons involved. For example, the law that in industrial organizations the conditions of work and wages will influence the quality and quantity of production, will prove to be true wherever it is tested.
4. *The Principles of Industrial Psychology are Valid*: Upon verification and even re-verification the principles of Industrial psychology prove to be valid. Their validity can be tested by anyone and at any time. For example, the fact that there is always some dissatisfaction, repression or maladjustment at the root of all labour tension, can be tested anywhere.
5. *Industrial Psychology Analyses Cause-effect Relationships*: Industrial psychology discovers the laws of behaviour and explains the causal relations existing between them. In Industries, the psychologist tries to discover the causal relations underlying human relationships, advertisement and development, etc. He can thus discover very useful facts and laws. In this way Industrial psychology aims at finding out not only the 'what' of behaviour but also its 'how'.
6. *Industrial Psychology can Make Predictions*: Because Industrial psychology can find out the causal relations that exist in human behaviour, it can make predictions about it, and these predictions also turn out to be true. For this reason, in all modern industrial nations, the predictions made by industrial psychologists are taken into account by the industrialists in solving industrial problems and disputes. These predictions have proved of much value.

It is clear from the above explanation that Industrial psychology is an exact science, but one must no conclude from it that it is as exact as the physical sciences. In fact, it is a mistake to expect the same degree of precision and exactness from every science, because in every science the precision depends upon the nature of its subject matter. Obviously, a science which studies human behaviour in industrial conditions cannot be as exact as a science which studies physical things, because human behaviour is a complex, dynamic and changeable phenomenon. Hence, in calling Industrial psychology an exact science it is necessary to keep in mind its limitations, although these limitations cannot be fixed or determined with precision. And it is hoped that the precision of Industrial psychology will improve with the development of more modern techniques of study.

What is Industrial Psychology?

Industrial psychology, as the name indicates, is that branch of psychology which studies human behaviour under industrial circumstances. Psychology is a normative science of behaviour which can be observed in the social, economic, educational and other spheres. In the modern period the different branches of psychology have developed during the study of human behaviour in these various fields. Educational psychology has been developed to study human behaviour in the field of education while social psychology is concerned with the study of human behaviour in a social environment. This is an age of industrial progress, in which each progressive nation is expanding the scope of its industries. But industries cannot be made to function without human beings, because individuals are required in the capacity of managers, administrators, programmers, etc. And, wherever there are human beings, their behaviour will be influenced by their relationships. If, in the industrial field, human relations deteriorate, then the result is strikes and lockouts which have a widespread impact upon its industrial development and progress, this particular field of human behaviour becomes extremely important. It is the aim of Industrial Psychology to study the principles governing behaviour in the industrial field and to undertake research.

A Branch of Practical Psychology

Psychology is not merely a theoretical science for it not only enunciates general laws concerning human behaviour but also tries to improve human life by applying these principles. Like any other science, therefore, psychology also has two aspects the theoretical and the practical. Industrial psychology is naturally a branch of practical psychology because it is fundamentally a study evolved for the improvement of human relations in the industrial sphere. The knowledge provided by it is used to solve the problems of people who work in industry, as well as to solve those non-human problems which emerge from time to time in industries. Nowadays psychologists are appointed to study the problems which arise in the field of Industrial psychology. A glance at the history of Industrial psychology will show us that universities have been responsible for the research concerned with it, but even more important research has been carried out in big industries under actual conditions. It is, therefore, more appropriate to consider Industrial Psychology as a branch of practical psychology. This aspect of the subject can be even better understood by studying the following definitions.

DEFINITIONS OF INDUSTRIAL PSYCHOLOGY

Some of the main definitions of industrial psychology are the following:

1. **Blum.** According to Blum, the psychologist, 'Industrial Psychology is simply the application or extension of psychological facts and principles to the problems concerning human relations in business and industry.' Blum shows in this definition that psychological facts and principles are used in human relations in the field of business and industry and this constitutes Industrial Psychology. By using them the industrial psychologist tries to solve the problems that arise in the industrial sphere. As Blum says further, 'Industrial psychology provides practical solutions to the problems that arise in the industrial society and its economic organization.
2. **Harrell.** Harrell has defined the subject in his book entitled *Industrial Psychology* in the following words, '*Industrial psychology is the study of people at work in industry and business.*' In his opinion, then the industrial psychologist makes a study of the behaviour of people working under conditions of business and industry. Harrell has further clarified that the subject matter of the industrial psychologist is always the human being, because it is the human being who is the object of a psychological study. Even in a business or industrial environment this continues to be true. Just as social psychology studies the human being under social circumstances, Industrial Psychology studies the individual in a business environment. As Harrell himself has put it, 'Industrial Psychology is a complicated study of a number of things, but it is always primarily the study of people as individuals or in groups-in the work situation.' It need hardly be explained that the industrial psychologist focuses his attention upon human beings.
3. **Smith.** Smith has defined industrial psychology thus, 'For practical purposes Industrial Psychology may be defined as the study of conduct of those who exchange the work of their hands and brains for the means to live.' Defined in this way, industrial psychology becomes concerned with the study of all people in an industry, whether they work by hand or by brain. Here it has been called the study of conduct, but it would be better to substitute the word 'behaviour' for this term because conduct is more properly the concern of ethics, not of psychology.

SCOPE OF INDUSTRIAL PSYCHOLOGY

Pointing out the scope of Industrial psychology Harrell has laid stress on the following things:

1. Industrial psychology is concerned with the physical aspect of the environment of work, for example, the effect of light and temperature on work and safety.
2. It is primarily a study of the principles and behaviour of human relationships.
3. It is a study of the causes that lead to indifference and disinterest and the motives and attitudes that influence zeal and high morale.
4. It is a study of the methods by which neurotic people can be brought back to level of normal mental health.

5. It is a study of the factors that create cooperation between labourers and the management, a study of the relations between the supervisor and his sub-ordinates and of industrial conflicts.

It is clear from the above exposition that industrial psychology studies, apart from the physical environment, the principles of human relationships, the factors which lead to and maintain mental health, and bases of high morale. Briefly, then, the scope of industrial psychology is the following :

1. **Economic, Social and Psychological Aspects of Industry.** Industrial psychology is concerned with human behaviour in the entire industrial environment. Consequently, it studies the economic, social and psychological aspects of human behaviour. In the modern age most economic factors have workers living in an industrial environment also influence the psychology of the worker. Industrial psychology studies this also.
2. **Study of the Physical Aspect of Works Environment.** In an industry the worker is greatly influenced by the conditions under which he works. If the conditions are to his liking the worker feels satisfied and remains healthy while on the other hand if the conditions are not good the number of accidents goes up and workers become dissatisfied. Working conditions include a number of factors such as clean air and water, arrangement for necessary rest, less noise, clean atmosphere, sufficient light, good relations between the worker and the management. In all these, guidance by the psychologist can prove of immense value. For example, it is better to consult the psychologist about the arrangement for lighting, about the quantity or intensity of the light and the angle from which it should come. Even the colour of the walls, floors and ceilings of the factory psychologically influence the worker. It has been seen in experiments that if the colour scheme of the environment is good there are fewer accidents and the atmosphere remains good. And it is for the psychologist to say what should be the colour of the machines, roofs, floors and ceilings. It can thus be said that industrial psychology studies the physical working conditions in industrial environment.
3. **Principles of Human Relationships.** Irrespective of the automation introduced in any industry, the human element cannot be eliminated. Even the biggest and the most efficient machine needs an engineer to run it, and because the engineer is a human being the importance of the psychological element of the man will depend very. In the last century most industrialists behaved like autocrats and considered the workers as most industrialists behaved like autocrats and considered the workers as nothing more than tools. But in that period the level of efficiency was never very high. It has been seen that an industrialist can achieve a higher rate of production if he behaves sympathetically with his employees. In the present age, the industrialist can no longer do as he will, because of the existence of labour unions. An industrialist who cannot maintain good and cordial relations with his worker does not succeed for long. Being the science of behaviour, Industrial psychology tries to discover principles for improving human relationships in an industrial environment. At the root of most of the lockouts and strikes, two common forms of expressing discontent seen so frequently in most industries today, are only distorted and injured human relationships. Industrial psychology helps to solve these problems.

4. **Study of Attitudes and Motives.** As in any other circumstance, human behaviour in the industrial environment is influenced and formed by attitudes and motives. Behaviour changes with the change in stimuli. Hence it is necessary to study the rules pertaining to correct attitudes and motives. Industrial psychology pursues this kind of study. One example of study of this kind is the study conducted by the Hawthorne Works Western Electric Company into the effect of the attitudes of workers upon production. This study is known as the Hawthorne Studies.
5. **Study of Principles of Mental Health.** Today, all intelligent people realize the importance of maintaining the proper health of workers. The worker's mental health is profoundly influenced by the conditions under which he works and by the attitude of other people towards him. Industrial psychology studies the factors influencing the mental health of industrial workers and tries to discover principles for maintaining their mental health. Industrial psychology also gives suggestions for improving the mental health of those who are suffering from mental disease or are otherwise unbalanced.
6. **Study of Human Relations.** Industrial psychology is the study of human behaviour in an industrial context. As has been pointed out earlier, the physical conditions of work have a direct and strong influence upon human behaviour. The manner in which the supervisor or the manager behaves towards the worker has a direct influence upon the efficiency, attitude and motives of the worker. Some employees try to spread maladjustment among industrial workers for purely personal reasons. Even this is a problem of human relations. Being a branch of psychology Industrial psychology is particularly concerned with the observation and study of human relations about which it reaches conclusions through experiment and other study. On the basis of these conclusions it tries to discover general principles which can help in improving social relations between the workers and the management.

Briefly, all industrial situations are within the scope of industrial psychology because every one of them influences human behaviour. The scope of industrial psychology expands with expansion in the sphere of industrial activity.

PROBLEMS OF INDUSTRIAL PSYCHOLOGY

In his book Industrial psychology and its Social Foundations the psychologist Blum has stated, *Industrial Psychology offers a dynamic solution to the perplexing problems which confront an industrial society and economic system.* What are these problems concerned with industry or profession? These are the problems psychological in nature that arise in any sphere of industry. Briefly, the problems of Industrial psychology are as follows :

1. **Selection of the Right Man for the Right Job.** If success is to be achieved in any industry, it is essential that the right man should be found and appointed to the right job. This involves first an accurate work study and also the selection of the most qualified individual from among the applicants to suit that particular job. This is basically a problem for the psychologist because the selection involves many kinds of psychological tests to discover the various abilities of the individuals. It also happens sometimes that an individual

working on a particular post cannot work efficiently for personal reasons, even though he is otherwise perfectly qualified to hold that post. In such a situation the industrial psychologist is faced with the problem of giving suggestions which will once again render the individual fit for work.

2. **Training of Workers.** Although different individuals have varying degree of ability to perform different kinds of functions, training can be useful improving these abilities to such an extent that the individual becomes capable of doing work which he could not have done without training. The kind and length of training required to train a particular individual to bring him up to a certain level of efficiency can be determined by the psychologist. Hence another problem for the industrial psychologist is the training of workers.
3. **Morale in Industry.** Despite the best possible working conditions in an industry the highest efficiency cannot be achieved unless the workers also have a high morale. Morale can be seen on the one hand in the enthusiasm and zeal with which work is tackled and on the other hand in the mutual cooperation extended to others in group activities. How a proper morale can be maintained in industry and what steps are necessary to create it is a problem for psychology, and it is the industrial psychologist who solves it.
4. **Human Relations in Industry.** The problem of human relations in industry has assumed greater importance an complexity with the formation of trade unions, which have channeled the power of the workers into a single direction. Now, no industry can run successfully and smoothly for any length of time in the absence of good relations between the management and the workers' union. If the relations deteriorate, the level of production falls, accidents increase, and lockouts and strikes are the result. This problem of human relations is primarily of concern of social psychology and the person best equipped to solve it is the industrial psychologist.
5. **Fatigue and Boredom.** In industry, as in any other sphere of human activity, individual become tired and bored after a long spell of mechanical work. Their psychological fatigue increases with this. Fatigue is both psychological and psychological. Scientifically viewed, the work and the instruments used in an industry should be so designed and planned as to result in the least possible amount of fatigue and the highest possible quantity of work. Specialists of engineering psychology have designed various kinds of machines and tools with this objective in view. They have also given many suggestions about the improvement of methods of work. Industrial psychologists also have planned many experiments on mental fatigue and boredom, and given many valuable suggestions on the basis of their results. It has been observed, for example, that if there is arrangement for music and light entertainment in certain kinds of mechanical work, the extent of fatigue and boredom is greatly reduced.
6. **Industrial Accidents.** If we want a machine to function without any accident, two things are necessary. In the first place the machine itself should be good working order. In the second place, the worker manipulating it should be using it correctly, and his mental condition must be normal. For the first factor engineering psychologists have given useful suggestions

for keeping the machines functioning properly and without accidents. Regarding the second factor they have given some suggestions for the development of safety habits, proper maintenance and the maintenance of normal health. Hence, one important problem before industrial psychology is the prevention of accidents.

7. **Responses Towards Physical Environment.** It has already been pointed out that the physical conditions existing in an industry, conditions such as the quantity, quality and direction of light, arrangement for fresh and clean air, proper ventilation, hygiene, level of noise, the amount of humidity in the air, etc., have an important influence upon the efficiency of the worker. In order to find out the kind of conditions that should exist in a particular industry, it is necessary to find out the workers' response to their environment. Clearly, it is the industrial psychologist who can find out and determine the quantity and quality of these physical conditions which are desirable.

8. **Problems of Production.** Maximum production in any industry can only be achieved under certain circumstances. Even if the machines are the best, it is essential that the workers handling them must also be capable. How can this ability be tested? In every factory many machines are installed? How can one find the particular person best suited to operate each particular machine? And out of the many people who apply for a job in a factory how can one discover the few who may prove to be really capable? In order to achieve maximum production it is necessary that machines should be so designed as to induce the minimum fatigue and the lighting so arranged as to give the least possible strain to the workers. Besides, most people soon become bored with their work. How can their enthusiasm be reawakened ? How should the factory work be designed so as to reduce the number of accidents? Psychology is needed to solve all these problems which beset every industry.

9. **Problems of Selling.** The work of an industry does not end with the production of things, but carried on till the produced goods are sold. If one did not get success in selling the final produce, its quality and quantity matter less than nothing. And in order to sell things, it is necessary that people should be acquainted with the product, its qualities and should develop the need to buy them. Advertisement serves this purpose and successful advertisement is based on appeal. Hence, the value of psychology in the field of advertisement can hardly be disputed.

10. **Prevention and Solution of Industrial Conflicts.** No industry is completely free from quarrels and conflicts of a minor or major kind. At times these conflicts get out of hand and lead to strikes by the workers or lockouts by the management. There are extreme cases in which such conflicts lead to widespread arson, murder and willful destruction of public and private property. Although some economic demands or political factors may be at the root of such industrial conflicts, the most important factor influencing the actions of workers and management alike is the psychological element. That is why sometimes even great issues are overlooked so that no conflict occurs while relatively insignificant incidents like the impolite words of a manager to a worker may lead to strikes and violent conflicts. It is

the psychological factor which results in strikes and conflicts becoming extremely violent. If, then, such conflicts are to be resolved, the mere satisfaction of economic demands is not enough. It is necessary also to remove those factors which, from the psychological standpoint, are responsible for the occurrence of such conflicts. If these psychological factors are kept in view from the beginning, it is possible to reduce the number of conflicts. And it is the task of Industrial psychology to study these factors.

11. **Problems of Personal Conduct.** While the majority of workers are inspired to revolt and conflict because of some defect in the environment, there are a few workers in whom the root cause of misconduct and conflict is some defect of personality and character. In such cases, it is necessary to consult the industrial psychologist who can trace the cause of the individual's maladjustment and offer solution.

The importance and value of the industrial psychologist's advice in big industrial complexes is evident from the above exposition of his role in solving various problems of industry. It is for this reason that in all progressive countries industrial psychologists are employed in all large industries.

OBJECTIVES OF INDUSTRIAL PSYCHOLOGY

"The aim of industrial psychology," according to Myers, *is not primarily to obtain greater output but to give the worker greater ease at his work. Ease does not mean mere physical ease but also mental ease*. As a branch of applied psychology, industrial psychology has the following objectives :

1. **Personnel Selection.** Industrial psychology tries to find out how a suitable individual can be selected to perform a particular task. If this can be done, then the work gets the correct worker while the worker himself gets the work he can do best.
2. **Care of Worker's Health.** If the worker does not have good mental and physical health, the work of the industry cannot progress smoothly. His mental and physical health is profoundly influenced by the conditions under which he is required to work and by his relations with the management. The objective of industrial psychology is to discover the ideal conditions in which the best mental and physical health of the worker can be maintained.
3. **Protection of Worker's Economic Interests.** Mental health cannot be maintained unless a person's economic interests are secure. Besides, the worker cannot be encouraged to give of his best if he is uncertain about his economic condition. Hence industrial psychology evaluates the efficiency of the worker and determines an adequate salary or suggests scientific principles on the basis of which an adequate salary can be determined.
4. **Search of Proper Methods of Work.** One important reason of accidents and mishaps in factories is the improper methods of work. Improper working also promotes fatigue and boredom. Hence, another objective of industrial psychology is to find out the proper methods of work so that accidents are prevented and fatigue and boredom reduced to the minimum.
5. **Removing Maladjustment.** Another important factor which causes industrial conflicts is the lack of adjustment between the worker and his circumstances and the conditions in

which he works. This maladjustment is primarily psychological in nature. It is the task of the industrial psychologist to locate the cause of maladjustment and to suggest means of rectifying it. This is another objective of industrial psychology.

6. **Reform of Working Conditions.** It is the task of the industrial psychologist to find out the ideal conditions in which the highest efficiency can be attained and the worker maintained at the peak of mental and physical health. The most important working conditions are arrangement for adequate and proper lighting, proper ventilation, absence of noise, provision for periodical rest, normal conveniences for the male and female employees, etc.
7. **Reform in Machines.** The worker and the machine are equally responsible for the number of accidents and amount of fatigue induced in the worker. Prevention of accidents and reduction in fatigue can be achieved by the proper designing of machines. Industrial psychologists give useful suggestions for the improvement of machines and tools.
8. **Reform in Human Relationships.** In order to maintain a proper atmosphere and a high degree of morale among the workers in an industry it is necessary to have proper and cordial human relations between the workers and the management. One objective of the industrial psychologist is to sugest means of improving human relations.
9. **Humanistic Approach in Industry.** Psychological studies have established that human relations in industry cannot be good unless a humanistic approach is adopted. Hence the relations existing between the management and the various levels of workers should be improved and the barriers between them removed. Industrial psychologists' help in spreading the humanistic approach in industry.

VALUE OF INDUSTRIAL PSYCHOLOGY

Progress in the field of industry depends not only on advances in technology but also upon the cordiality and pleasantness of human relations. In the field of industry these human relations are also the industrial relations, and are fundamentally psychological in nature. They depend upon the interests, motives, sentiments and passions of individuals. If their nature is to be understood and they are to be made more profitable, it is necessary to undertake a study of interests, motives, sentiments an passions, which is the task of psychology. For this reason, psychological study in the sphere of industry is of great value. The following facts can be pointed out about the contribution of industrial psychology to industry :

1. **Solution of Labour Problems.** Conflicts between management and workers is almost a normal feature of every industry and can be caused by almost any factor. Often they become so violent that they result in severe losses in terms of money and lives to both the management and the workers. At the root of all such conflicts are some psychological tensions. It is the task of psychology to study these conflicts and for that reason psychology can help in the solution of these problems. Most of the means adopted today to improve the relations between the management and the worker are in fact evolved from psychological observation and testing under actual industrial conditions over a long period. They cannot

be changed by the wish of any conditions over a long period. They cannot be changed by the wish of any one individual. The truth of the matter is that a conflict can be resolved only if the various factors inherent in it are separated and analyzed. Even in the sphere of industrial conflicts, only the psychologist can do this. One major cause of conflict, for example, is the individual differences between individuals which are studied by psychology. Just as a doctor is consulted in the case of bodily disease and the sociologist consulted about social problems, the industrial psychologist should be considered a specialist on psychological problems in industry and his help should be sought.

2. **Prevention of Accidents.** Psychology has provided valuable suggestions not only in the solution of conflicts but also in the prevention of accidents. Psychologists have discovered the kinds of machines that should be designed, the manner in which they should be operated and the plan according to which they should be arranged in a factory. The purpose of this study is to find means of preventing accidents. The psychologist finds out how much accident-prone the workers are and suggests methods of getting rid of this propensity.
3. **Study of Aptitude.** Irrespective of the quality and nature of the physical conditions prevailing in a factory, it depends upon the worker's aptitude to make the best use of them. If the worker has favourable attitude towards the work it will be done but if his aptitude is not suitable then even the best conditions cannot persuade the worker to work. The study and measurement of aptitude is the subject of psychology and it is the psychologist who can help the industrialist here.
4. **Maintaining Morale.** In order to maintain a certain level of production and to improve the quality of production, it is necessary in every industry and profession to maintain a high level of morale among the workers. Morale is influenced by a large number of psychological factors such as affection and freedom, the desire to make sacrifices, availability of proper suggestions for maintaining morale.
5. **Creating Proper Leadership.** The study of leadership is the responsibility of social psychology. In the field of industry the supervisor must not only be an official but also a capable leader because otherwise he cannot guide the workers properly and encourage them to work hard. Social psychology can help in the field of industry by pointing out the qualities that are necessary for leader shop and by explaining how such qualities can be developed. It can also tell the industrialist about the person who has such qualities or who is capable of developing them.
6. **Measurement of Individual Differences.** Success in industry or a profession can be achieved only if the most capable workers are assigned jobs which they are best capable of performing. If this can be done, the workers perform their functions with greater interest and can thus increase production and improve its quality. And individual differences can only be discovered by a wide variety of psychological tests. Hence, the assistance of the psychologist can prove of great value in this sphere.
7. **Study Efficiency.** In an industry all the workers do not have the same degree of efficiency. Nor is this required, because there are many different kinds of functions to be performed,

for which varying levels of efficiency are needed. The psychologist finds out which person has the requisite efficiency to perform a particular job. In addition to this the psychologist can also give suggestions for improving efficiency by removing those obstacles which hinder efficient working.

8. **Use of Psychological Tests.** In the present day psychological tests are being extensively employed to select the most qualified individuals for particular jobs in industry. The chief tests are those of intelligence, interest, aptitude and personality. Sometimes several of these tests are included in a single test battery. Some of these tests are used on individuals while others are used to study the group qualities of workers. All of these tests have their own limitations but even then they are successfully used in the recruitment of employees in industry.

9. **Motion and Time Studies.** Different people take varying amounts of time to complete a specific job because they work at different speeds. Today time and motion studies are conducted to find out the efficiency of individuals and even of machines. These studies have also been used to find out means by which a specify work can be done better in a shorter time. Labour and time are saved by analyzing motion studies so that the essential movements can be isolated and concentrated upon. Time studies help in economizing upon the time spent in a particular operation. In modern factories the machines, the specific places at which particular workers sit and the positions in which they sit are so arranged as to save time and improve efficiency. All this is done to eliminate all unnecessary movement and duplication of work.

10. **Aid in Industrial Training.** It is now accepted that the efficiency of a worker can be appreciable improved by the proper kind of training and that the expense involved in training is paid off double fold. Training people can avoid accidents while the quality and quantity of their production is far higher than that of untrained people. Hence, different kinds of training programmes for different jobs are now called for. At the same time training programmes for different jobs are now called for. At the same time training programmes for workers at all levels are now organized regularly. The industrialist stands to gain by all such training imparted to his employees. Such training programmes can be devised only by the psychologist, who can point out the basis of such training and the methods employed in it.

11. **Suggestions concerning Motives.** An employee must be motivated if he is to progress in his job, this motivation can be supplied through increase in wages, promotion, praise or in many other ways. In the absence of the workers' output both suffer. The special study of motivation is the task of psychology. Only a psychologist can point out how a worker can be motivated to improve the quality and quantity of this product, how the worker's motives can be prevented from leading them to strike, how motivation can be improved even without constituting a permanent motive. All these suggestions tremendously help in the working of an industry.

12. **Studies of Fatigue and Monotony.** The most important obstacle in the way of increasing production is fatigue and monotony. Psychologists have conducted extensive studies into the ways and means of eliminating them. These suggestions can be of great help in removing fatigue and monotony from industrial work.
13. **Vocational Guidance.** Vocational guidance involves the finding out of an individual's capabilities through psychological tests and suggesting the profession for which the individual is best suited. It is the suggestion given by a psychologist, which, if acted upon by the worker, will help him to exploit his own talent to the greatest extent. In most of these progressive nations an individual is given vocational guidance about the various professions he can enter profitably, even before he has completed his education. The chief benefit of this method is that the individual can then pursue a course of studies which will train him for the right profession.
14. **Advertisement and Selling.** In the sphere of industry the psychologist's advice is not limited only to suggesting methods of improving production but is also concerned with suggesting methods of advertisement and selling. Advertisement is based upon the psychology of appeal. It then gives suggestions about the subject matter and the layout of the advertisement so that it can attract the attention of the greatest possible number of people. One example of this is the use of neon signs for advertisement during the night. Apart from advertisement, modern industries try to make use of psychological ideas in selling so that they can convince the customer of the utility of the goods an persuade him to buy it. Psychologists have analysed the process of buying and selling things and have given useful suggestions about selling, they not only explain how the salesmen should persuade the customer to buy his stock but also how the customer should avoid being trapped into unnecessary expenses by the salesman.

It is clear from the above explanation that psychology has great importance for industry and that this importance is increasing.

Experimental Method is Used in Industrial Psychology

Industrial psychology, which is a branch of applied psychology, makes a study of human behaviour under industrial conditions. Hence, basically it makes use of the same methods as are used in applied psychology. In psychology the most scientific technique is the experimental method because the conclusions gained from experiment under controlled circumstances are the most valid and reliable. Industrial psychology also makes use of the experimental method because it is the most scientific. But it also makes use of other psychological methods such as observation, interview, questionnaire, etc.

EXPERIMENTAL METHOD

An experiment is a question asked methodically. In this the experimenter is faced with a question which he tries to answer by conducting an experiment. This question is based on his hypothesis, which itself is based on his own experience, the results of the experiment either prove or disprove the hypothesis. If the hypothesis is proved to be valid, it is used as the basis for some scientific law which can be used in other spheres. In every industry there are certain problems which are discovered through experience. Industrial psychology begins with certain hypothesis which are the various possible solutions to those people. This can be better explained by an example. From his experience Taylor learnt of the difficulties of increasing production and in trying to overcome them he created the principle of scientific organization, later called after him. He observed that every worker goes through certain motions in performing his functions. He came up with the hypothesis that if these motion are scientifically performed through the proper organization of machines and training of the workers then time can be saved and more production achieved in less time. In order to test the truth of this hypothesis he made an experiment upon the labourers of the Bethlehem Iron Company which deals in iron. He studied their movements and conditions of work and then explained his idea to the labourers and persuaded them to apply it. When the idea was put into practice, it was found that production increased three and four-fold. Hence, his principle of scientific organization was proved correct. Gilbreth, a student of Taylor, made more experiments on the same principle in the brick industry and came up with conclusions which supported Taylor's principle. Later on, many other psychologists applied Taylor's principle of scientific organization to test its validity in many other industries. Finally, this principle was accepted as valid. It will be obvious from this example that in industrial psychology many hypotheses are tested through experiment. Those hypotheses which prove valid and correct are used as a base to make general scientific laws. These laws are valid because in an experiment the scientist himself controls the circumstances under which the tests are conducted. For this reason the experiment is being extensively used in industrial psychology.

PSYCHOLOGICAL MEASUREMENT

In industrial psychology the most important problem is the selection of the right person for a particular job. Many kinds of psychology:

(*i*) **Intelligence Tests.** The intelligence of an individual or a group of individuals is tested by getting answers to some questions or by making them perform certain tasks. Different intelligence tests are used for different age levels, and they may be verbal or non-verbal, individual or collective. They are chosen according to the situation in which they are to be used. In industry it is essential to know the intelligence quotient of the workers, for on the basis of intelligence quotient they can be graded and suitable work found for them.

(*ii*) **Tests of Special Abilities.** Certain jobs require a particular set of mental abilities. Special tests are used to discover these mental abilities in individuals. One example of tests of this kind is the test battery used by the Psychological Corporation of America which includes tests concerned with verbal arguments, numerical ability, abstract argument, internal relationships, mechanical argument, writing speed, reality, linguistic ability. Thurston's S.R.A. tests for primary mental abilities are well known as tests of special abilities.

(*iii*) **Aptitude Tests.** Among the aptitude tests, one of the most famous is the Minnesota mechanical adjustment test for measuring the mechanical aptitude of a person. Another famous test is the Bennet test for mechanical aptitude.

(*iv*) **Interest Test.** According to the principles of industrial psychology every worker should be given work which he finds interesting. Hence tests of interest are very common in the field of industry.

(*v*) **Personality Tests.** Certain traits of personality are essential for particular jobs in industry. Personality tests are administered to the candidate to find out whether he possesses such traits. The chief methods of testing personality are case history method, interview method, questionnaire method, etc., by using these methods, one can find out the traits of each individual personality.

MEASUREMENT OF APTITUDES

Studies have been conducted to find out the aptitudes of the workers, managerial staff and the industrialists—to find out their aptitudes towards the conditions of work, the condition of wages and many kinds of reforms and improvements. Three kinds of standards are used to measure aptitudes :

(*i*) **Opinion Scale.** Examples of opinion scales are Thurston's standard, Likert's standard and Gutmann's standard. By using these measures one can find out the opinions of people and then their aptitudes can be discovered indirectly. In these methods there are differences of construction and kinds.

(*ii*) **Rating Scale.** In these the evaluation of aptitudes does not depend upon the opinions and decisions of the workers themselves but upon the scientist's own decision. Rating is done on the basis of non-verbal behaviour, verbal behaviour, clinical interview, private essays, projection techniques and immediate experience, etc.

(*iii*) **Indirect Scales.** In these the workers are not aware that their aptitudes are being tested. In 1938 Ash, Block and Hurzmann studied changes of opinions among industrial groups through suggestions or hinds.

TIME AND MOTION STUDIES

Apart from the above methods used in industrial psychology, there are certain other methods which are used in the solution of specific problems. One important method, for example, much used in industrial psychology, is the time and motion study in which all the movements made by a worker are studied and the time consumed by him is calculated. From this one can find out those movements which can be eliminated. It is also possible to find out those motions which can help in increasing production. Many time and motion studies have been conducted in industrial spheres recently.

Briefly, the methods used in industrial psychology are growing along with the number of new problems being brought up for research. In the future too, one can hope for the evolution of new methods which provide more valid results.

JOB ANALYSIS

Aims of Job Analysis

It has been pointed out before that the main objective of job analysis is selection of personnel. But it can also have other objectives such as improvements in the methods of working training of employees, promotion of employees, obviating accidents and protection of health, etc.

What is Job Analysis?

Defining job analysis Blum has remarked, "A job analysis is an accurate study of the various components of a job. It is concerned not only with an analysis of the duties and conditions of work, but also with the individual qualifications of the worker." It is evident that job analysis will reveal the duties of individuals in a particular job or profession, as also the conditions in which they will be required to work. It will also bring out the qualities required of an individual aspiring to perform some definite function or piece of work. According to J.D. Hackett, in the process of job analysis, the fundamental elements of a job are established and clarified, while simultaneously the abilities desirable in the worker are known, the abilities that will help him to perform his function skillfully. Thus, job analysis has two aspects, one the analysis of duties and conditions of work and the other, the analysis of qualities desired in the worker or employee.

Advantages of Job Analysis

Job analysis concurs many advantages. On the basis of 401 essays concerned with job analysis, Zerga pointed out twenty advantages and utilities of job analysis. One is the increase in efficiency, as well as increase in the mutual feelings of workers since everyone is happy to be employed in the job he cherishes. Job analysis can help to determine the salary or wages accruing to the employee for a particular function performed by him. Job analysis helps, in the classification of professions and occupations, it thereby becoming possible to determine the qualities and abilities required for them. Through job analysis it also becomes possible to determine the extent of training necessary for a specific individual to be given a particular job of work. Job analysis determines the duty of everyone in his own job by determining the responsibility inherent in any kind of work.

Various Components of a Job

Now, the first thing to be mentioned in connection with job analysis is the presence of various components in a job. Headings of information collected in this connection are the following:

1. Identification of the Job
2. Number Employed
3. Statement of Duties
4. Machines Used
5. Analysis of Operations
6. Conditions of Work.
7. Pay and Incentives
8. Relation to Other Allied Jobs
9. Opportunities for Transfer and Promotion
10. Time and Nature of Training
11. Personal Requirements:
    (*a*) General—Age, Sex, Nationality, Marital Status
    (*b*) Physical
    (*c*) Educational
    (*d*) Previous Experience
    (*e*) General and Special Abilities
    (*f*) Temperamental and Character Requirements.

As is evident from the above list, there is extensive collection of data regarding job analysis.

Methods of Job Analysis

Of the many methods employed in job analysis the main are the following:

1. Individual Psychographic Method
2. Questionnaire Method
3. Job Psychographic Method
4. Job Analysis by Text
5. Motion Study Method.

These methods will now be described in brief:

1. *Individual Psychographic Method*: In this method, the mental peculiarities of an individual successful in a particular kind of job are examined, a list of these peculiarities prepared and this list transcribed in figure form on graph. This provides some standard of judgment in future recruitments for the same job.
2. *Questionnaire Method*: A list of questions is prepared on the basis of the different qualities of personality concerned with the job. This list is then provided to the individuals doing that job, and they are asked to answer these questions. An analysis of the answers received helps to reveal the special qualities necessary for the job, a list of which can now be prepared. This, too, helps in the future selection of candidates for the job in question.

3. *Job Psychographic Method*: According to Vitals, there are three things essential to job psychographic method:
   (*a*) Accurate classification of mental qualities
   (*b*) Valid method of evaluation
   (*c*) Direct examination or analysis by trained examiners.

   In this manner, in this method, some specialist analysis study the work and they evolve a valid and standard method of evaluation. They prepare a very accurate list in which the various mental qualities required for the job are properly and reliably classified. A graph of these qualities is prepared so that selection of candidates for the job may become easier.
4. *Job Analysis by Test*: In the test method, some reliable and valid tests are performed on the basis of essential qualities and abilities; the candidates are tested for selection and suitability by these tests.
5. *Motion Study Method*: Under this method, the speed of an individual worker in performing some job and time consumed therein are both noted. Similar examinations being performed on other individuals doing the same work, the results obtained are compared. Such a study of speed and time helps in job analysis and classification of the workers.

Job analysis can be done by any one or more of these methods, the choice of method being governed by the situation or circumstances.

WORKER'S ANALYSIS

Essential Elements in Worker's Analysis

The second step in personnel selection is that of worker's analysis. In worker's analysis, as is apparent from the term used to denote it, detailed information regarding the applicant's qualities, abilities, experience and other factors is obtained. Roughly speaking, worker's analysis requires information under the following heads:

1. Age
2. Caste
3. Sex
4. Nationality
5. Physical Health and Characteristics
6. Education and Training
7. Experience
8. Level of Intelligence
9. Mental Abilities and their Level
10. Interests and Aptitudes
11. Personality Traits.

Having gathered the above information regarding a particular applicant, it becomes possible to determine the kind of job he is likely to prove proficient in and the kind of job in which he tends to be failure. Worker's individual will require before he can successfully enter a particular profession. Worker's analysis can also help to make a rough estimate of the remuneration. Worker's analysis can also help to make a rough estimate of the remuneration that can justifiably be paid to the worker, for the job in which he is expected to excel. Worker's analysis prepares a picture of an individual's personal excellence, by virtue of which it is also called individual analysis.

Method of Worker's Analysis

Worker's analysis is now a matter of science, so that it has come to use certain specific methods. Broadly speaking, the following are the various methods used in worker's analysis:

1. Application Blank
2. Letters of Recommendation
3. Academic Record
4. Psychological Test
5. Group Tests
6. Rating
7. Interview.

It is not essential that all the above methods be used to analyse the abilities of any individual worker, a selection of any one of them being required to meet the need in a particular case. It will be in keeping with the context to glance briefly at these methods.

1. *Application Blank*: Nowadays, the first step in the worker's analysis is the filling in of a blank by the applicant. This application blank can be designed to reveal much information of varied kind, sometimes being so successful as to reveal the individual's entire background. In the application blank, the individual provides information regarding his age, sex, caste, nationality, earlier or past level of education, training, personal experience, history, etc. What kind of information should be provided in the application blanks is determined differently in different professions. Professions that are likely to be influenced by the workers attitudes, mental inclinations, interest, etc., require that information regarding them should also be provided in the application blank. Many advertisers do not make a detailed report of what the applicant is expected to include in his application; they make a brief mention of a very few things. Application blanks should preferably contain detailed enquiries regarding all important facts and details. Research in this direction can help to form outlines of application blanks for various professions, an according to that outline blanks can be provided to the various applicants and aspirants. Often, evidence is required to substantiate the facts detailed in the application.
2. *Letters of Recommendation*: Letters of recommendation also help in worker's analysis. In this method, the aspirant produces various recommendations, recommendations from his previous employer, the principle of his school or college, or from some respective

stalwarts of society, etc. In these letters, in addition to the natural commendation, some degree of ability is also evidenced, but often these letters are seen to contain many confusing and incorrect piece of information regarding the individual. One of the simplest ways of misleading the intended employer is to include mention of many qualities that the aspirant does not possess, or to overemphasize the qualities that he is fortunate enough to possess. As a general rule, such letters of recommendation usually prove to be hindrances rather than helps to the process of job analysis, but if they are valid and justified, reliable and temperate, they can definitely promote job analysis or rather worker's analysis.

3. *Academic Records*: Different professions require different levels of education as an essential qualification. Academic records are evidences of the individual's educational progress and proficiency. These sometimes include cumulative records of the universities.
4. *Psychological Tests*: But the most important and valid method of worker's analysis is that psychological testing in which the applicant's mental ability, interest, personality and particularly attitude is tested. Results of these tests should be employed with exemplary caution since they can also lead to very serious mistakes.
5. *Physical Tests*: There are some jobs that require physical fitness of various kinds as an essential pre-requisite; for example, the eye-sight of a railway guard should be normal and not impaired. And for satisfaction on this point, different physical tests have been devised to suit various professions and their requirements. Nowadays, physical or medical tests have become an essential part of examinations for governmental jobs.
6. *Group Tests*: There are some professions in which many workers have to work collectively but even if they work individually they are constantly thrown together in the process of their work. Hence in their case, it is essential for them to possess certain group qualities which are otherwise not taken into consideration. And it is with the intention of evaluating such qualities of collective behaviour in the individual that the employees or applicants are tested in group. In other words, their conduct in the group is judged.
7. *Rating*: One of the many aspects of worker's analysis is the rating given to the individual by his Principal in school or college or by psychologist. This rating is sometimes taken into consideration by the worker analyst.
8. *Interview*: Finally, in most of the industries today, the applicant is personally interviewed by the employer and some other specialists, during which he is questioned by them on various topics so that they can form some estimate of him as an individual. Every examiner or individual of the board of interviewers asks some or the other question, but even while the applicant is engaged in answering it, the rest of the board is very minutely observing his reactions and conduct. Interview as a method of judging personality has advantages over other methods in that it reveals certain aspects of the individual that cannot be brought to light otherwise. It helps to form an estimate of the individual in respect of his self-confidence, self-control, response to discipline, presence of mind, dynamically, interests, manner of dressing, conduct, behaviour, manners, attraction of personality, if any, etc., besides many

other intangible things that make an impression on the mind of a viewer. But for this method to yield valid and desirable results it is essential that the interviewers themselves be educated, trained and unbiased since, otherwise, such an interview can lead to many misunderstandings and misjudgments.

The method of personnel selection is evident from the detailed description of its two aspects, job analysis and worker's analysis. Following job analysis and worker's analysis, all that remains to be done in the way of personnel selection is to provide the individual with work for which he has been found and pronounced most able.

BOREDOM AND MONOTONY

Meaning of Boredom and Monotony

In the context of psychological fatigue, insofar as it pertains to industry, the words boredom and monotony are used in addition to fatigue. Monotony is a mental condition which is produced by the constant repetition of some function over a long period of time. On the other hand, boredom is a mental condition in which the individual evinces negative attitudes and aptitude for a particular work. In other words he does not want to do that work. Both boredom and monotony contribute to fatigue but neither is the result of physical fatigue. Both of them are caused by mental attitudes. Boredom is caused more by the personality of the worker, his aptitude, his emotional condition and the apparent importance of the function he is performing. When these factors are varied one person will feel no boredom in some particular function which bores another person. Some people become bored rapidly with some work requiring repetition but many other people adapt themselves very quickly to such work. For these reasons the workers have completely divergent opinions about work which is boring and other work which is not.

1. *Study by Wyatt, Langdon and Stock*: Some important facts connected with this subject were revealed in the study of S. Wyatt, J.H. Langdon and F.G.L. Stock. This study was conducted on ten individuals and five kinds of work. Each individual was required to do each kind of work for one month, and at the end of the period each individuals was required to point out the extent of boredom experienced in each kind of work. The worker was to award zero points to the work which contained no boredom and five points to the work in which he felt consistently bored. When this evaluation was analysed it was seen that all the workers considered two kinds of work consistently boring, although some awarded five points to one work and some awarded them to the other. Apart from this the ten individuals showed no unanimity of opinion. The average evaluation for the five kinds of work was 4.2, 2.4, 2.3 and 1.7. It is evident that different individuals differences. The scientists conducting the study pointed out that boredom was evinced by workers with a higher intelligence quotient and an extrovert tendency. But this fact has not been substantiated by other studies.

CAUSE OF BOREDOM AND MONOTONY

Factors which cause boredom and monotony have been revealed through many studies. Some of the factors leading to boredom and monotony, briefly stated, are:

1. **Individuality of the Worker.** As has already been demonstrated boredom and monotony are closely connected with the individual traits of the individual workers. It is commonly seen that particular kind of work will strike some people as boring while others will find no boredom in doing it. In an experiment on 400 students of Munsterberg's college, it was seen that boredom depends upon the individual's particular personality traits, not upon the nature of the work. Different individuals take interest in different kinds of work and that is why the pattern of boredom in each case is different.

2. **Intelligence of the Worker.** Among the different qualities that make up individual differences, intelligence is important and it has a close relation with boredom and monotony. As has been pointed out earlier, the more intelligent individual is inclined to be bored by mechanical repetition of some activity. On the other hand, the less intelligent individual makes a better adjustment with his work. But in this connection it would be better to give a brief review of some of the studies conducted on this subject. The more important studies are the following :

   (*i*) *Thomson's Study*: Thomson experimented upon 32 people and came to the conclusion that boredom has nothing to do with intelligence.

   (*ii*) *Viteles' Study*: Viteles conducted an experiment on girls working in the salary section and concluded that the more intelligent girls experience more boredom with the result that majority of such girls are among those who leave this kind of job.

   (*iii*) *Komhauser's Research*: A.W. Kornhauser conducted an experiment on office workers and supported the contention of Viteles. He also found that the more intelligent people soon become bored with the work and run away. The less intelligent continue to retain their interest in their work.

   (*iv*) *Burnett's Study*: Burnett came to the same conclusion when he conducted an experiment on four girls. He also concluded that the less intelligent girls achieved higher production than the more intelligent girls.

   (*v*) *Studies by Wyatt, Fraser and Stock*: These psychologists also came to the same conclusion. It was observed by them that the less intelligent girls take more interest in their work than the average of exceptionally intelligent girls.

   (*vi*) *Study by A Pound*: In this book **'The Iron Man in Industry'** A. Pound has remarked, A more one trained in habits of doing regularly and obedience, is *for many practical purposes, more valuable to his boss for good production than one in higher mental state.*

3. **Attitude to the Work.** Many studies have established that workers with a negative attitude to their work experience boredom and monotony much sooner than those with a

positive attitude. People with a positive attitude can maintain their concentration in their work for a much longer time.

4. **Satiation.** Some people soon become fed up with doing work that needs recall, and they do not want to continue doing it. Their attention in the work gradually decreases as their mind becomes more and more satiated. As a result the quantity and quality of the production also declines. Satiation is a psychological condition in which physical fatigue is at a very low level. A. Karsten conducted an experiment in this connection with some college students. When they had become completely bored with the work of writing they were asked to write names on a sheet of paper, in which they experienced no difficulty at all. In an experiment with poetry it was seen that some individuals who did not want to utter one more line of poetry were willing to continue talking for a long time when the subject was changed. They, too, did not experience any fatigue. It is evident from both these experiments that only those muscles were being exercised which already appeared to be fatigued. But this apparent fatigue was due to boredom and when the subject was changed they again began to function normally because the boredom was removed. Obviously, the difficulty in working was not due to muscular fatigue but due to satiation, a psychological condition. Satiation is caused by doing the same kind of work. It does not imply fatigue. This was also proved by the fact that some workers complaining of fatigue resumed their work when they were allowed to change their position.
5. **Feeling of Progress.** Many experiments have also yielded the fact that if the worker is aware of the progress he has made in his work, he does not experience boredom or monotony. In fact, as the work progresses the worker becomes excited at the respect of achieving his target and works with renewed energy. An individual becomes bored very quickly with some work the end of which he cannot see or which leads to no tangible result. For this reason it is always better to have recognizable targets at short intervals in any work. The desire to finish the day's work can itself be an aim. In such a case one can observe the increase in the speed of working. But the feeling of having achieved some target or of being near the end also depends upon the individual's attitude. If the attitude is negative this feeling of achievement is weal. Fairly often the boredom of the individual can be reduced if he can be convinced of the value and importance of his work for others.
6. **Other Qualities.** In addition to the above, individual qualities of the worker also influence boredom. The more important ones are leading of attention, emotional condition, peculiarities of nature. If these are in favour of the work, the work will produce less boredom. But is these are negative the individual will soon become bored with his work.
7. **Feeling of Leaving Something Incomplete.** One particular worker was lying on his death bed. He was asked to mention the last wish he would like to have fulfilled. He said that he would like to have a board on which the screws were only half tightened. He wanted to complete the work of tightening those screws. This individual had spent all his life fixing screws on a board and half tightening them. But he was always filled with the desire to tighten these screws fully. Similar phenomena have been observed in many

studies. A worker feels dissatisfied and deprived if he is not allowed to complete his task. In another example, it was seen that one foreman ordered a worker to leave the work in hand and go on to something else. The worker did not want to leave his work incomplete, so he refused to obey the foreman. Using his position the foreman ordered him to leave it. This led to an exchange of words and a scuffle in which the worker pushed the foreman who fell against a machine and was killed. The only thing at the root of this incident was that the foreman wanted to complete. It is also seen that many workers do not want to start some fresh assignment near the end of the day. They know that they will not be able to complete it and it is against human psychology to leave some work incomplete. A refusal in such conditions does not amount to disobedience, disrespect or obstinacy and should not be interpreted as such. Man has a natural desire to finish anything that he has begun and if he is prevented from doing so, he loses his balance, a fact which has been established by many psychological experiments. When the worker enters the factory, he first of all wants to complete the previous days work before going on to something fresh. While working, an individual enters a psychological state in which he wants to leave some work only after he has completed it. This motivation can differ in degree from person to person and from work to work. And providing an opportunity to complete the work is an important element in job satisfaction. This tendency of completing unfinished work is seen more particularly in those kinds of work which influence the emotions, irrespective of their inherent interest or the lack of it. If the worker is indifferent towards his work, he will show no desire to complete it. A worker is seen working rapidly only because he is pressed by the desire to finish it. For this reason the desire to finish some work has an important influence upon boredom or monotony. If this desire is present the individual does not become bored. In this way this tendency is directed against boredom because it creates motivation. In industrial conditions it is desirable that the work should be derived in such a way among the workers that they get an opportunity to complete their part of the work. This increases motivation and reduces boredom.

8. **Conditions of Work.** From the above account of the causes of boredom and monotony it should not be taken for granted that only individual and personal factors are responsible while the external environment plays no part at all. In fact, the truth of the matter is that the manager or the employer can do more to remove boredom and monotony by changing the external conditions of work than he can be trying to condition the worker's mind or to control his attitudes. Monotony can be reduced and production increased by making adequate changes in the working conditions. This can be done by making the following changes :

   (i) *Provision for Rest*: Boredom or monotony increase in the absence of any rest period. In a study conducted by Mayo it was seen that the workers in a cloth mill suffered from boredom because they did not have any rest interval in their working hours. When provision was made for rest, an immediate decline in the level of boredom was soon noticed. This has also been substantiated by the research of other psychologist.

   (ii) *Arrangements for Wages*: The salary system plays an important part in creating interest among the workers. They feel dissatisfied and bored if the wages are not paid at the correct time or at the correct rates. Shaaz sawn his studies that the worker experiences less boredom and achieves a higher level of production if he gets proper wages.

(*iii*) *Working Method*: Wyatt, Frazer and Stock studied the work technique of three girls working in a factory making cigarette boxes. One of these girls had to work three times as much as the third girl, with the result that they regularly exchanged their positions. The scientist, instead of allowing one girl to work at one position for the whole day, made the girls interchange their respective positions six times a single day. It was noticed that their boredom grew less and they produced an extra ten percent of work.

9. **Nature of Work.** One cause of boredom is the nature of the work because if a particular function does not vary at all the worker becomes bored very soon and experiences monotony. If the work is varied and changed frequently the worker's interest in it is maintained. Many experimental results have confirmed this view. Wyatt and Frazer conducted experiments in which six girls were asked to pack soap, fold handkerchiefs, gather cycle chains and to do a variety of other kinds of work. It was noticed that production went up and monotony declined.
10. **Social Factors.** Boredom and monotony also depend to a large extent upon some social factors because the worker works in a social environment which has a decided influence upon his mental condition. If the mutual exchange upon the management and the worker is entertaining and cooperative then the boredom is quickly done away with. Then the worker takes an interest in his work. As long as conversation and laughter do not interfere with the performance of work, the workers should be allowed to indulge in conversation. This helps to maintain the worker's interest in his work. It has also been noticed that less boredom occurs if men and women work together. On the contrary if the atmosphere is one of mutual suspicion and distrust in which the management goes out of the way to scold the worker, the worker soon loses his interest in the work, thus adversely affecting production.

REMEDIES TO BOREDOM AND MONOTONY

Many psychological means have now been evolved in industrial psychology to relieve boredom and monotony. Since monotony depends upon the nature of the work and upon the individual differences of each worker, different means are adopted to remove monotony from different kinds of work. But even then the following general measures can be useful in eliminating boredom:

1. **Exchanging Job.** The most important single measure in removing boredom is to exchange the jobs of the workers among them. Since different kinds of work exhaust different muscles of the body, a change of job helps to maintain the novelty of the work and thus monotony is avoided. Again, the worker also gets an opportunity to gain experience about different kinds of work, while repetition of the same work does not provide any variety of experience. In addition to an exchange of jobs, the worker should be allowed to do the

same job in many different ways since this helps to reduce mental and physical fatigue and maintain interest in the work. In the case of girls working in a telephone exchange it was seen that they took more interest in their work and complained of boredom less frequently when they were allowed to exchange their jobs. By his studies J.R.P. French has shown that job exchange has a positive and beneficial influence upon morale. In his study the working girls were allowed to change the rate and method of working.

2. **Relating the Job to the Large Picture.** Some people become bored with their jobs only because their function is not connected with a comprehensive picture of the job. If a woman who cleans dishes treats each dish as nothing more than another dish, she will soon become bored and will experience monotony. Norman R. F. Maier has described the case of a subnormal boy who cleaned all the dishes in the house, irrespective of the number of guests. And as there were already fifteen members in the household, he should ordinarily have become bored and tired very soon. But he never required any help in this task because, for him each dish had individual characteristics and he could indentify each dish by some mark on it. He treated each dish as a friend and found pleasure in cleaning the face of each friend. Some of them he liked more than others and therefore he had reserved special places for them. He found interest in this work because had reserved special places for them. He found interest in this work because he experienced the feeling that he was rapidly meeting one friend after another.
3. **Knowledge of Work.** It has been seen that working girls soon become bored in their office work if they do not have interest in it. On the other hand, a typist will not experience monotony if he finds the official correspondence interesting or if the office's functions interest him. For this reason it is desirable that all the workers should have sufficient knowledge of the work of their organization. As long as they are ignorant of this they cannot gauge the importance of their own contribution to it. Once they reaslise this importance of their own job can be seen in the right perspective as part of the larger picture. Then the sense of responsibility increases and better work is done. Sometimes the worker is told instead to mind his own business and to carry out orders as they are given to him, without taking interest in the working of the organization. The consequence of this kind of management is that the worker is not interested in the quality of his own work and neither does he make any effort to improve his method of working.
4. **Use of Sub-Goals.** In order to reduce monotony it is desirable to create sub-goals within the work which can be achieved quickly. One such goal is the completion of the day's work with the result that the worker feels he is making progress as the day wears on. If the goal is too far away or can be achieved only after a long time, it does not serve to inspire the worker in this way. In addition to this goal of completing the day's work, the rest intervals can also be made sub-goals. The worker is inspired to complete his work because he feels that soon he will get the chance to rest. It is often seen that the speed of working increases as the time of rest comes nearer. In this way the rest period provides relaxation and removes monotony.

5. **Division of Work into Large Units.** Another way of creating goals all with the intention of finishing it chapter by chapter, then the book can be completed without loss of interest or creation of boredom. Besides, the reader experiences a feeling of progress as he moves from one chapter to the next.
6. **Distribution of Units.** In order to enhance this sense of achievement in industry, the various units of production should be distributed among the workers and each one should be encouraged to complete his own unit. Production can thus be increased by making production itself a goal. The unit of production is between two periods of rest and the desire and enthusiasm to complete the unit tends to reduce monotony.
7. **Use of Pacing Method and Automatic Work Habits.** Psychological analyses have revealed that monotony is repeated activity. It is not caused by recall but by repeating the work. Nowadays efforts are made to turn all repetitive functions into automatic activities, as far as is possible. When this is done the work becomes natural and continues to be done without any attention being paid to it so that the worker can allow his mind to wander here and there. Work of this kind does not cause monotony. For example, people do not notice the distance they walked if they are talking to another person at the same time. But if the individual concentrates his attention on the activity of walking he will soon find it monotonous. Hence, if the work is of the same nature as walking, then the worker should have the liberty to talk to others or to day dream, if he so desires. Many studies have shown that, given the liberty to day dream, monotony can be kept at a low level.
8. **Rhythmic Activity.** Improvement in performance can be seen when some repeated activity is made rhythmic. It has been seen that when many workers are performing the same function they tend to follow a rhythm. Men who carry heavy loads can be seen working in this way. Similarly, less boredom is experienced when walking in step rather than in walking without any rhythm.
9. **Provision of Industrial Music.** Another means of reducing boredom is to provide music to the workers in industry. This measure has proved of great value in all work which does not require the constant attention of the worker. And it should be noted that instrumental music proves more useful than vocal music.
10. **Increase of Experience of Completion.** The awareness of having completed some work provides natural motivation and stimulation. For this reason boredom can be reduced by allowing the worker to have a greater sense of having completed his work. The managers should try to avoid interruption of the worker at his work and in particular not to interfere with him before he has completed his task. The consciousness of completion is created when the worker is aware of the progress he has made. Leaving the work in hand as soon as ordered is not assign of effective administration or obedience in industry. No intelligent manager will stress that the worker should suspend his work as soon as he is ordered. The manager will allow the worker to complete the work in hand and then ask him to report. By doing this the manager can help to maintain the motivation of the worker and avoid boredom. In addition to this the work can be divided into small units so that it gives more

frequent experience of completion and achievement. These smaller units themselves become the goals for the worker and he gets a feeling of completion and the satisfaction when he achieves even this smaller goal. The total work and the working hours should be divided in such a manner that there should be the satisfying experience of completing each unit. The job of preparing records and maintaining accounts can be made more satisfying by dividing the work into separate files so that the worker can feel relieved after finishing work on one file. Job satisfaction increases as the work is seen coming to an end.

11. **Attending to Individual Differences.** In dividing the work among the workers attention should be paid to their individual differences. If this is done the incidence of disinterest and boredom will be less. As far as possible a worker should be given a task which suits his intelligence, attitudes, spheres of attention, nature and emotional condition.
12. **Improvement of Working Conditions.** Generally, boredom and monotony can be kept in control by providing a properly timed and sufficiently long period of rest, payment of wages at the correct time, by introducing the proper method of working, permitting freedom to laugh and enjoy and generally improving the working conditions.
13. **Proper Social Environment.** Finally, the most important method of reducing boredom is to maintain an atmosphere of love and confidence, cooperation and faith among the workers and the management. If the social environment is encouraging and pleasant, boredom normally does not occur.

Chapter **2**

HAWTHORNE EFFECT

The **Hawthorne effect** is a form of *reactivity* whereby subjects improve an aspect of their behaviour being experimentally measured simply in response to the fact that they are being studied, not in response to any particular experimental manipulation.

The term was coined in 1955 by Henry A. Landsberger when analyzing older experiments from 1924–1932 at the *Hawthorne Works* (a *Western Electric* factory outside Chicago). Hawthorne Works had commissioned a study to see if its workers would become more productive in higher or lower levels of light. The workers' productivity seemed to improve when changes were made and slumped when the study was concluded. It was suggested that the productivity gain was due to the motivational effect of the interest being shown in them. Although illumination research of workplace lighting formed the basis of the Hawthorne effect, other changes such as maintaining clean work stations, clearing floors of obstacles and even relocating workstations resulted in increased productivity for short periods. Thus the term is used to identify any type of short-lived increase in productivity.

The term gets its name from a factory called the *Hawthorne Works*, where a series of experiments on factory workers were carried out between 1924 and 1932.

(*a*) This effect was observed for minute increases in illumination.

(*b*) Evaluation of the Hawthorne effect continues in the modern era.

Most industrial/occupational psychology and organizational behaviour textbooks refer to the illumination studies. Only occasionally are the rest of the studies mentioned. In the lighting studies, light intensity was altered to examine its effect on worker productivity.

RELAY ASSEMBLY EXPERIMENTS

In one of the studies, experimenters chose two women as test subjects and asked them to choose four other workers to join the test group. Together the women worked in a separate room over the course of five years (1927–1932) assembling telephone relays.

Output was measured mechanically by counting how many finished relays each dropped down a chute. This measuring began in secret two weeks before moving the women to an experiment room and continued throughout the study. In the experiment room, they had a supervisor who discussed changes with them and at times used their suggestions. Then the researchers spent five years measuring how different variables impacted the group's and individuals' productivity. Some of the variables were:

- Changing the pay rules so that the group was paid for overall group production, not individual production.
- Giving two 5-minute breaks (after a discussion with them on the best length of time) and then changing to two 10-minute breaks (not their preference). Productivity increased, but when they received six 5-minute rests, they disliked it and reduced output.
- Providing food during the breaks.
- Shortening the day by 30 minutes (output went up); shortening it more (output per hour went up, but overall output decreased); returning to the first condition (where output peaked).

Changing a variable usually increased productivity, even if the variable was just a change back to the original condition. However it is said that this is the natural process of the human being to adapt to the environment without knowing the objective of the experiment occurring. Researchers concluded that the workers worked harder because they thought that they were being monitored individually.

Researchers hypothesized that choosing one's own coworkers, working as a group, being treated as special (as evidenced by working in a separate room) and having a sympathetic supervisor were the real reasons for the productivity increase. One interpretation, mainly due to *Elton Mayo*, was that "the six individuals became a team and the team gave itself wholeheartedly and spontaneously to cooperation in the experiment." (There was a second relay assembly test room study whose results were not as significant as the first experiment).

Interviewing Program

The workers were interviewed in attempt to validate the Hawthorne Studies. The participants were asked about supervisory practices and employee morale. The results proved that upward communication in an organization creates a positive attitude in the work environment. The workers feel pleased that their ideas are being heard.

BANK WIRING ROOM EXPERIMENTS

The purpose of the next study was to find out how payment incentives would affect group productivity. The surprising result was that productivity actually decreased. Workers apparently had become suspicious that their productivity may have been boosted to justify firing some of the workers later on. The study was conducted by Mayo and *W. Lloyd Warner* between 1931 and 1932 on a group of fourteen men who put together telephone switching equipment. The researchers found that although the workers were paid according to individual productivity, productivity decreased because the men were afraid that the company would lower the base rate. Detailed observation between the men revealed the existence of informal groups or "cliques" within the formal groups. These cliques developed informal rules of behaviour as well as mechanisms to enforce them. The cliques served to control group members and to manage bosses; when bosses asked questions, clique members gave the same responses, even if they were untrue. These results show that workers were more responsive to the social force of their peer groups than to the control and incentives of management.

INTERPRETATIONS AND CRITICISMS OF THE HAWTHORNE STUDIES

H. McIlvaine Parsons (1974) argues that in the studies where subjects had to go for long drives with no toilet breaks, the results should be considered biased by the feedback compared to the manipulation studies. He also argues that the rest periods involved, possible *learning* effects, and the fear that the workers had about the intent of the studies may have biased the results.

Parsons defines the Hawthorne effect as "the confounding that occurs if experimenters fail to realize how the consequences of subjects, performance affect what subjects do" [*i.e.*, learning effects, both permanent skill improvement and feedback-enabled adjustments to suit current goals]. His key argument is that in the studies where workers dropped their finished goods down chutes, the "girls" had access to the counters of their work rate.

It's possible that the illumination experiments were explained by a *longitudinal learning effect*. It is notable however that *Parsons* refuses to analyze the illumination experiments, on the grounds that they haven't been properly published and so he can't get at details, whereas he had extensive personal communication with Roethlisberger and Dickson.

But Mayo says it is to do with the fact that the workers felt better in the situation, because of the sympathy and interest of the observers. He does say that this experiment is about testing overall effect, not testing factors separately. He also discusses it not really as an experimenter effect but as a management effect: how management can make workers perform differently because they feel differently. A lot to do with feeling free, not feeling supervised but more in control as a group. The experimental manipulations were important in convincing the workers to feel this way: that conditions were really different. The experiment was repeated with similar effects on *mica* splitting workers.

Richard E. Clark and Timothy F. Sugrue (1991, p.333) in a review of *educational research* say that uncontrolled novelty effects cause on average 30% of a *standard deviation* (SD) rise (*i.e.*, 50%–63% score rise), which decays to small level after 8 weeks. In more detail: 50% of a SD for up to 4 weeks; 30% of SD for 5–8 weeks; and 20% of SD for > 8 weeks, (which is <1% of the variance).

A psychology professor at the *University of Michigan*, Dr. *Richard Nisbett*, calls the Hawthorne effect 'a glorified anecdote.' 'Once you've got the anecdote,' he said, 'you can throw away the data.'

Harry Braverman points out in "Labor and Monopoly Capital" that the Hawthorne tests were based on industrial psychology and were investigating whether workers' performance could be predicted by pre-hire testing. The Hawthorne study showed "that the performance of workers had little relation to ability and in fact often bore an inverse relation to test scores...". Braverman argues that the studies really showed that the workplace was not "a system of bureaucratic formal organization on the *Weberian model*, nor a system of informal group relations, as in the interpretation of Mayo and his followers but rather a system of power, of class antagonisms". This discovery was a blow to those hoping to apply the behavioural sciences to manipulate workers in the interest of management.

The Hawthorne effect has been well established in the empirical literature beyond the origina studies. The output ("dependent") variables were human work, and the educational effects can b expected to be similar (but it is not so obvious that medical effects would be). The experiment stand as a warning about simple experiments on human participants viewed as if they were onl material systems. There is less certainty about the nature of the surprise factor, other than it certainl depended on the mental states of the participants: their knowledge, beliefs, etc.

Research on the *demand effect* also suggests that people might take on pleasing th experimenter as a goal, at least if it doesn't conflict with any other motive, but also, improving thei performance by improving their skill will be dependent on getting feedback on their performance and an experiment may give them this for the first time. So you often won't see any Hawthorn effect-only when it turns out that with the attention came either usable feedback or a change i motivation.

Adair (1984): warns of gross factual inaccuracy in most secondary publications on Hawthorn effect and that many studies failed to find it. He argues that it should be viewed as a variant o Orne's (1973) experimental *demand effect*. So for Adair, the issue is that an experimental effec depends on the participants' interpretation of the situation; that this is why *manipulation check* are important in social sciences experiments. So he thinks it is not awareness per se, nor specia attention per se, but participants' interpretation must be investigated in order to discover if/how th experimental conditions interact with the participants' goals. This can affect whether participant believe something, if they act on it or don't see it as in their interest, etc.

In a currently unpublished working paper, economists John List and *Steven Levitt* claim tha in the illumination experiments the variance in productivity is partly accounted for by other factor such as the weekly cycle of work or the seasonal temperature, and so the original conclusions wer overstated. If so, this confirms the analysis of SRG Jones's 1992 article examining the rela experiments.

Unit II

Chapter 3 MOTIVATION

Motivation includes all those conditions which being an activity or sustain it. Motive is different form stimulus because it is there even before the stimulus. In the absence of internal motive there cannot be any response, however intense the external stimulus may be. Motive includes those internal factors which control the activity of the living being. It does not include mechanical or reflex actions because they depend on the physical structure and the external environment such mechanical behaviour is observed in less developed animals. Their changing physical and mental conditions control their behaviour. It is said that the horse can be taken to the water, but no amount of effort can make it drink. In spite of the presence of the water, the horse will drink only when it feels thirsty. Motives depend on the changing physical conditions and past experience. A burnt child dreads the fire because the memory of burning in always present in his mind. Thus it is clear that motivation explains the 'why' of behaviour. Why a certain man behaves in a particular way can be known by an enquiry into his internal motivating factors. Sometimes this 'why' can be inferred from external behavoiur also. For example, the influence of the sex motive can be inferred by a particular behaviour of a pair of male and female. The cause of a particular behaviour towards the child show tender motive in the mother. There can be one motive behind different actions and different motives behind the same action. A man may throw a rupee towards a beggar due to disgust and also due to pity. A soldier may save a person from drowning due to altruistic motive and also to take him to gallows. Social psychology explanation the real motives behind the behaviour and experience of the individual in social situations.

WHAT IS MOTIVATION?

According to Woodworth, *A motive is a state or a set of incentives which disposes him for certain behaviour and for seeking certain goal.* In this way one finds goal-oriented behaviour in motivation. The aim of this behaviour is to achieve certain specific goals. By analysis of motivation one can find out why man works. No individual can achieve something solely due to motivation when it is beyond his capacity to achieve it. Hence the power to do something due to motivation is limited by ability or capacity. Motivation is the method of giving expression to an individual's abilities. The condition of motivation has two aspects the subjective and the objective. In the subjective aspects is contained that condition of the individual which is called need desire or derive. And the objective aspect is the incentive or the goal due to which individual acts. A situation in which the incentive is one for which some need is experienced is a motivation situation. For example, an individual gets some salary if he works in some industry. Now if the money received as salary is a means by which an individual can fulfil his desires then he will work in order to get the salary. Obviously then motivation changes when the incentive and the need both change. Hence in order to create motivation in activity it is desirable that the incentive should be concerned with some or the other need of the worker. If for example, an individual does not need money, then the incentive of money will not form sufficient motivation by which he will be impelled to work. In such a case non-financial incentives like social prestige, proper utilization of one's time, etc., may form sufficient motives to induce a man to work.

CHARACTERISTICS OR MOTIVATE BEHAVIOUR

The analysis of the place of motive in experience and behaviour as given above, clarifies the general characteristics of motivated behaviour. Roughly speaking, these characteristics are as follows:

1. **Energy Motivation.** The first and the most important characteristic of the motivated behaviour is energy mobilization. Even the most peaceful animal becomes frightening in times of emergency. This is due to the mobilization of energy. This process of the mobilization of energy is chemical as well as physical. This process cannot be perceived directly, but when there is some difficulty in the attainment of the object of motive this process is seem in the form of extra energy. The animal tries to attain the object with as much energy as is the impetus of the motive behind it. A hungry dog takes the bread even while beaten. The labour which a student puts into attain a first division in the examination is never seen in his ordinary life. It is often observed that some of the persons brought up in the poor families are very persevering and laborious. Some men perform such inhuman actions due to the sex urge which they would never do in ordinary conditions. When the need is excessive the process of metabolism in the body is also increased in the same proportion and the nervous energy also increases in the same ratio.
2. **Persistence.** Another characteristic of motivated experience or behaviour is persistence. The man cannot leave its work without achieving the goal of its motive. A nomad wandering in search of food keeps on roaming so long as he does not get it. The fighting persons keep on fighting till either of them is down runs away. Sometimes some motivated actions go on for years. A young man in search of a job on labouring for several years till he gets a suitable one. A lover determined to conquer his beloved, does not leave her even in the face of great difficulties. Even in the motivated behaviour of cripples and weak persons much patience and persistence is observed.
3. **Variability.** Third characteristic of the motivated behaviour is variability. A motivated person has a goal, hence he continuously changes his activities with the view of attainment of goal. A person trapped in a house on fire tries new devices to come out

of it. Sometimes he tries this way, some times that and this change of behaviour goes on till he succeeds in coming out of the house. A man with the goal of earning money tries many ways for it. Sometimes he purches a lottery ticket while at other times he is busy in some business. In fact the motivated person goes on changing his ways till he arrives at the way successful for the achievement of the aim. In the beginning his behaviour is trial and error, but after he knows the successful way he always follows it.

4. **Restlessness for the Attainment of the Goal.** The motivated behaviour is goal-directed. The restlessness observed in such a behaviour persists so long as the goal is no achieved. For example the goal of hunger is food. Till the food is taken, there is persistant restlessness due to hunger. After the food is taken this restlessness disappeaes, the goal may be conscious or unconscious. Sometimes the man knows the goal of his motive, but at other times it is only after long efforts and trial and error that he knows the real object which will bring his restlessness to an end. The physical and the mental motives have physical and mental goals respectively. It is this goal which distinguishes between mechanical and the motivated behaviour.
5. **Extinction of Restlessness After the Attainment of the Goal.** The fifth characteristic of motivated behaviour is the extinction of restlessness after the achievement of the goal. The restlessness of the motivated behaviour exhibits itself in following way of the fulfillment of some internal want or desire and extinguishes as soon as that want or desire if fulfilled. A thirsty man roams in search of water. As he gets water and drinks it the restlessness is gone.

There are only two ways to get rid of the restlessness of the motive. Either the tension should be removed or it should be changed. The tension should be removed by the attainment of the object. Sometimes conflicts are observed due to tensions between more than one motives at the same time. Some tensions may be removed immediately while some take days or years to be extinguished.

MOTIVATION IN LEARNING

Motivation as much affects learning. In the absence of motivation either there will be no learning or very little learning and the learned activity shall be forgotten very soon. On the other hand, sufficient motivation will release energy in the process of learning. The motive gives energy for the contribution of the process of learning. It is due to the motive that a student goes on studying attentively for weeks, months and years. Just look at a boy, desirous of learning how to cycle and you can very easily see the role of motivation is this activity. He tries to learn cycling with perfect attention and with all his energy. He falls several times and gets cuts and bruises, but he does not cease to make effort. If he does not succeed one way he adopts another way. So long as he does not learn cycling, a restlessness is seen in him, so much so that he often dreams of cycling. After he learn, cycling he seems to be very happy and is seen cycling now and then. here and there. This importance of motivation in learning has been widely utilsed in education. A good teacher tries to incite motive in the student before beginning some new chapter or before asking them to learn something new. As he succeeds in doing so, half of the work is over, because now he has only to guide the student, for the rest the student learns himself. Learning is a voluntary activity. The more difficult the subject of learning is the more efforts will be necessary to learn it and consequently the more motivation is required for it.

Motivation is not only required in teaching but also in learning for one self. Hence the intelligent student develops motivation in his studies. By motivation the learning the learning becomes active. In it, the interest and attention are spontaneous. Motivation has same place in learning as energy in mechanical function.

VARIETIES OF MOTIVES

Different classifications of motives have been affected from different viewpoints *e.g.,* psychological and physiological, innate and acquired, personal and social. They have been given different names also *e.g.,* needs, motives, propensities, etc., the theory of instincts is included in this. Two types of classification of the motives are the more popular-innate and acquired. The innate motives include instincts, physiological and psychological needs and personal propensities while the acquired motives account for the social and the learned personal needs.

Woodworth [Woodworth R.S., an Marquis D.G., Psychology, Methuren & Co.Ltd., London, (1949)] has divided motives into the following three categories:

1. **Organic Needs.** Those motives which are aroused by the bodily condition, *e.g.,* hunger, thirst, etc.
2. **Emergency Motives.** Those motives which are aroused when the environmental conditions demand a strong and quick reaction, *e.g.,* the motive of escape.
3. **Objective Motives.** The object of these motives is behaviour towards people and the objects in the environment. This class of motives is comprehensive.

Other psychologists have classified motive under primary and complex needs, while some classify them as innate and acquired. The later classification will be the one on the basis of which the following description will be made, because it is the simples classification.

INNATE MOTIVES

Innate motives are not learned, they are inborn. They are the primary, vital, physiological and biological needs which the person brings with him upon his entry into this world. Their fulfillment is indispensable and of primary importance. They are also necessary for the protection of life. The equilibrium of the body and the mind is disturbed, if they remain frustrated, and it can be restored only when these needs are satisfied. The microscopic cells of the body led the psychologists to a hypothesis of drives, which are internal motor activities.

ACQUIRED MOTIVES

So far we have treated of innate motives which are also called primary motives because they are directly related to the biological needs of the organism. These motives are active almost throughout life though the methods of satisfying them are modified with age and experience. These motives are universal because they are hereditary. A major share of them are directly or indirectly related to the physiological condition of the organism. Though most of the motives depend upon the physical condition of the organism it is not correct to conclude that all the motives are physical or innate. The innate motives originate within the organism but there are other motives which are related to objects outside the organism. Woodworth calls them objective tendencies. Some motives are the result of social situations. Gregariousness is a social motives. A child is unable to fulfil his physiological needs unaided. He learns the ways of the fulfillment from others. Thus a developed individual fulfils his needs in accordance with the laws of society. This leads to a socialization of his needs, a process in which the individual develops many needs and motives, causes of which are difficult to trace. An example of this is the difficulty in location physiological causes of the lust for money, search for fame and literary and aesthetic tendencies of the modern man. It is apparent that many of the motives and needs of the individuals are learned in society. They may be called secondary or non-vital motives.

MOTIVATION IN INDUSTRY

It is apparent from the above description that both an understanding of human wants and a knowledge of industrial incentives are necessary for understanding the importance of motivation in industry. Broadly, human wants are of two kinds-natural or internal and acquired. The inner needs include hunger, thirst, maternal instinct, sex needs, sleep etc. The category of acquired needs includes needs like love, sympathy, social prestige and innumerable others which are products of modern culture. Acquired needs change according to past experience and the individual's own traits. The most important among them are social needs. And one of the major social needs is the desire to maintain one's respect in society and the desire to be a kingpin among other men. In addition to this, human beings have the need to get something with which they can identify themselves and get satisfaction.

Different individuals have their own level of ambition and if these are not achieved the individuals feel frustrated. People who have a high level of ambition make very great efforts to achieve it. In one of the studies conducted by Coch and French a production level of 60 units was assumed to be the average. The result was that those who were producing less than this, between 55 and 59 units, immediately increased their production and achieved the average, but those who could not achieve it left their jobs. When the level of ambition is low the individual does not make any effort to exploit his own capabilities to the fullest extent. On the other hand, a person with a high level of ambition often tries to achieve much that is beyond his capabilities.

INFLUENCE OF EXTERNAL CIRCUMSTANCES

External circumstances influence the motivation of an individual only when they have some effect on his internal motivation. This internal motivation has its well spring in the individual's egoistic needs. If a person feels respected in his job, he will motivated to do well in it. If, on the other hand, he feels neglected, he will not be motivated in work. For this reason group motivation has very great influence.

INTERNAL MOTIVES IN INDUSTRY

Considering the importance of various motives in the industrial context, T.W. Harrell has laid stress on three motives which he believes to be most important-sex, self-respect and social prestige. But the motives of remaining active, the desire to work, and hunger are also important motives. It is a common fact that the majority of people work to earn their bread. By working most people can earn enough to satisfy the physical needs of the family and can lead a married life. But some individuals continue to work even after these needs have been fulfilled because work gives them social prestige which satisfies their desire for respect in society. And yet some people continue to work even after both these needs have been satisfied. That is because they want to remain active, because activity is the nature of life. It is difficult to spend life in completely inactive state. Hence most work is done without any financial or non-financial incentives. It is done for the sake of working.

INTERNAL DRIVE

In connection with internal motives, internal drive is mentioned along with needs. Needs include such physical needs as hunger, thirst, sex desire, excretion, respiration and homeostasis, etc. If these needs are not satisfied than the balance of the body is destroyed with the result that mental adjustment is endangered. Drives pertain to more powerful and intense needs the nonfulfilment of which leads to anxiety. Conditions of such anxiety can be seen in the case of dissatisfaction of the sex instinct. A similar condition can also be seen when hunger and thirst are not satisfied. If these drives are not satisfied, the individual's balance is upset.

CONFLICT IN MOTIVES

Sometimes many motives in an individual come into conflict. In such a condition work suffers and production falls. In the sphere of industry care must be taken to avoid such a situation where motives come into conflict. This must be kept in mind while creating motivation. Conflict always leads to mental conflict and the worker cannot decide what to do. Therefore, only those motives should be created which clearly show him the way. In that case he does not have to think very much and he can continue to work at peace. Nowadays variety of methods are used to create motivation among the workers. As far as internal motivation is concerned, it is entirely a matter of the individual worker's mental state. Only external motives can be provided in an industry, and these are called incentives.

Chapter 4 MEANING AND DEFINITION OF JOB SATISFACTION

When an employee joins an enterprise and performs his duties, he wants to satisfy his economic, social and psychological needs. When an employee does not feel satisfy with his job, negative attitudes towards the work develops in his mind. In this case he tries to change the job. This way, he finds himself unable in concentrating to his work. On the contrary, if an employee is satisfied with his job he will perform his duties with his whole hearted efforts. He will contribute his best efforts to the best of his efficiency and capability towards the achievement of pre-determined objectives of the enterprise. A satisfied employee proves to be an asset for the organization. Many factors affect job satisfaction, like salaries, designation, working conditions, the environment, family problems, efficiency of the employee to do his work, his interests in the work and human relations in the industries, etc. Thus, it is clear that job satisfaction of an employee is the result of many attitudes and factors. The term job satisfaction has been defined as under:

Dale Yoder, "*Job satisfaction is regarded as the composite of attitudes of individual employees towards their jobs and relationship, they create.*"

Thus, it may be concluded that job satisfaction is the result of many attitudes. These attitudes include the nature of job, working conditions, individual characteristics and capabilities and the employee and some specific attitudes developed by the circumstances prevailing out of the enterprise.

There are three major theories of job satisfaction:

(*i*) Herzberg's motivation - Hygiene theory

(*ii*) Need fulfillment theory

(*iii*) Social reference group theory.

Herzberg's theory has already been discussed earlier. Under the need—fulfillment theory it is believed that a person is satisfied if he gets what he wants and the more he wants something, or the more important it is to him, the more satisfied he is when he gets it and the more dissatisfied he is when he does not get it. The social reference group theory is similar to need fulfillment theory except that it takes into account not the desires, needs and interests of the individual, but rather the point of view and opinions of the group to whom the individual looks for guidance. Such groups are defined as the **"Reference Group"** for the individual in that they define the way in which he should look at the world and evaluate various phenomena in the environment (including himself). It would be protected, according to his story, that if a job meets the interests, desire and requirements of a person's reference group, he will like it any if it does not, he will not like it. A good example of this theory has been given by C.L. Hulin. He measured the effects of community characteristics on job satisfaction of female clerical workers employed in 300 different catalogue order offices (Journals of applied psychology 196 and 50). He found that with job conditions held constant job satisfaction was less among persons living in a will to do neighbourhood then among those whose neighbourhood was poor. Hulin thus provides strong evidence that frames of reference for evaluation may be provided by one's social groups and general social environments. However, it is obvious that this theory gives an incomplete explanations since while some people may go along with group opinions and group evaluation of organizational phenomena, many people are independent of these pressures.

In summary two theories respectively tell us that:

(i) Job satisfaction is a function of, or is positively related to, the degree to which one's personnel needs are fulfilled in the job situations.

(*ii*) Job satisfaction is a function of, or is positively related to the degree to which the characteristics of the job meet with approval and the desire of the group to which the individual looks for guidance in evaluating the world and defining social reality.

FACTORS AFFECTING JOB SATISFACTION

Factors affecting job satisfaction may be divided into two parts as follows: (1) Individual factors (2) Job factors. Detailed descriptive of these factors is as under:

1. Industrial Factors

(*i*) *Level of Education*: Level of education effects the feeling of job satisfaction among the employees. It has been seen that educated employees feel more satisfied with their jobs than uneducated employees.

(*ii*) *Intelligence*: There is a direct co-relation between intelligence and satisfaction. It has been the experience that intelligent employees feel satisfied with their jobs.

(*iii*) *Health*: Health of the employees is an important factor affecting job satisfaction among the employees. The employees having sound health, feel satisfied with their jobs.

(*iv*) *Age*: Age also affects job satisfaction among the employees. Generally, it is not seen that young employees feel satisfied with their jobs because they always try to get better and better job while the employees of more age feel more satisfied with their jobs.

(*v*) *Interest*: The employees who take interests in their work, feel more satisfied with their work.

(*vi*) *Sex*: Generally it has been the experience that ladies feel more satisfied with their jobs than gents because ladies are learnt ambitious than gents.

(vii) *Family Condition*: Family conditions of the employees affect job satisfaction to a great extent. The employees who are satisfied with their family conditions and atmosphere, feel more satisfied with their work.

2. Job Factors

(i) *Nature of Job*: Nature of job has its own affect on the job satisfaction of the employees. Employees feel dissatisfied if they have to do the work of similar nature for a long time. On the contrary, if the work of an employee is of different types, it gives more satisfaction.

(ii) *Working Conditions and Working Environment*: Working conditions and working environment also affect the job satisfaction of the employees feel more satisfied. If the working conditions of the enterprise are not suitable, the employees feel dissatisfied. The working conditions include arrangement of light, heat, water, machine, etc.

(iii) *Stability of Job*: If the employees feel stability in their job, they feel more satisfied, on the other hand if they feel that their job is not stable, they will remain dissatisfied.

(iv) *Training Arrangements*: Arrangements of training also satisfy the employees because trained employees can do work easily and more efficiency.

(v) *Freedom to Work*: If the employees feel that they are free to do their job in the manner they like, they will feel more satisfied because it will provide them an opportunity to take the relevant decisions.

(vi) *Promotion Opportunities*: If there are challenging opportunities open before the employees, they will made their best efforts to avail the opportunities that will provide them more satisfaction.

(vii) *Effective Supervision*: An efficient and capable supervisor satisfied his subordinates much more than an inefficient supervisor.

(viii) *Proper Remuneration*: Remuneration is the main base of job satisfaction. If proper remuneration is given to the employees in return to their job they will feel more satisfied.

(ix) *Social Aspects*: If the work of an employee is socially recognized, it will give him more job satisfaction.

(x) *Human Relation in the Enterprise*: If there are cordial relations in the enterprise and the labour problems are solved in democratic manner, it increases the feeling of job satisfaction among employees.

HOW CAN JOB SATISFACTION BE INCREASED

Following efforts must be made to increase the job satisfaction among the employees of an enterprise:

1. **Right Job for the Right Person.** The very first suggestion to increase the job satisfaction among employees is that the allocation of work among the employees must be made on scientific basis so that right job may be allocated to the right person.

2. **Proper Remuneration.** Remuneration bears a close and direct relation to job satisfaction of employees. Therefore, the remuneration must be adequate and proper so that the employees may feel they are being duly rewarded for their job.
3. **Security of Job.** The jobs of employees must be secured so that they may feel stable in their jobs.
4. **Promotion Opportunities.** Promotion opportunities must be available to the employees so that they may contributes their best efforts to achieve the targets.
5. **Proper Working Conditions.** Working condition must be sound and proper so that employees may not feel any difficulty in discharging of their duties properly.
6. **Labour Welfare Schemes.** Various schemes for labour welfare must be introduced like accommodation, medical facilities, insurance facilities, recreation facilities and prevented need, etc.
7. **Democratic Supervision.** Supervision of the enterprise must be based on democratic principles. The supervisors must adopt Y theory of supervision.
8. **Effective Communication System.** Communication system must be sound so that the orders and instruction may easily be communicated to the employees and the opinions, suggestion, feelings and problems of employees may be communicated to the management.
9. **Establishment of Friendly Human Relations.** Friendly human relations must be established in the enterprise so that the employees may feel themselves an important part of the enterprise.
10. **Freedom to Work.** Adequate freedom must be granted to the employees to do their work so that they may satisfy their ego.

Chapter 5 STRESS MANAGEMENT

DEFINITION

Stress is defined as a feeling of emotional or physical tension. Emotional stress usually occurs when situations are considered difficult or unmanageable. Therefore, different people consider different situations as stressful.

Physical stress refers to a physiological reaction of the body to various triggers. The pain experienced after surgery is an example of physical stress. Physical stress often leads to emotional stress, and emotional stress is frequently experienced as physical discomfort (*e.g.*, stomach cramps).

The term stress in medicine and biology today is used in a number of different ways. It may refer to external forces or conditional experienced by the organisms, or to the reaction of the organism to these. When applied to external forces the term stress is similar to its use in physics and applies to an external, stimulus or force which is strain/producing or potentially strain producing to the person to whom it is applied. Anything may be considered a stress if it threatens the biological integrity of the organism, whether directly by its physical or chemical properties indirectly because of its symbolic meaning.

Selye used the term 'a state of stress' to denote a specific syndrome occurring in the body in response to certain agents to which he refers as 'stresses.'

In medicine and psychiatry the term stress is usually used to denote various psychosocial situations which can produce disorganisation of behaviour, including physical and mental illnesses.

A convenient definition of stress is any stimulus or in the external or internal environment which disturbs homeostasis which under certain conditions, can result in illness. According to Coleman, "Stress, like a motive, may be partly or wholly unconscious, though the presence of uneasiness or anxiety may be the clue that stress is present. Stress is inevitable and sometimes chosen voluntarily, mental health results not from lack of stress but ability to cope with it satisfactorily."

Stress cannot be considered in isolation. We need to know what stimuli or situations are potentially stressful and we need to the effect produced by such stresses on the organism and finally, the pathways and mechanisms mediating the organism's response to stresses.

STRESS, DISTRESS AND DISEASE

According to W. L. Linford Rees, "Stress can be defined as stimulus or change in the external or internal environment of such a degree in terms of strength or intensity or duration as to tax the adaptive capacity of the organism to its limit and which, in certain circumstances, can lead to a disorganisation of behaviour or a dysfunction which may lead to disease. What may constitute a stress may consist of physical stimuli, infections (bacterial, viral or fungal) or allergic reactions, or may refer to a whole series of stimuli or change in the social or psychological spheres of life".

COPING MECHANISM AND STRESS

Selye's (1950) defamation of a stress is one which evokes the manifestation of a General Adoption Syndrome. Thus this is a physiological response, and the effect of the stress can be measured in terms of action on the hypothalamus; the adrenal cortex, the sympathetic adrenomedullary system and the secretion of different hormones. Physiological stresses differ from psychical stresses in that the power or force of the psychosocial stress will be determined not on1y' by its inherent threat but also by the way in which the individual perceives and appraises the significance of the potentiality challenging event and what degree of threat he perceives as appertaining to the stimulus situation. When an event is perceived as being harmful or threatening, a variety of coping mechanisms may be used as a defense. Reality may be discounted by denial, which is a very common mode of dealing with distressing events, including illnesses leukemia and myocardial infection. The degree of subjective distress may be modified by displacement, *e.g.*, anxiety or hostility into smiling or laughter, into sleep, or into eating, drinking or smoking. Other coping mechanisms are rationalisation and self-deception (which are merely manifestations of denial) and withdrawal from the stressful stimulus or situation. These coping mechanisms can ameliorate the experience or distress as well as its bodily concomitants. According to W. L. Linford Rees, "Distress denotes an unpleasant emotional experience which may arise in response to environment influent or to changes in some internal environment, or as a reaction to some diseasc or disability." To quote W. L. Linford Rees, again, "Disseat is a notoriously difficult term to define, but for pragmatic purposes the term disease is used to denote disability arising from bodily or mental malfunction which imposes difficulties in coping with everyday work and responsibilities, interferes with well-being and produces distress."

We will consider the ways in which stresses or stressors produce distress in the individual and in which, in certain circumstances, they may produce disease, which in turn can also cause distress by the threat of the illness itself, or the disability it causes.

Sequences of Events

The sequence of events which occur in the mediation of the effects of stimuli which may be physical or may be psychological stresses on the individual. The individual's response to such stimuli will be influenced by genetic-constitutional factors and by the environmental modification of his genetic make up.

Previous Experience

Previous experiences, particularly in childhood may also influence the susceptibility to respond to psychosocial stresses. These stimuli; acting on the individual, give rise to bodily changes involving hypothalamic pituitary control of adrenal and other endocrine glands and a variety of biochemical and physiological changes which may constitute the precursors of disease, and these in turn, if they continue, lead to disease. These changes may be modified at all stages.

Coping Mechanisms

We have noted the effect of coping mechanisms. It is sometimes possible to modify the response of the individual by changing the internal environment, *e.g.*, at the premenstrual phase. It is possible to modify the mechanisms involved in the precursors of disease by psychotropic drugs or psychological means to prevent the changes actually leading to disease.

Stress and Life Changes

Holmes and Rahe quantified life events giving point value to life changes that require adaptation. They found that there was a critical level at which too many of these events happening during a one year time span to one person, put that person at great risk of illness. Of those people who accumulated 300 points in one year were 80 per cent at risk of illness in the near future, with 155 to 299 points; 50 per cent became ill in the near future.

Of those with fewer than 150 stress points 30 per cent became ill shortly after the life events.

SOCIAL RE-ADJUSTMENT SCALE

Event	Points
1. Death of Spouse	100
2. Divorce	73
3. Marital Separation from Mate	65
4. Detention in Jail or other Institution	63
5. Death of Close Family Member	63
6. Major Personal Injury or Illness	53
7. Marriage	50
8. Being Sacked from Work	47
9. Requirement from Work	45
10. Changing to Different Type of Work	26

It has been found that situations relating to occupation, marriage and parenthood were the most likely to produce anxiety and depression. The life changes affected both sexes but women were more vulnerable, also the poor and disadvantaged groups were more vulnerable. The change created significant strain when it was unexpected and when it not only involved adjustment to a loss, for example a job, but the need to adjust a new status that involved further hardships and problems.

Loss of work constitutes a stress and may tax the adaptive capacity of the person to the maximum, particularly, if it means marked loss of financial status, marked loss of prestige, or creates additional problems with the family.

STRESS AT WORK

How to Reduce and Manage Job and Workplace Stress?

In this difficult economy, you may find it harder than ever to cope with challenges on the job. Both the stress we take with us when we go to work and the stress that awaits us on the job are on the rise - and employers, managers and workers all feel the added pressure. While some stress is a normal part of life, excessive stress interferes with your productivity and reduces your physical and emotional health, so it's important to find ways to keep it under control. Fortunately, there is a lot that you can do to manage and reduce stress at work.

Coping with Work Stress in Today's Uncertain Climate

For workers everywhere, the troubled economy may feel like an emotional roller coaster. "Layoffs" and "budget cuts" have become bywords in the workplace, and the result is increased fear, uncertainty, and higher levels of stress. Since job and workplace stress grow in times of economic crisis, it's important to learn new and better ways of coping with the pressure. The ability to manage stress in the workplace can make the difference between success or failure on the job. Your emotions are contagious, and stress has an impact on the quality of your interactions with others. The better you are at managing your own stress, the more you'll positively affect those around you and the less other people's stress will negatively affect you.

How to Manage Job Stress?

There are a variety of steps you can take to reduce both your overall stress levels and the stress you find on the job and in the workplace. These include:

- Taking responsibility for improving your physical and emotional well-being.
- Avoiding pitfalls by identifying knee jerk habits and negative attitudes that add to the stress you experience at work.

- Learning better communication skills to ease and improve your relationships with management and coworkers.

Warning Signs of Excessive Stress at Work

When people feel overwhelmed, they lose confidence and become irritable or withdrawn, making them less productive and effective and their work less rewarding. If the warning signs of work stress go unattended, they can lead to bigger problems. Beyond interfering with job performance and satisfaction, chronic or intense stress can also lead to physical and emotional health problems.

Signs and Symptoms of Excessive Job and Workplace Stress:

- Feeling anxious, irritable, or depressed
- Apathy, loss of interest in work
- Problems sleeping
- Fatigue
- Trouble concentrating
- Muscle tension or headaches
- Stomach problems
- Social withdrawal
- Loss of sex drive
- Using alcohol or drugs to cope.

Common Causes of Excessive Workplace Stress

- Fear of layoffs
- Increased demands for overtime due to staff cutbacks
- Pressure to perform to meet rising expectations but with no increase in job satisfaction
- Pressure to work at optimum levels - all the time.

Reducing Job Stress by Taking Care of Yourself

When stress on the job is interfering with your ability to work, care for yourself, or manage your personal life, it's time to take action. Start by paying attention to your physical and emotional health. When your own needs are taken care of, you're stronger and more resilient to stress. The better you feel, the better equipped you'll be to manage work stress without becoming overwhelmed.

Taking care of yourself doesn't require a total lifestyle overhaul. Even small things can lift your mood, increase your energy and make you feel like you're back in the driver's seat. Take things one step at a time, and as you make more positive lifestyle choices, you'll soon notice a noticeable difference in your stress level, both at home at work.

Make Food Choices That Keep You Going and Make You Feel Good

Eating small but frequent meals throughout the day maintains an even level of blood sugar in your body. Low blood sugar makes you feel anxious and irritable. On the other hand, eating too much can make you lethargic.

Drink Alcohol in Moderation and Avoid Nicotine

Alcohol temporarily reduces anxiety and worry, but too much can cause anxiety as it wears off. Drinking to relieve job stress can also start you on a path to alcohol abuse and dependence. Similarly, smoking when you're feeling stressed and overwhelmed may seem calming, but nicotine is a powerful stimulant—leading to higher, not lower, levels of anxiety.

Get Enough Sleep

Stress and worry can cause insomnia. But lack of sleep also leaves you vulnerable to stress. When you're sleep deprived, your ability to handle stress is compromised. When you're well-rested, it's much easier to keep your emotional balance, a key factor in coping with job and workplace stress.

REDUCING JOB STRESS BY PRIORITIZING AND ORGANIZING

When job and workplace stress surrounds you, you can't ignore it, but there are simple steps you can take to regain control over yourself and the situation. Your growing sense of self-control will also be perceived by others as the strength it is, leading to better relationships at work. Here are some suggestions for reducing job stress by prioritizing and organizing your responsibilities.

Time Management Tip for Reducing Job Stress

- **Create a Balanced Schedule.** Analyze your schedule, responsibilities and daily tasks. All work and no play is a recipe for burnout. Try to find a balance between work and family life, social activities and solitary pursuits, daily responsibilities and downtime.
- **Don't Over-Commit Yourself.** Avoid scheduling things back-to-back or trying to fit too much into one day. All too often, we underestimate how long things will take. If you've got too much on your plate, distinguish between the "shoulds" and the "musts." Drop tasks that aren't truly necessary to the bottom of the list or eliminate them entirely.
- **Try to Leave Earlier in the Morning.** Even 10–15 minutes can make the difference between frantically rushing to your desk and having time to ease into your day. Don't add to your stress levels by running late.

- **Plan Regular Breaks.** Make sure to take short breaks throughout the day to sit back and clear your mind. Also try to get away from your desk for lunch. Stepping away from work to briefly relax and recharge will help you be more, not less, productive.

Task Management Tips for Reducing Job Stress

- **Prioritize Tasks.** Make a list of tasks you have to do and tackle them in order of importance. Do the high-priority items first. If you have something particularly unpleasant to do, get it over with early. The rest of your day will be more pleasant as a result.
- **Break Projects into Small Steps.** If a large project seems overwhelming, make a step-by-step plan. Focus on one manageable step at a time, rather than taking on everything at once.
- **Delegate Responsibility.** You don't have to do it all yourself, whether at home, school, or on the job. If other people can take care of the task, why not let them? Let go of the desire to control or oversee every little step. You'll be letting go of unnecessary stress in the process.

REDUCING WORKPLACE STRESS BY IMPROVING EMOTIONAL INTELLIGENCE

Even if you're in a job where the environment has grown increasingly stressful, you can retain a large measure of self-control and self-confidence by understanding and practicing emotional intelligence. Emotional intelligence is the ability to manage and use your emotions in positive and constructive ways. It's about communicating with others in ways that draw people to you, overcome differences, repair wounded feelings and defuse tension and stress.

Emotional Intelligence in the Workplace

Emotional intelligence in the workplace has four major components:

- **Self-Awareness.** The ability to recognize your emotions and their impact while using gut feelings to guide your decisions.
- **Self-Management.** The ability to control your emotions and behaviour and adapt to changing circumstances.
- **Social Awareness.** The ability to sense, understand and react to other's emotions and feel comfortable socially.
- **Relationship Management.** The ability to inspire influence and connect to others and manage conflict.

REDUCING STRESS IN THE WORKPLACE WITH EMOTIONAL INTELLIGENCE

The more emotional intelligence you have, the more stress you can avoid in the workplace. Fortunately, emotional intelligence is not something we're born with; it's something we can learn and develop.

The skill set that enables you to acquire these capabilities can be learned but requires the development of emotional and nonverbal ways of communicating that include:

- Learning to recognize your particular stress response and become familiar with sensual cues that can rapidly calm and energize you.
- Staying connected to your internal emotional experience so you can appropriately manage your own emotions. Knowing what you are feeling will not only add to yourself confidence and improve yourself control but enhance your understanding of others and help you build more satisfying relationships.
- Learning to recognize and effectively use the nonverbal cues that make up 95–98% of your communication process including eye contact, facial expression, tone of voice, posture, gesture and touch. Its not what you say but how you say it that impacts others for better or worse.
- Developing the capacity to meet challenges with humor. There is no better stress buster than a hardy laugh and nothing reduces stress quicker in the workplace than mutually shared humor. But, if the laugh is at someone else's expense, you may end up with more rather than less stress.
- Learning to navigate conflict by becoming a good listener and someone who can face conflict fearlessly with the expectation that differences resolved will strengthen the relationship.

Reducing Workplace Stress by Breaking Bad Habits

As you learn to manage your job stress and improve your work relationships, you'll have more control over your ability to think clearly and act appropriately. You will be able to break habits that add to your stress at work - and you'll even be able to change negative ways of thinking about things that only add to your stress.

ELIMINATE SELF-DEFEATING BEHAVIOURS

Many of us make job stress worse with patterns of thought or behaviour that keep us from relieving pressure on ourselves. If you can turn around these self-defeating habits, you'll find employer-imposed stress easier to handle.

- **Resist Perfectionism.** No project, situation, or decision is ever perfect and you put undue stress on yourself by trying to do everything perfectly. When you set unrealistic goals for yourself or try to do too much, you're setting yourself up to fall short. Do your best, and you'll do fine.

- **Clean up your Act.** If you're always running late, set your clocks and watches fast and give yourself extra time. If your desk is a mess, file and throw away the clutter; just knowing where everything is saves time and cuts stress. Make to do lists and cross off items as you accomplish them. Plan your day and stick to the schedule - you'll feel less overwhelmed.
- **Flip your Negative Thinking.** If you see the downside of every situation and interaction, you'll find yourself drained of energy and motivation. Try to think positively about your work, avoid negative-thinking co-workers, and pat yourself on the back about small accomplishments, even if no one else does.

Find Ways to Dispel Stress

- **Get Time Away.** If you feel stress building, take a break. Walk away from the situation. Take a stroll around the block, sit on a park bench, or spend a few minutes meditating. Exercise does wonders for the psyche. But even just finding a quiet place and listening to your iPod can reduce stress.
- **Talk it Out.** Sometimes the best stress-reducer is simply sharing your stress with someone close to you. The act of talking it out and getting support and empathy from someone else - is often an excellent way of blowing off steam and reducing stress.
- **Cultivate Allies at Work.** Just knowing you have one or more co-workers who are willing to assist you in times of stress will reduce your stress level. Just remember to reciprocate and help them when they are in need.
- **Find Humor in the Situation.** When you or the people around you start taking things too seriously, find a way to break through with laughter. Share a joke or funny story.

WHAT MANAGERS OR EMPLOYERS CAN DO TO REDUCE STRESS AT WORK?

It's in a manager's best interest to keep stress levels in the workplace to a minimum. Managers must act as positive role models, especially in times of high stress. All of the tips mentioned in this article are twice as important for managers to follow. If someone that we admire remains calm, it is much easier to remain calm ourselves and vice versa! There are also organizational changes that managers and employers can make to reduce workplace stress.

Improve Communication

- Share information with employees to reduce uncertainty about their jobs and futures.
- Clearly define employees' roles and responsibilities.
- Make communication friendly and efficient, not mean-spirited or petty.

Consult Your Employees

- Give workers opportunities to participate in decisions that affect their jobs.
- Consult employees about scheduling and work rules.
- Be sure the workload is suitable to employees' abilities and resources; avoid unrealistic deadlines.
- Show that individual workers are valued.

Offer Reward and Incentives

- Praise good work performance verbally and institutionally.
- Provide opportunities for career development.
- Promote an "entrepreneurial" work climate that gives employees more control over their work.

Cultivate a Friendly Social Climate

- Provide opportunities for social interaction among employees.
- Establish a zero-tolerance policy for harassment.

Make management actions consistent with organizational values.

Chapter 6 ORGANIZATIONAL CULTURE

Organizational culture is an idea in the field of Organizational studies and management which describes the psychology, attitudes, experiences, beliefs and values (personal and cultural values) of an organization. It has been defined as "the specific collection of values and norms that are shared by people and groups in an organization and that control the way they interact with each other and with stakeholders outside the organization."

This definition continues to explain **organizational values** also known as "beliefs and ideas about what kinds of goals members of an organization should pursue and ideas about the appropriate kinds or standards of behaviour organizational members should use to achieve these goals. From organizational values develop organizational norms, guidelines or expectations that prescribe appropriate kinds of behaviour by employees in particular situations and control the behaviour of organizational members towards one another."

Organizational culture is not the same as **corporate culture.** It is wider and deeper concepts, something that an organization 'is' rather than what it 'has'.

Corporate culture is the total sum of the values, customs, traditions and meanings that make a company unique. Corporate culture is often called "the character of an organization" since it embodies the vision of the company's founders. The values of a corporate culture influence the ethical standards within a corporation as well as managerial behaviour.

Senior management may try to determine a *corporate culture*. They may wish to impose corporate values and standards of behaviour that specifically reflect the objectives of the organization. In addition, there will also be an extant internal culture within the workforce. Work-groups within the organization have their own behavioural quirks and interactions which, to an extent, affect the whole system. Roger Harrison's four-culture typology and adapted by Charles Handy, suggests that unlike organizational culture, corporate culture can be 'imported'. For example, computer technicians will have expertise, language and behaviours gained independently of the organization, but their presence can influence the culture of the organization as a whole.

STRONG/WEAK CULTURES

Strong culture is said to exist where staff respond to stimulus because of their alignment to organizational values. In such environments, strong cultures help firms operate like well-oiled machines, cruising along with outstanding execution and perhaps minor tweaking of existing procedures here and there.

Conversely, there is **weak culture** where there is little alignment with organizational values and control must be exercised through extensive procedures and bureaucracy.

Where culture is strong people do things because they believe it is the right thing to do there is a risk of another phenomenon, Groupthink. "Groupthink" was described by Irving L. Janis. He defined it as "...a quick and easy way to refer to a mode of thinking that people engage when they are deeply involved in a cohesive ingroup, when members' strivings for unanimity override their motivation to realistically appraise alternatives of action." This is a state where people, even if they have different ideas, do not challenge organizational thinking and therefore there is a reduced capacity for innovative thoughts. This could occur, for example, where there is heavy reliance on a central charismatic figure in the organization, or where there is an evangelical belief in the organization's values, or also in groups where a friendly climate is at the base of their identity (avoidance of conflict). In fact group think is very common, it happens all the time, in almost every group. Members that are defiant are often turned down or seen as a negative influence by the rest of the group, because they bring conflict.

Innovative organizations need individuals who are prepared to challenge the status quo-be it groupthink or bureaucracy, and also need procedures to implement new ideas effectively.

TYPOLOGIES OF ORGANIZATIONAL CULTURES

Several methods have been used to classify organizational culture. Some are described below: It is demonstrated that there are national and regional cultural groupings that affect the behaviour of organizations.

Hofstede looked for national differences between over 100,000 of IBM's employees in different parts of the world, in an attempt to find aspects of culture that might influence business behaviour.

Hofstede identified five dimensions of culture in his study of national influences:

- **Power Distance.** The degree to which a society expects there to be differences in the levels of power. A high score suggests that there is an expectation that some individuals wield larger amounts of power than others. A low score reflects the view that all people should have equal rights.
- **Uncertainty Avoidance.** Reflects the extent to which a society accepts uncertainty and risk.
- **Individualism vs. Collectivism.** Individualism is contrasted with collectivism and refers to the extent to which people are expected to stand up for themselves, or alternatively act predominantly as a member of the group or organization. However, recent researches have shown that high individualism may not necessarily mean low collectivism and vice versa. Research indicates that the two concepts are actually unrelated. Some people and cultures might have both high individualism and high collectivism, for example. Someone

who highly values duty to his or her group does not necessarily give a low priority to personal freedom and self-sufficiency.

- **Masculinity vs. Femininity.** Refers to the value placed on traditionally male or female values. Male values for example include competitiveness, assertiveness, ambition and the accumulation of wealth and material possessions.
- **Long vs. Short Term Orientation.** Describes a society's "time horizon," or the importance attached to the future versus the past and present. In long term oriented societies, thrift and perseverance are valued more; in short term oriented societies, respect for tradition and reciprocation of gifts and favors are valued more. Eastern nations tend to score especially high here, with Western nations scoring low and the less developed nations very low; China scored highest and Pakistan lowest.

Deal and Kennedy

Deal and Kennedy defined organizational culture as the way things get done around here. They measured organizations in respect of:

- ***Feedback.*** Quick feedback means an instant response. This could be in monetary terms, but could also be seen in other ways, such as the impact of a great save in a soccer match.
- ***Risk.*** Represents the degree of uncertainty in the organization's activities.

Using these parameters, they were able to suggest four classifications of organizational culture:

- *The Tough-Guy Macho Culture*: Feedback is quick and the rewards are high. This often applies to fast moving financial activities such as brokerage, but could also apply to a police force, or athletes competing in team sports. This can be a very stressful culture in which to operate.
- *The Work Hard/Play Hard Culture* is characterized by few risks being taken, all with rapid feedback. This is typical in large organizations, which strive for high quality customer service. It is often characterized by team meetings, jargon and buzzwords.
- *The Bet your Company Culture,* where big stakes decisions are taken, but it may be years before the results are known. Typically, these might involve development or exploration projects, which take years to come to fruition, such as oil prospecting or military aviation.
- *The Process Culture* occurs in organizations where there is little or no feedback. People become bogged down with how things are done not with what is to be achieved. This is often associated with bureaucracies. While it is easy to criticize these cultures for being overly cautious or bogged down in red tape, they do produce consistent results, which is ideal in, for example, public services.

Charles Handy

Charles Handy (1985) popularized the 1972 work of Roger Harrison of looking at culture which some scholars have used to link organizational structure to organizational culture. He describes Harrison's four types thus:

- A *Power Culture* which concentrates power among a few. Control radiates from the center like a web. Power Cultures have few rules and little bureaucracy; swift decisions can ensue.
- In a *Role Culture,* people have clearly delegated authorities within a highly defined structure. Typically, these organizations form hierarchical bureaucracies. Power derives from a person's position and little scope exists for expert power.
- By contrast, in a *Task Culture,* teams are formed to solve particular problems. Power derives from expertise as long as a team requires expertise. These cultures often feature the multiple reporting lines of a matrix structure.
- A *Person Culture* exists where all individuals believe themselves superior to the organization. Survival can become difficult for such organizations, since the concept of an organization suggests that a group of like-minded individuals pursue the organizational goals. Some professional partnerships can operate as person cultures, because each partner brings a particular expertise and clientele to the firm.

Edgar Schein

Edgar Schein, an MIT Sloan School of Management professor, defines organizational culture as:

"A pattern of shared basic assumptions that the group learned as it solved its problems of external adaptation and internal integration, that has worked well enough to be considered valid and, therefore, to be taught to new members as the correct way you perceive, think and feel in relation to those problems".

According to Schein, culture is the most difficult organizational attribute to change, outlasting organizational products, services, founders and leadership and all other physical attributes of the organization. His organizational model illuminates culture from the standpoint of the observer, described by three cognitive levels of organizational culture.

At the first and most cursory level of Schein's model is organizational attributes that can be seen, felt and heard by the uninitiated observer - collectively known as *artifacts.* Included are the facilities, offices, furnishings, visible awards and recognition, the way that its members dress, how each person visibly interacts with each other and with organizational outsiders, and even company slogans, mission statements and other operational creeds.

The next level deals with the professed culture of an organization's members - the values. At this level, local and personal *values* are widely expressed within the organization. Organizational behaviour at this level usually can be studied by interviewing the organization's membership and using questionnaires to gather attitudes about organizational membership.

At the third and deepest level, the organization's tacit assumptions are found. These are the elements of culture that are unseen and not cognitively identified in everyday interactions between organizational members. Additionally, these are the elements of culture which are often taboo to discuss inside the organization. Many of these 'unspoken rules' exist without the conscious knowledge of the membership. Those with sufficient experience to understand this deepest level of organizational culture usually become acclimatized to its attributes over time, thus reinforcing the invisibility of their existence. Surveys and casual interviews with organizational members cannot draw out these attributes--rather much more in-depth means is required to first identify then understand organizational culture at this level. Notably, culture at this level is the underlying and driving element often missed by organizational behaviourists.

Using Schein's model, understanding paradoxical organizational behaviours becomes more apparent. For instance, an organization can profess highly aesthetic and moral standards at the second level of Schein's model while simultaneously displaying curiously opposing behaviour at the third and deepest level of culture. Superficially, organizational rewards can imply one organizational norm but at the deepest level imply something completely different. This insight offers an understanding of the difficulty that organizational newcomers have in assimilating organizational culture and why it takes time to become acclimatized. It also explains why organizational change agents usually fail to achieve their goals: underlying tacit cultural norms are generally not understood before would be change agents begin their actions. Merely understanding culture at the deepest level may be insufficient to institute cultural change because the dynamics of interpersonal relationships (often under threatening conditions) are added to the dynamics of organizational culture while attempts are made to institute desired change.

Arthur F Carmazzi

The Blame Culture: This culture cultivates distrust and fear, people blame each other to avoid being reprimanded or put down, this results in no new ideas or personal initiative because people don't want to risk being wrong.

Multi-Directional Culture: This culture cultivates minimized cross-department communication and cooperation. Loyalty is only to specific groups (departments). Each department becomes a clique and is often critical of other departments which in turn creates lots of gossip. The lack of cooperation and Multi-Direction is manifested in the organization's inefficiency.

Live and Let Live Culture: This culture is Complacency, it manifests Mental Stagnation and Low Creativity. People here have little future vision and have given up their passion. There is average cooperation and communication and things do work, but they do not grow. People have developed their personal relationships and decided who to stay away from, there is not much left to learn.

Brand Congruent Culture: People in this culture believe in the product or service of the organization, they feel good about what their company is trying to achieve and cooperate to achieve it. People here are passionate and seem to have similar goals in the organisation. They use personal resources to actively solve problems and while they don't always accept the actions of management or others around them, they see their job as important. Most everyone in this culture is operating at the level of Group.

Leadership Enriched Culture: People view the organization as an extension of themselves, they feel good about what they personally achieve through the organization and have exceptional cooperation. Individual goals are aligned with the goals of the organization and people will do what it takes to make things happen. As a group, the organization is more like family providing personal fulfillment which often transcends ego so people are consistently bringing out the best in each other. In this culture, Leaders do not develop followers, but develop other leaders. Most everyone in this culture is operating at the level of Organization.

Carmazzi's model requires application of his directive communication psychology to evolve the culture. While the idea of having a leadership enriched organization is inspirational, it would require substantial leadership resources to develop. The concept of evolving the culture assumes that "every individual in the organization wants to do a good job" and the behaviours that result in poor performance are manifestations of psychology the group or organization has created through policies, leadership and poor communication.

Robert A. Cooke

The Organizational Culture Inventory: Culture Clusters

Robert A. Cooke, PhD, defines culture as the behaviours that members believe are required to fit in and meet expectations within their organization. The Organizational Culture Inventory measures twelve behavioural of norms that are grouped into three general types of cultures:

- *Constructive Cultures,* in which members are encouraged to interact with people and approach tasks in ways that help them meet their higher-order satisfaction needs.
- *Passive/Defensive Cultures*, in which members believe they must interact with people in ways that will not threaten their own security.
- *Aggressive/Defensive Cultures*, in which members are expected to approach tasks in forceful ways to protect their status and security.

The Constructive Cluster

The constructive cluster includes cultural norms that reflect expectations for members to interact with others and approach tasks in ways that will help them meet their higher order satisfaction needs for affiliation, esteem and self-actualization.

The four cultural norms in this cluster are:

- Achievement
- Self-Actualizing
- Humanistic-Encouraging
- Affiliative.

Organizations with constructive cultures encourage members to work to their full potential, resulting in high levels of motivation, satisfaction, teamwork, service quality, and sales growth. Constructive norms are evident in environments where quality is valued over quantity, creativity is valued over conformity, cooperation is believed to lead to better results than competition, and effectiveness is judged at the system level rather than the component level. These types of cultural norms are consistent with (and supportive of) the objectives behind empowerment, total quality management, transformational leadership, continuous improvement, reengineering and learning organizations.

The Passive/Defensive Cluster

Norms that reflect expectations for members to interact with people in ways that will not threaten their own security are in the Passive/Defensive Cluster.

The four Passive/Defensive cultural norms are:

- Approval
- Conventional
- Dependent
- Avoidance.

In organizations with passive/defensive cultures, members feel pressured to think and behave in ways that are inconsistent with the way they believe they should in order to be effective. People are expected to please others (particularly superiors) and avoid interpersonal conflict. Rules, procedures and orders are more important than personal beliefs, ideas and judgment. Passive/Defensive cultures experience a lot of unresolved conflict and turnover and organizational members report lower levels of motivation and satisfaction.

The Aggressive/Defensive Cluster

The Aggressive/Defensive Cluster includes cultural norms that reflect expectations for members to approach tasks in ways that protect their status and security.

The Aggressive/Defensive cultural norms are:

- Oppositional
- Power
- Competitive
- Perfectionistic.

Organizations with Aggressive/Defensive cultures encourage or require members to appear competent, controlled and superior. Members who seek assistance, admit shortcomings, or concede their position are viewed as incompetent or weak. These organizations emphasize finding errors, weeding out "mistakes," and encouraging members to compete against each other rather than competitors. The short-term gains associated with these strategies are often at the expense of long-term growth.

Elements

G. Johnson described a cultural web, identifying a number of elements that can be used to describe or influence Organizational Culture:

- *The Paradigm*: What the organization is about; what it does; its mission; its values.
- *Control Systems*: The processes in place to monitor what is going on. Role cultures would have vast rulebooks. There would be more reliance on individualism in a power culture.

- *Organizational Structures*: Reporting lines, hierarchies and the way that work flows through the business.
- *Power Structures*: Who makes the decisions, how widely spread is power and on what is power based?
- *Symbols*: These include organizational logos and designs, but also extend to symbols of power such as parking spaces and executive washrooms.
- *Rituals and Routines*: Management meetings, board reports and so on may become more habitual than necessary.
- *Stories and Myths*: build up about people and events and convey a message about what is valued within the organization.

These elements may overlap. Power structures may depend on control systems, which may exploit the very rituals that generate stories which may not be true.

Organizational Culture and Change

There are a number of methodologies specifically dedicated to organizational culture change such as Peter Senge's *Fifth Discipline* and Arthur F Carmazzi's *Directive Communication.* These are also a variety of psychological approaches that have been developed into a system for specific outcomes such as the *Fifth Discipline's* "learning organization" or Directive *Communication's* "Corporate Culture Evolution." Ideas and strategies, on the other hand, seem to vary according to particular influences that affect culture.

Burman and Evans (2008) argue that it is 'leadership' that affects culture rather than 'management', and describe the difference. When one wants to change an aspect of the culture of an organization one has to keep in consideration that this is a long term project. Corporate culture is something that is very hard to change and employees need time to get used to the new way of organizing. For companies with a very strong and specific culture it will be even harder to change.

Cummings and Worley (2005, p. 491 – 492) give the following six guidelines for cultural change, these changes are in line with the eight distinct stages mentioned by Kotter (1995, p. 2)3:

1. Formulate a clear strategic vision (stage 1,2 & 3 of Kotter, 1995, p. 2).

   In order to make a cultural change effective a clear vision of the firm's new strategy, shared values and behaviours is needed. This vision provides the intention and direction for the culture change (Cummings & Worley, 2005, p.490).

2. Display Top-management commitment (stage 4 of Kotter, 1995, p. 2).

   It is very important to keep in mind that culture change must be managed from the top of the organization, as willingness to change of the senior management is an important indicator (Cummings & Worley, 2005, page 490). The top of the organization should be very much in favour of the change in order to actually implement the change in the rest of the organization. De Caluwé & Vermaak (2004, p 9) provide a framework with five different ways of thinking about change.

3. Model culture change at the highest level (stage 5 of Kotter, 1995, p. 2).

   In order to show that the management team is in favour of the change, the change has to be notable at first at this level. The behaviour of the management needs to symbolize the kinds of values and behaviours that should be realized in the rest of the company. It is important that the management shows the strengths of the current culture as well, it must be made clear that the current organizational does not need radical changes, but just a few adjustments. (See for more: (Deal and Kennedy, 1982; Sathe, 1983; Schall; 1983; Weick, 1985; DiTomaso, 1987).

4. Modify the organization to support organizational change.

   The fourth step is to modify the organization to support organizational change.

5. Select and socialize newcomers and terminate deviants (stage 7 and 8 of Kotter, 1995, p. 2).

   A way to implement a culture is to connect it to organizational membership, people can be selected and terminate in terms of their fit with the new culture (Cummings & Worley, 2005, p. 491).

6. Develop ethical and legal sensitivity.

   Changes in culture can lead to tensions between organizational and individual interests, which can result in ethical and legal problems for practitioners. This is particularly relevant for changes in employee integrity, control, equitable treatment and job security (Cummings and Worley, 2005, p. 491).

Change of culture in the organizations is very important and inevitable. Culture innovations is bound to be because it entails introducing something new and substantially different from what prevails in existing cultures. Cultural innovation is bound to be more difficult than cultural maintenance. People often resist changes hence it is the duty of the management to convince people that likely gain will outweigh the losses. Besides institutionalization, deification is another process that tends to occur in strongly developed organizational cultures. The organization itself may come to be regarded as precious in itself, as a source of pride and in some sense unique. Organizational members begin to feel a strong bond with it that transcends material returns given by the organization and they begin to identify with in. The organization turns into a sort of clan.

ENTREPRENEURIAL CULTURE

Stephen McGuire defined and validated a model of organizational culture that predicts revenue from new sources. An Entrepreneurial Organizational Culture (EOC) is a system of shared values, beliefs and norms of members of an organization, including valuing creativity and tolerance of creative people, believing that innovating and seizing market opportunities are appropriate behaviours to deal with problems of survival and prosperity, environmental uncertainty and competitors' threats and expecting organizational members to behave accordingly.

Elements of Entrepreneurial Culture

- People and empowerment focused.
- Value creation through innovation and change.
- Attention to the basics.
- Hands-on management.
- Doing the right thing.
- Freedom to grow and to fail.
- Commitment and personal responsibility.
- Emphasis on the future.

CRITICAL VIEWS

Writers from critical management studies have tended to express skepticism about the functionalist and unitarist views of culture put forward by mainstream management thinkers. Whilst not necessarily denying that organizations are cultural phenomena, they would stress the ways in which cultural assumptions can stifle dissent and reproduce management propaganda and ideology. After all, it would be naive to believe that a single culture exists in all organizations, or that cultural engineering will reflect the interests of all stakeholders within an organization. In any case, Parker has suggested that many of the assumptions of those putting forward theories of organizational culture are not new. They reflect a long-standing tension between cultural and structural (or informal and formal) versions of what organizations are. Further, it is perfectly reasonable to suggest that complex organizations might have many cultures, and that such sub-cultures might overlap and contradict each other. The neat typologies of cultural forms found in textbooks rarely acknowledge such complexities, or the various economic contradictions that exist in capitalist organizations.

One of the strongest and widely recognised criticisms of theories that attempt to categorize or 'pigeonhole' organizational culture is that put forward by Linda Smircich. She uses the metaphor of a plant root to represent culture, describing that it drives organizations rather than vice versa. Organizations are the product of organizational culture, we are unaware of how it shapes behaviour and interaction (also recognised through Scheins (2002) underlying assumptions) and so how can we categorize it and define what it is?

ORGANIZATIONAL COMMUNICATION PERSPECTIVE ON CULTURE

The organizational communication perspective on culture is divided into three areas:

- **Traditionalism** views culture through objective things such as stories, rituals and symbols.
- **Interpretivism** views culture through a network of shared meanings (organization members sharing subjective meanings).

- **Critical-Interpretivism** views culture through a network of shared meanings as well as the power struggles created by a similar network of competing meanings.

There are many different types of communication that contribute in creating an organizational culture:

- **Metaphors** such as comparing an organization to a machine or a family reveal employees' shared meanings of experiences at the organization.
- **Stories** can provide examples for employees of how to or not to act in certain situations.
- **Rites and ceremonies** combine stories, metaphors and symbols into one. Several different kinds of rites that affect organizational culture—
    - o *Rites of Passage*: employees move into new roles.
    - o *Rites of Degradation*: employees have power taken away from them.
    - o *Rites of Enhancement*: public recognition for an employee's accomplishments.
    - o *Rites of Renewal*: improve existing social structures.
    - o *Rites of Conflict Reduction*: resolve arguments between certain members or groups.
    - o *Rites of Integration*: reawaken feelings of membership in the organization.
- **Reflexive comments** are explanations, justifications and criticisms of our own actions. This includes—
    - o *Plans*: comments about anticipated actions.
    - o *Commentaries*: comments about action in the present.
    - o *Accounts*: comments about an action or event that has already occurred.

  Such comments reveal interpretive meanings held by the speaker as well as the social rules they follow.
- **Fantasy Themes** are common creative interpretations of events that reflect beliefs, values, and goals of the organization. They lead to rhetorical visions, or views of the organization and its environment held by organization members.

Schema

Schemata (plural of schema) are knowledge structures a person forms from past experiences allowing them to respond to similar events more efficiently in the future by guiding the processing of information. Schemata are created through interaction with others and thus inherently involve communication.

Stanley G. Harris argues that five categories of in organization schemata are necessary for organizational culture:

- *Self-in-Organization Schemata*: a person's concept of themselves within the context of the organization, including their personality, roles and behaviour.
- *Person-in-Organization Schemata*: a person's memories, impressions and expectations of other individuals within the organization.

- *Organization Schemata*: subset of person schemata, a person's generalized perspective on others as a whole in the organization.
- *Object/Concept-in-Organization Schemata*: knowledge an individual has of organization aspects other than other people.
- *Event-in-Organization Schemata*: a person's knowledge of social events within an organization.

All of these categories together represent a person's knowledge of an organization. Organizational culture is created when the schemata's of individuals within an organization come to resemble each other. This is primarily done through organizational communication as individuals directly or indirectly share knowledge and meanings.

MERGERS, ORGANIZATIONAL CULTURE AND CULTURAL LEADERSHIP

One of the biggest obstacles in the way of the merging of two organizations is organizational culture. Each organization has its own unique culture and most often, when brought together, these cultures clash. When mergers fail employees point to issues such as identity, communication problems, human resources problems, ego clashes and inter-group conflicts, which all fall under the category of "cultural differences". One way to combat such difficulties is through cultural leadership. Organizational leaders must also be cultural leaders and help facilitate the change from the two old cultures into the one new culture. This is done through cultural innovation followed by cultural maintenance.

- **Cultural Innovation Includes:**
  - o *Creating* a new culture: recognizing past cultural differences and setting realistic expectations for change.
  - o *Changing* the culture: weakening and replacing the old cultures.
- **Cultural Maintenance Includes:**
  - o *Integrating* the new culture: reconciling the differences between the old cultures and the new one.
  - o *Embodying* the new culture: establishing, affirming, and keeping the new culture.

Chapter 7

LEADERSHIP

WHAT IS LEADERSHIP?

Before entering upon a detailed study and discussion of it, it is necessary to determine what, leadership is. As usual, different scholars have defined it differently, each according to his own propensity. An investigation into these definitions will make the nature of leadership clear. Some important definitions are the following:

1. **According to Sprott.** "Any one who acts as a model to others is often called a leader." Sorott, W.G.H., Social Psychology, (1949) p. 71. According to this definition, leadership is attributed of that person who is an ideal for the other members of the group of wrestlers, while only a person acquainted with political techniques and means can lead a group of politicians. In both circumstances the term leader is used only for that individual who guides the others, or who is the ideal of others. It is only because he is the ideal that the other members of the group follow him naturally and it is due to this that he wields so much influence upon the other members. The followers of the leader acquiesce to the wishes of the leader. They want to apply his teachings, in their lives. They are even prepared to lay down their lives at his wish. According to Freud, the leader becomes the ego-ideal of the followers.
2. **According to Lapiere and Fransworth.** "Leadership is a behaviour that affects the behaviour of other people, more than their behaviour affects that of the leader." Laprere and Franworth, Social Psychology, (1949), p. 254. In every group every member bears some relation to the others all them influence and affect each other. In these mutual relationships and the mutual influences the individual who exerts the greater influence it is, in his turn, not influenced quite so much becomes the leader. In this way, then this definition sheds light upon the interaction between the leader and his followers. The leader leads, suggests, orders and guides. Other people follow him.

Putting it briefly; leader is that individual in the group who performs special tasks, makes suggestions, orders and shows the way, who appears before the others as the ideal, who is respected by all the others and whose suggestions and orders are implemented. Leadership is the term which denotes the behaviour or functions of this leader. In this way, the leader affects other individuals in such a way that they surrender themselves and follow his dictates. The process, of domination or dictatorship differs from that of leadership. In his book, Leadership or Domination, Pigors writes,

"Leadership is a process of control in which by the assumption of superiority a person or group regulates the activities of others for purposes of his own choosing." Pigors, Leadership or Domination (1935).

NATURAL OF LEADERSHIP

The nature of leadership is expressed and clarified by the various definitions given to it. An investigation to the status and the functions of the leader with in the group will be conducive to a better understanding of the nature of leadership. In this connection, it would be in keeping with the context of study to differentiate between a leader and an officiating individual or between a leader and the senior official.

Status and Functions of Leader within the Group

The leader occupies a special place within the group bears some specific relations to his followers. The important facts in this connection are the following:

1. *Leader is the Ideal of the Followers*: As has been stated earlier, only that person assumes the station of leader in any group who is the ideal of the other constituents and he retains his leadership only as long as the people continue to look upon him as the ideal.
2. *Leader is a Respected and Revered Person*: In order that he may be the ideal of the people of the group, it is essential that the leader be a person who commands respect and reverence. Generally the leader is as respected and revered as he is great.
3. *Leader is Shown Regard*: In the mutual behaviour and interaction between the leader and the followers, the latter manifest much regard for him and are even prepared to lay down their lives in preventing the leader from suffering, any injury. He does not have to coax or to persuade the followers to act on I his decisions. His word is law to them. This show of regard also has the effect of encouraging the leader and is constant reminder to him of his duty towards those who have placed so much trust in him.
4. *The Leader's Order is a Command*: Just is the child cannot disregard the order of the parent, the followers in a group cannot disregard the orders of the leader.
5. *Leader and the Followers Influence Each Other*: In studying the mutual behaviour between the leader and his followers it must be kept in mind that the influence is not entirely one sided. Both mutually influence each other, though of course in this mutual affect, the influence exerted by the leader is by far the greater. From this another fact that emerges is that a successful leader should make a constant note of the psychology of his followers. He should respect them and do nothing that can injure their feelings. It should be his constant endeavour to win their hearts rather than trying to display his power and influence. Only then can he hope to be their loved leader.
6. *Leader Determines the Group's Conduct*: All the members of the group obey and carry out the orders of the leader. In this way, the position of the leader in the group is central and the most superior. His followers are always turning to him and constantly attending to him. Whenever any difficulty is posed they turn to him expectantly for the solution and do

whatever he sees fit, It is in elucidating this very point that Seeman and Morris write, "One tentatively adoptable definition of leadership emphasizes its influence aspect, leadership acts are acts by persons which influence other persons in shared direction."

7. *Leader Controls the Other Members of the Group*: Every group is composed of many members. The process of leadership is determined by their specific kinds of relationships. In the words of Pigors, "Leadership is a concept applied to the personality-environment relation to describe the situation when a personality is so placed in the environment that his will, feeling and insight direct and control others in pursuit of a common cause."

8. *Leadership and office*: The foregoing treatment of the station and the functions of a leader in his group is enough to make it clear that leadership is dependent upon some personal and individual qualities and that it is distinct from office. It cannot be denied that an individual can became a leader with facility if he is occupying a high and important post. As Shartle and Stogdill have written, "Persons who occupy positions which are commonly presumed to demand leadership ability are proper and likely subjects for the study of leadership." But merely by his occupying an office that demands the qualities of leadership it cannot be concluded that the individual possesses the qualities usually found in a leader. It is, of course, necessary that if he is to continue in that post for long he must possess the requisite qualities. For example, if a person lacks the qualities of all army general he cannot successfully lead the army for long. On the other hand, the individual who possesses these qualities can become the general. It is only due to this difference in leadership and office that many so-called leaders are divested of their status, generals are murdered by their own armies while new persons come to the forefront in the leadership.

Difference between Leader and Officiating Head

In this way, leader differs from the officiating head. Roughly speaking, the difference between the two is the following:

1. *Difference in the Basis of Influence*: Both the leader and the official head influence other people but the basis of this influence in the two cases is different. The influence or authority of the officiating individual is, as is evidently indicated by his designation, by virtue of the office he occupies. Not so is the case with the leader. All the authority hat he weilds is only by virtue of his qualities of leadership.
2. *Difference in the Basis of Authority*: The leader, no less than the officiating head, weilds authority but this authority is obtained by the two through different media. The officiating head retains his authority by appointing individuals of his party at main and important centres and implementing his plans through them. On the other hand, the leader maintains his benevolent and loving authority over the constituents of his group by winning their hearts.
3. *Difference in Relation with Other Members of the Group*: Neither the leader nor the officiating head is an isolated entity. Both have relations with other people. The natures of these relationships are different. The officiating head only issues orders and does not

invite suggestions or take advice from others. The successful leader on the other hand, is suitably influenced by the views of other members of the group and is actively aware of them.

4. *Difference of Social Distance*: The social distance between the officiating head and his subordinates is considerable, due to which they go in awe of him. Not so .is the leader. Despite the respect and reverence lie is accustomed and entitled to demand, he mixes with his subordinates and does not maintain any social distance between them and himself. The officiating head tries to maintain this social distance while the leader tries to annihilate it if it dose exist.
5. *Difference in the Control of the Group*: Both the leader and the officiating head perform the task of controlling other individuals but the nature of this control differs. The control exercised by the officiating head is generally of a dominating nature whereas the leader of the group seeks to control his subordinates by demanding co-operation of them.
6. *Difference in Determining the Objectives of the Group*: It falls to the lot of the leader as well as the officiating head to formulate the objectives of his respective group but whereas the officiating head does not solicit the advice of even those to be affected by them the leader decides upon only such objectives that have the implicit sanction of his group and these are likely to be treated by the members of the group as the objectives near to their own hearts.

Types of Leadership

Different types of leadership have been described by different scholars, and this classification of leadership is made on bases which differ. The following are some of the main bases ?

(1) Origin of leadership

(2) Purpose of leadership

(3) Nature of leadership

(4) Nature of the relation of the leader with the followers.

The different types of leader in these various classes will now be described.

1. ***Classification on the Basis of Origin.*** The following types of leadership have been accepted in the classification based on origin. It need not be pointed out that a perusal of them will throw light on to , origin of leadership.

   (*a*) *Executive Appointed Leadership*: As is evident from the name given to this particular type of leader, he is appointed by the executive and his leadership stems from the office or post to which he is appointed by the executive. The class of government officers is of this type.

   (*b*) *Leader Appointed by Group*: These leaders are elected by the group. In India, the public leaders of panchayats, local groups, the Lok Sabha and the Rajya Sabha are elected by the group.

(*c*) *Self Appointed Leader*: But there are some leaders whose authority derives neither from the executive nor the group because it is not vested in them by these groups. They advance because of their individual qualities and having attained the central position, lead the people. They are also recognised as such because of their qualities. Leaders like Mahatma Gandhi, who were liked by the public, belong to this class. Here one may be assailed by the doubt that the self appointed leader may impose himself upon the public scene inspired by the desire for leadership. But, in actual fact, this is not inevitably so. Hence, the term self-appointed is employed merely to point to the fact that leadership or authority is not bestowed upon them by any electoral body but their leadership is accepted because of their personal qualities.

2. ***Classification on the Basis of Purpose.*** Leadership can also be classified on the basis of the purpose for which it is meant. Different groups make efforts for the achievement of different aims in their respective individual spheres. The individuals who appear to be the most qualified and the most resourceful in the attainment of these purposes are accepted as leaders in these respective spheres. There can undoubtedly be any number of spheres of this kind but here only the intellectual, the artistic and the executive will be described. In this way, this classification includes the following types of leadership:

(*a*) *Intellectual Leadership*: Intellectual leadership is needed in the intellectual field. In the fields of philosophy, science, etc., the greatest thinkers can be said to be the intellectual leaders because they show the way and the others follow them. Freud and Shankaracharya were leaders of this category.

(*b*) *Artistic Leadership*: In the field of art, only the great artists can provide the leadership. Artists like Tansen, Premchand and Ravindra Nath Tagore can be said to be leaders.

(*c*) *Executive Leadership*: In the sphere of administration it is the, authoritative personality who becomes the leader. For example, the District magistrate in every district is the leader of the district in the sphere of administration, and his orders are respected and carried out by every one.

3. ***Classification on the Basis of Nature of Leadership.*** Leadership, as found in different individuals is also classified on the basis of its nature. For example, some leaders are exclusively authoritarian while some others are more faithful to the democratic ideal. The following Ore the classes into which leadership is deviled on the basis of its nature -

(*a*) *Authoritarian Leader*: The authoritarian leader is an individual who likes to assert his authority. Hence, he conducts himself as his fancy takes him. He does not consult anyone else in taking decisions and leads by creating fear into the hearts of his followers and subordinates. He does not solicit co-operation but prefers to issue orders and punishes those who disobey him while those who fall into line with him are rewarded. He keeps all his authority in his hand and appoints reliable subordinates at crucial positions. Evidently, the leader of this kind is an officer and an authoritarian. And to be accurate, he should not be called a leader.

(*b*) *Democratic Leader*: This type of leader is of a democratic mould in his thoughts, modes of action and conduct. He takes advice from every one and is always anxious to enlist the co-operation of any one who is willing to give it. His leadership is based upon sympathy, belief and affection. He does not call himself a leader and neither dos he take all the authority into his own hands. With the authority vested in him he speaks of himself as the humble servant of the public.

4. ***Classification on the Basis of Nature of Relation with Followers.*** Leadership is classified also on the basis of the nature of the relation of the leader to his followers. The relations of the leader with his followers depend on the leader. They differ from leader to leader. Some leaders are connected with the executive, others are leaders because of their important position in the group, some are leaders because of their ability, efficiency or capability while others lead because of their ability in getting work done by their power of persuasion. The following are their classes

(*a*) *Institutional Leader*: In every institution, there is some individual who occupies the highest post, just as there is the Vice. Chancellor in a University who is looked upon as the highest official or supreme authority. His orders are appreciated and implemented because of the authority vested in his chair. Actually, the institutional leader is not leader but the officiating head.

(*b*) *Dominant Leader*: The dominant leader is so called because he maintains a relation of does and dominance with his followers or subordinates. He does not rule over them, however successful he may appear because of his power and authority.

(*c*) *Expert Leader*: In many spheres it is not unusual to see the most efficient and capable individuals becoming the leaders in their, own specialized field. The basis of their contact with their followers and subordinates is their special ability and efficiency. Leaders of this type do not put any premium on maintaining social contact with their followers, understanding them or even knowing their thoughts. Being specialists, people come to them for advice from time to time, respect their opinions and these experts show the way when difficulties crop up in others paths. Expert leaders are experts, and should not be considered as leaders.

(*d*) *Persuasive Leader*: The persuasive leaders win the heart of their followers and do their best to maintain the closest social contact with them. These are the real leaders. It is only this kind of individual who really exhibits all the qualities of leadership.

Qualities of Leadership

In the analysis of leadership, the greatest importance, from the practical viewpoint, is that of the qualities of leadership. While this knowledge of the qualities of a leader on the one hand reveals the kind of person the leader is, it also on the other hand, shows the qualities that an individual should posses if he wants to become a leader. Once again, different scholars have attributed different qualities to leaders. Some of the important views will be described here.

Constituents of Leadership

In connection with leadership, Pigors regards the following Constituents as indispensable-

1. Common cause 2. Leader

3. Follower 4. Present situation

Qualities of Leadership According to All Port:All port has included the following in the qualities of leadership

1. Trait of Ascendence 2. Physical power 3. High mobility 4. Erect, Aggressive carriage 5. Tonus 6. Tenacity 7. Face to face mode of address 8. Reinforcement of energy 9. Restraint 10. Inscrutability 11. Expansiveness in the field of action 12. High intelligence 13. Understanding 14. Keenly susceptible to social stimulation 15. Tact 16. Zeal 17. Social participation 18. Character. 19. Drive.

Coffin's classification-Charles Bird has recounted no less than 79 qualities in a leader, but in this long list many of the qualities have been repeated. Coffin has tried to place these qualities in some limited classes. According to Coffin, the qualities of a leader can be included *i.e.,* following classes-

1. *Intelligence*: Sliarp intellect, insight, intellectual for sighted nees, skill and acuity.
2. *Moral Sensitivity*: Honesty, justice, proper decision, benevolent viewpoint, moral outlook, selflessness, idealism and love of truth.
3. *Imagination*: Originality, imagination, foresight, curiosity, comprehensive interests and mental flexibility.
4. *Restraint*: Restraint, self-control and profundity.
5. *Drive and Determination*: Inspiration, enthusiasm, mobile or dynamic personality, candidness, aggression, desire of name and fame, bravery, determination, patience, concentration, the tendency to pursue to an end.
6. *Responsibility*: Respected, candid, charactered, believable, organised, aware of duties, lover of work, concentrated.
7. *Self Reliance*: Awareness of purpose and direction, self reliance, confidence, the ability to take decision, enthusiasm and, unvarying decision.
8. *Dynamic Physical Characteristics*: Physical power, shape, ability, tonus, straight body, etc.
9. *Imperturbability*: balance, optimism, benevolence, patience, decisiveness, energy and positive nature.
10. *Social Responsiveness*: Adaptability of social motivation taking part in social activities, friendliness, affection, sociability, extrovert tendency and influence on others.
11. *Easy Maintenance of Good Relation with Others*: Acuity, sympathy, co-operation, humanity and a knowledge of human nature.

Coffin has further made these 11 classes even more brief by dividing all the qualities into the following classes-

1. *Planning*: 1. The ability to know problems. 2. The ability to evolve plans for solving these problems.
2. *Organization*: 3. The ability to organise the necessary objects and individuals to ensure the success of these plans. 4. The ability to organise the entire system and have it function as one unit. 5. The ability to introduce sudden changes.
3. *Persuation*: 6. The ability of distributing responsibility among different individuals for the implentation of the plan. 7. The ability of successfully examining the entire plan. 8. The ability of keeping his own control on the entire organization.

All Qualities are Needed for Leadership

From the various opinions on the different qualities of leadership which have been hither to described, it is evident that it is not efficient for the leader to be the master of only physical qualities. Here it must be remembered that in the animal world the most powerful animal is the leader but in human society physical prowess alone 1, not sufficient. Yet, the importance of the qualities of physical Power and an attractive personality is not inconsiderable. One can often see intellectual ability and an attractive physical personality going together in the human leader. By his studies, Partridge has proved that all the individuals who scored the highest in the army Alpha tests were tall, attractive and of an independent nature. This view, held by Partridge is one-sided, because one often finds a complete lack of physical charm in intellectual giants and leaders. One only need be reminded of Socrates and Chanakya. On the other hand, it would, be equally incorrect and baseless to state that in the modern world only intellectual achievements are enough to bring leadership to an individual. Actually in order to become a leader, an individual should be possessed of many qualities of the personality and in particular, skill in behaving, in addition to physical and intellectual qualities.

Education for Leadership

But the mere fact of the existence of these qualities in an individual is not a sufficient insurance of successful leadership. It is true that the leader possesses in innate form the qualities of leadership, but Plato observed correctly that lie also requires to be educated. In a democracy, leaders can be discovered and created through education and public programmes. For this, responsible tasks should be entrusted to the men and women of the younger generation. They should be given the opportunity of coming forward and expressing themselves. Youth festivals should be organised in order that the youngsters, may be able to display their qualities. In this way, when there will always be new leaders to replace the older and retiring leaders, the society and the nation will be able to progress constantly and at a fast pace.

Chapter 8 GROUP DYNAMICS

GROUP

It is significant to say that a same group has been an important research area for a social psychologist, because it has been realized that social psychological problems arising from the larger society will not be formidable, if the problems of small groups are solved. From another point of view, the importance of groups is clear. Our relations with other individuals take place within a group.

Study of the group is concerned with the problem of how "the behaviour of an individual is altered by the actual presence of others".

There are variety of definitions regarding the constitution of groups but all of them agree that some degree of interaction must be there in the group. An example can be given from Sharif as follows: a group is a social unit which consists of a number of individuals who stand in definite status and role relationships to one another and which possess a set of values or norms of its own regulating the behaviour of individual members, at least in matters of consequence to the group.

In the above definition, the term 'status' and 'role' have been used these require artification. Status applies to position in the social group and the other to the behaviour that goes along with that position. For example, a father "as head of a household" has a role iron mode of behaviour which he must act out in that status.

Burgess has given briefer definition than that of above definition of Sharif, he regards the group as a "unity of interacting personalities."

The definition given by Newcomb occupies middle position between the above two definitions. Newcomb says, "A group consists of two or more persons who share norms about certain thins with one another and whose social roles are closely interlocking."

It is manifest from the above definition, that group is made up of two or more individuals who interact in order to achieve a goal. They have their own personalities, statuses auld role which have no meaning apart from the group of which individuals are members.

As regards *classification of groups*, it can be said at the outset that Gestalt psychologists were opposed to the classification of groups because they felt that they were obstacles in scientific thinking. But Dr. Brown' presented a contrary notion by lying that descriptive classifications are the starting point in science. Thus, in describing social groups, we find that they can be classified in many ways:

1. *Size* can be the basis of classification. For example, the groups may be of two individuals or it may be as large as the nation.
2. *Permanence* can be the basis of classification as groups may be permanent and they may be temporary. In the former the importance is given to mutual cooperation while it is absent in the latter. Example of permanent group is state or city while that of temporary group is crowd or mob.
3. *Determinants* can be the basis of classification. Say, blood relationship is the arsis as family. In the determinant features may be oddly characteristics as on the basis of age and sex.
4. *Organization* is the basis of classification. It may be psychological and social. According to Krech and Crutchfield, the criteria for the psychological group are two: (1) "All the members exist as a group in the psychological field of each individual *i.e.,* be perceived and reacted to as a group; (2) the various members must be in dynamic infection with one another." on the other hand, social organizations are groups "characterized by the possession of the following: (1) Cultural products such as buildings, robes, prayers, magic formulas, songs); (2) collective name or symbol; (3) distinctive action patterns; (4) a common belief system ; and (5) enforcing agents or techniques."
5. *Specific kinds of interpersonal techniques* are the bases for categorizing groups. One such classification has been presented by Krout on the lines of the sociologist park: (*a*) parasitism-a predatory relationship, examples are found in animal societies; (*b*) commensalisms-association without contractual relationships such as people who "eat the same table", and students in college class; (*c*) mutualism-a contractual relationship, namely servant and master in a household; and (*d*) sociality-interdependence and intercommunication of equals, as in marriage, friendship or a business partnership, (the highest form of social grouping and the one best manifested consensus, esprit de corps and morale).
6. *Primary and Secondary Groups Classification*: This type of classification has been proposed by Cooley (social organization, 1909). By the primary groups he means those groups which are characterized by intimate face-to-face cooperation found in the family, neighbourhood and play group. In primary groups there is close physical proximity and warm emotional tone. Secondary groups refer to those groups where contact between individuals is more impersonal more indirect, less frequent, or removed in space or time. Examples are one's political party, state or nation.

   The primary and secondary groups can be contrasted from the point of view of relative characteristics as follows: Primary groups are: small in size, there is face-to-face relationship in them, there is close intimacy among members while in the secondary group we find that they are large in size, there is indirect relationship among members, there is lack of intimacy of relationship, there is no identity of ends and relations of.. members are impersonal.

In modern sociology/ the distinction between primary and secondary group recurs again and again. Durkheim has spoken or 'mechanistic society' which represents blood group or primitive society where ties are based on kinship or on some other intimacy. But, in the 'organic society' formalized aspects of secondary groups are seen, and behaviour is controlled by laws. In the former, the membership is involuntary, while in the latter it is a matter of free choice.

7. *In-groups and Out-Groups Classification*: This classification has been suggested by Sumner. These may be called majority and minority groups. Many years ago, Sumner coined the term 'ethnocentrism' for the view that one's group is the centre of everything, it is superior and that its folkways are the only right ones. The equivalent term for ethnocentrism is patriotism. The group to which the individual is patriotic and accepts its norm is know as in-group to him. Thus the group to which the person belong and with which he identifies himself is known as in group, Other identified people are as members of out-groups. The boundaries are further sharpened if the interests of groups come in conflict so that in-group and the out-group come into competition. Feuds between family group and political battles between. Parties in power and the party seeking power represent in- group-out-group conflict. Caste and class distinction are fundamentally based on in-and out-grouping. In the Second World War, the Britishers used to say, "We are the short, selected few and let rest be damned." This statement exemplifies in-and out-group destination.
8. *Membership and References Groups*: A new distinction has been made between 'membership' and 'references' groups. The distinction was first proposed by Hyman. Membership groups are those groups to which the child actually belongs, like his family or play group. Reference group are those to which he aspires or 'refers', himself which may or may not be the same as the membership groups. Hyman: (The Psychology of Status, 1942) A child is motivated by the desire to be-long and to gain prestige among his peers, he learns or introjects the group norms and standards. These determine the structure of his ego and the nature of his ego-involvements, which in turn affect his personality and his relationship to other persons and groups.

CHARACTERISTICS OF GROUPS

Groups have many properties or characteristics; structure, structure status patterning, in-group feelings and role expectancy. In addition to these characteristics of groups are below: (1) Size, (2) Conformity, (3) Cohesiveness, and (4) group effectiveness .

Size. It can be said without hesitation that size of a group determines its structuring and functioning to a large extent. One study was made by Simmel on the dyad (twosome) as compared to tryad'(threesome). He found that the group of three was unstable because of tendency for two to combine their forces against a third party. After this conflict, the two would show greater bond because of common object of opposition. Later on, Mills wanted to test this hypothesis. He arranged for groups of three to work on given intellectual task, he saw that there was a tendency for the trial to break down in a power structure with a dyad working against a third party. It is important to realize that size of the group can be related to the purposes or function of the group.

Conformity. It has been seen that conformity is a fundamental need, whether it may be in manners, food, or politics. Kline berg proposes four main reasons for customary conformity:

(*a*) *Prestige*: Suggestion which means that the group has power and importance, and ideas coming from it will be accepted.

(*b*) The individual often knows no other customs than those of his own community.

(*c*) The individual who does not practice the customary behaviour related to the social and economic life of the group will soon be regarded as outside the system of- reciprocal rights and duties upon which life in the community may depend.

(*d*) There may be punishment for violation. This punishment may be coercive in nature.

These four factors together make it possible to understand why individuals conform, without the necessity of assuming that custom itself has power and authority.

GROUP COHESIVENESS

This is most significant ingredient in group structure. The principal element in this unit consensus among members. Consensus may be thought of not only a 'thinking together' but also working together, joint involvement on the part of members of group. Cohesiveness is also a function of a number of factors, such as cooperativeness, affiliative needs, social facilitation, and other motives and processes. Determinants of cohesiveness may be physical as in a housing project studied, It was found that the occupants formed friendships on the basis of (1) physical distance with those living nearest them and (2) functional distance-direction of the adjacent home; preference being for those living opposite rather than alongside.

GROUP EFFECTIVENESS

Effectiveness may be defined in terms of productivity. It has been observed that productivity rises in a group setting because of social facilitation, In some cases, it has been seen that productivity may not lead to maximum satisfaction of group members, since their status or affiliative needs may not be satisfied. If the goal of a group is morale, or psychological wellbeing of the members, effectiveness may be differently defined from the way it is when productivity is the end result. However, morale and productivity are positively related.

SOCIOMETRY

Sociometry deals with one very important aspect of personality; how the person affects others. According to William James we have as many selves as there are people who recognize us. The reason is that our 'self' is in large part how we affect others. Later on, a psychologist Mark. May once defined personality as "social stimulus value."

Socially oriented psychiatrist, Moreno coined the tern sociometry for his technique. He used this technique for the betterment of interpersonal relations. He asked each girl at Hudson Training school to name the girls she preferred to eat with, work with, and live with, and which ones she wished to avoid. From the data obtained by him he constructed 'sociograms' showing the patterns of attractions and repulsions. Such sociograms revealed isolate and leaders. A simple example of a sociogram's given below:

The sociometric technique was found to be useful in many ways.

For example, by its use individuals could be rearranged into congenial groups for the sake of living, eating an working together. This technique was also found to be valuable or the study of leadership.

Many psychologists and social scientists have used Moreno technique for the study and improvement of social relations within groups. In recent years psychodrama and sociodrama have developed the technique of sociometry and they are very valuable techniques for depicting maladjustive roles and for producing better type of intragroup relationship.

GROUP DYNAMICS

Group dynamics is the study of the nature of groups. This field of investigation seeks 'to learn more about how groups develop and function and what factors affect the relationships which exit between groups and individuals, or other groups.

Social psychologists began to seek the effects of family, club, play group, gang and other groups upon the needs, attitudes, value and frustrations of their members, and upon their social behaviour. During war Lewin. Studied how food consumption habits might be changed by group discussion, as opposed to more traditional lecture method, compared experimental groups (group discussion) and control unit groups (Lecture) and found that ten times as many women in the former as letter changed their habits, on the basis of participation and discussion.

Group dynamics has developed out of Gestalt psychology, particularly through the work of Lewin. Now, it has become a fully grown movement, it was the belief of Lewin that life; by nature is dynamic, "flows on but keeps a recognizable form". Lewin opened a centre at the Michigan University. Its aim is to find out the laws of group behaviour, and other small groups with an idea to develop their productivity and efficiency.

Group dynamics is the study of groups, and also a general term for group processes. Relevant to the fields of psychology, sociology, and communication studies, a group is two or more individuals who are connected to each other by social relationships. Because they interact and influence each other, groups develop a number of dynamic processes that separate them from a random collection of individuals. These processes include norms, roles, relations, development, need to belong, social influence, and effects on behaviour. The field of group dynamics is primarily concerned with small group behaviour. Groups may be classified as aggregate, primary, secondary and category groups.

In Organizational Development (OD), or group dynamics, the phrase "group process" refers to the understanding of the behaviour of people in groups, such as task groups, that are trying to solve a problem or make a decision. An individual with expertise in 'group process, such as a trained facilitator, can assist a group in accomplishing its objective by diagnosing how well the group is functioning as a problem-solving or decision-making entity and intervening to alter the group's operating behaviour.

Because people gather in groups for reasons other than task accomplishment, group process occurs in other types of groups such as personal growth groups (*e.g.*, encounter groups, study groups, prayer groups). In such cases, an individual with expertise in group process can be helpful in the role of facilitator.

Well researched but rarely mentioned by professional group workers, is the social status of people within the group (*i.e.*, senior or junior). The group leader (or facilitator) will usually have a strong influence on the group due to his or her role of shaping the group's outcomes. This influence will also be affected by the leader's sex, race, relative age, income, appearance, and personality, as well as organizational structures and many other factors.

KEY THEORISTS

Gabriel Tarde's Les lois de I' imitation (1890) (translated as the Law oflmitation1903) conceives sociology as based on small psychological interactions among individuals (as in a chemical compound), the fundamental forces being imitation and innovation.

Gustave Le Bon was a French social psychologist whose seminal study, The Crowd: A Study of the Popular Mind (1896) led to the development of group psychology.

Sigmund Freud's Group Psychology and the Analysis of the Ego, (1922) based on a critique of Le Bon's work, led to further development in theories of group behaviour in the latter half of the twentieth century.

Kurt Lewin (1943, 1948, 1951) is commonly identified as the founder of the movement to study groups scientifically. He coined the term group dynamics to describe the way groups and individuals act and react to changing circumstances.

William Schutz (1958, 1966) looked at interpersonal relations from the perspective of three dimensions: inclusion, control, and affection. This became the basis for a theory of group behaviour that sees groups as resolving issues in each of these stages in order to be able to develop to the next stage. Conversely, a group may also devolve to an earlier stage if unable to resolve outstanding issues in a particular stage.

Wilfred Bion (1961) studied group dynamics from a psychoanalytic perspective, and stated that he was much influenced by Wilfred Trotter for whom he worked at University College Hospital London, as did another key figure in the Psychoanalytic movement, Ernest Jones. He discovered several mass group processes which involved the group as a whole adopting an orientation which, in his opinion, interfered with the ability of a group to accomplish the work it was nominally engaged in. His experiences are reported in his published books, especially Experiences in Groups. The Tavistock Institute has further developed and applied the theory and practices developed by Bion.

Bruce Tuckman (1965) proposed the four-stage model called Tuckman's Stages for a group. Tuckman's model states that the ideal group decision-making process should occur in four stages:

- Forming (pretending to get on or get along with others)
- Storming (letting down the politeness barrier and trying to get down to the issues even if tempers flare up)
- Norming (getting used to each other and developing trust and productivity)
- Peiforming (working in a group to a common goal on a highly efficient and cooperative basis).

Tuckman later added a fifth stage for the dissolution of a group called adjourning.

(Adjourning may also be referred to as mourning, *i.e.,* mourning the adjournment of the group). It should be noted that this model refers to the overall pattern of the group, but of course individuals within a group work in different ways. If distrust persists, a group may never even get to the norming stage.

M. Scott Peck developed stages for larger-scale groups (*i.e.*, communities) which are similar to Tuckman's stages of group development.AI Peck describes the stages of a community as:

- Pseudo-community
- Chaos
- Emptiness
- True Community.

Communities may be distinguished from other types of groups, in Peck's view, by the need for members to, eliminate barriers to communication in order to be able to form true community. Examples of common barriers are: expectations and preconceptions; prejudices; ideology, counterproductive norms, theology and solutions; the need to heal, convert, fix or solve and the need to control. A community is born when its members reach a stage of "emptiness" or peace.

DIMENSIONS OF GROUP PROCESS

Aspects of group process include:

- Patterns of communication and coordination
- Patterns of influence

- Roles / relationship
- Patterns of dominance (*e.g.*, who·leads, who defers)
- Balance of task focus vs social focus
- Level of group effectiveness how conflict is handled
- Emotional state of the group as a whole, what Wilfred Bion called basic assumptions.

Groups of individuals gathered together to achieve a goal or objective, either as a committee or some other grouping, go through several predictable stages before useful work can be done. These stages are a function of a number of variables, not the least of which is the self-identification of the role each member will tend to play, and the emergence of natural leaders and individuals who will serve as sources of information. Any individual in a leadership position whose responsibilities involve getting groups of individuals to work together should both be conversant with the phases of the group process and possess the skills necessary to capitalize on these stages to accomplish the objective of forming a productive, cohesive team.

Various theories of group development exist. The model below combines elements of theories by Jones (1973), Tuckman (1965), and Banet (1976). In this model, each phase of group development is looked at with respect to group members' concerns with task and personal relations (process) functions.

Phase	*Task Functions*	*Personal Relations Functions*
1	Orientation	Testing and Dependence
2	Organizing to Get Work Done	Intragroup Conflict
3	Information-Flow	Group Cohesion
4	Problem-Solving	Interdependence

APPLICATION

Group dynamics form a basis for group therapy, often with therapeutic approaches that are formed of groups such as family therapy and the expressive therapies. Politicians and sales personnel may use their knowledge of the principles of group dynamics to aid their cause. Increasingly, group dynamics are of interest in light of online social interaction and virtual communities made possible by the internet.

Unit III

Chapter 9

THE WORK ENVIRONMENT

In different factories, offices and other professional premises, the worker is compelled to work under certain conditions examples of which are innumerable. He may be required to continue his effort of a definite kind, in some specific place. His health stands to be influenced greatly by virtue of the fact whether his place of work is adequate and properly ventilated or not. Provision of adequate lighting is an essential condition, and one which justifiably occupies the worker's mind, since it will influence his eyesight, thereby his fatigue and consequently his efficiency and the quality of his output. It is well known that noise can be a disturbing element, and may put out off one's work. One of the conditions of work is that there be little if any noise; hence this must be taken into consideration. Temperature or the climate is another factor that influences the potential of a worker, as it is known that in certain temperatures a worker cannot work well while in a more moderate or suitable temperature his work takes a turn for the better. Temperature also must be taken into consideration when looking out for the place of work. In addition to these physical conditions, there are many other psychological conditions that also influence the worker and consequently his work. Of these, some are the behaviour of those in authority, mutual relationship among the workers, their respective family lives; incentives to work, etc.

In this manner, the conditions of work can be divided into two classes:

1. Physical conditions
2. Psychological conditions

Of the physical condition, the main ones are:

1. Intencity, location, distribution and colour of light
2. Temperature
3. Ventilation
4. Noise
5. Working Hours
6. Rest Pauses
7. Music
8. Other Physical Conditions.

Of the psychological conditions that affect work, the main are:

1. Behaviour of the Authorities
2. Mutual Relations of the Employees
3. Security
4. Satisfaction of Needs
5. Incentives.

PHYSICAL CONDITIONS OF WORK

1. **Intencity, Location, Distribution and Colour of Light.** The kind and intensity of light differs with the occupation that they have adopted. As a normal rule, individuals over 35 require light of a greater intensity than their younger counterparts. If the objects handled are minute, then, naturally, the light must be fairly birth while in work where objects handled are of a large size, and the workers are fairly young, intense light is not necessary. Light provided should never be intense enough to cause glare, and never dim enough to cause strain in concentrating upon an object to be worked. Work that requires light of high intensity also requires the use of special protective glasses, as is the case with welding where the light of a very high intensity is produced by the welding flame. Protection from its harmful effects is achieved by the use of coloured glasses.

   The source of light should be so located as to avoid falling directly upon the eyes; instead, it should fall on the instrument that is to be manipulated and then also in a manner to avoid all reflection into the eyes of the person handling it. Hence, light should be evenly distributed and for this, tubelighting has been found to be superior to bulb lamps, which are now considered obsolete.

   Daylight is naturally uniform in its distribution; it is only when the work is done at night that the problem of uniform and even lighting arises, and it is a problem that requires expert handling and planning.

   Besides the intensity and location of light, it is necessary to pay attention to its colour. It has been uniformly experienced in a large number of cases that light that resembles daylight very nearly is the best and most beneficial. Hence, white light has been considered the most superior. And in colour light, the best is a light yellow but a healthy yellow and not a sickly pale yellow. All other coloured lights harm the eyes in some measure.

2. **Temperature.** Temperature of the working premises has considerable and direct influence on the worker's health, it having been found that working in too high or too low temperatures leads to disease and accident. Proper temperature maintains good health in the workers, and reduces the number of accidents as external conditions do not divert the attention of the worker and thus reduce his efficiency. H.M.Vernon found that in the British mines, in temperatures about 70° Fahrenheit there were greater number of accidents while the

perception and sensibility of workers also adversely affected. Extreme temperatures in working areas cause discomfort to the worker, so much so that the quantity as well as quality of his output is reduced. Temperature further influences the ventilation in a room, as it is essential for proper ventilation and flow of air to have only an adequate temperature.

3. **Ventilation.** Inflow of fresh air is essential in a place of work, as its absence tends to increase the fatigue and laziness or drowsiness of the workers. Air easily becomes contaminated in places where a large number of individuals work together, such as mines, factories and offices. For this the use of exhaust fans is particularly desirable. Transport should be freely and easily available in places of work. Health is adversely affected if the percentage of oxygen in air is varied even within very narrow limits. According to Poffenberger, when the percentage of oxygen in air tends to fall below 10, the workers show signs of adverse effect. Ventilation also influences the body temperature of the workers, and if the body temperature varies it leads to fatigue and drowsiness. Another important factor is the presence as well as percentage of humidity in the air. Excessive humidity is undeniably a very harmful influence.
4. **Noise.** Excessive noise normally distracts attention and obstructs smooth working. It is for this reason that in every industry now attention is paid to the noise produced, and efforts are made to curb noises that distract attention. But noise of a continuous nature is often to be more soothing than disturbing, and when it is discontinued it disturbs the attention of people used to it. The truth of the matter is that only excessive noise is harmful and has the worst effect on the auditory system. Keeping in mind these observations, efforts should be made to regulate noise.
5. **Hours of Work.** Professions in which the hours of work are so long and so unhygienically planned that worker is completely fatigued by the time he stops working, find themselves confronted with the problem of continuously decreasing efficiency among their staff. In addition to this, these profession become prey to all kinds of very serious problems of human relationships. When a worker is compelled to work for long hours beyond his physical endurance limits, he becomes diseased and loses his efficiency. Besides, his irritability increases significantly. For this reason, in most progressive nations, the government promulgates certain orders whereby the hours of work for different occupations, for individuals of different ages and of different sexes, are determined. If need for more work arises, the employer is faced either with the alternative of indulging in illegal activity or remunerating the worker for his extra labour. But if he chooses to evade these laws, he incurs the displeasure of the law, and this is never to his advantage.
6. **Rest Pauses.** Whatever the ability and endurance of an individual, even if he be abnormal in this respect, he cannot work continuously for long periods of time. After a certain period of time he feels the need for a rest, and his need has been found to have psychological justification as it has been found that better results can be obtained by working in shifts and periods than by working continuously. Increases of between ten and twenty per cent in production have been found to occur as a result of provision of rest in between work. The

length and frequency of rest that is required depends upon the nature of work, the endurance and age of the worker and the general conditions of work. Hard work requires relatively longer and greater number of rest pauses. Similarly women, young children and old people require longer and greater number of rest pauses, than young men. Nowadays, in practically every profession and occupation, rests of 15 minutes to an hour are provide once or more so that the worker may be able to take refreshments and restore his vitality otherwise. Rest in between hours of work not only removes fatigue, it also eliminates the elements of monotony and boredom, there by regenerating enthusiasm and vitality.

7. **Music.** One of the conditions of work taken into consideration is music. From their experiments W.A. Keir and H.C. Smith concluded that music has a beneficial and desirable influence upon the mental condition of workers, and thus it helps to induce some increase in their productive capacity. And one often sees people singing at their work, a phenomenon particularly obvious in the case of Indian woman working at the grinder or in the fields or even when at their domestic chores. The rhythm in music has a beneficial effect on the rate of working. Tata in India provide music in their various factories. In western countries, particularly in the United States, the use of music in factories and other working places is steadily on the increase. Through a questionnaire H.C. Smith collected the views of one thousand workers regarding the provision of music in working places, and found that as many as 98 per cent of them were in favour of it, as they found considerable pleasure in it. The influence of music on routine work is as yet under extensive study.
8. **Other Physical Conditions.** In addition to these above conditions, there are other physical and material considerations which influence the worker and his work. For example, if there is good and clean provision of urinals, latrines, bathrooms, refreshment rooms, canteen, etc., the worker's time in the office becomes more pleasant, and many of his difficulties arc removed. A place of work should not be foul smelling, neither should it be dirty or dusty, as any of these conditions disgusts the worker.

PSYCHOLOGICAL CONDITIONS OF WORK ENVIRONMENT

Of the psychological conditions of work the more important have the following influences:

1. **Behaviour of Those in Authority.** A worker's mind is very susceptible of the behaviour of his boss. If the behaviour of authorities is desirable and good, the worker's enthusiasm and interest in his work is maintained, but if their behaviour is bad and inconsiderate, it is potentially a dangerous state as it can lead to conflict and unnecessary tension that has the worst effect upon production. Good behaviour does not imply laxity in administration and in dealing with the workers, as in such circumstances it is inevitable that the lazy and designing individuals in the organization will have a field day and do no work at all. It is essential that constant attention be paid to the worker's performance, but tact and diplomacy should be employed if it becomes necessary to point out his shortcomings. Senior officials

and employers who are in the habit of constantly haranguing and bickering with their staff, are very often faced with continuous conflict and non-co-operation. Employees are not inclined to respect and work for people who are irritable, highly inflammable and ingratiating types. Working under a considerate individual not only keeps the worker happy but also inspires him to work more and work better.

2. **Mutual Relations of Workers.** One of the psychological conditions of working is the nature of relations that exist between the workers themselves. Where the number of workers is fairly large, and that nature of work demands their constant cooperation, better results are obtained if the workers have happy relations. If the relations are not all can be desired, work suffers. And particularly work that requires comparative effort is a total loss as there is no cooperation.
3. **Security in Profession.** If the worker is confident that he is secure in his job, then his work shows definite improvements. If a profession that offers no security of employment, or in a position in which one can never be confident of remaining safe, a worker cannot work with enthusiasm or with his mind on the work. Hence, a profession must offer security of future employment. After a certain predetermined period of service has been completed, the worker should be made permanent in his position, as is now done in all government jobs and many laws regarding such employment procedure. Besides this minimal security of profession, other inducements are insurance during unemployment, old age insurance, and security of insurance in the event of accidents that render the individual incapable of further work. Nowadays, in all progressive states, government and other general employers make provision for these benefits, as in their absence it only natural for the worker to spend time in wondering about his future and making efforts to secure it, efforts that enfeeble him for his regular work.
4. **Satisfaction of Life's Needs.** Every individual has some personal and other family requirements, such as adequate food and housing for his family, and purchasing power to the extent of his other reasonable needs. Besides this, there are certain needs that foster self-respect, and these, too, cannot be neglected. Progress has made it necessary for employers to pay attention to these aspects of the human personality also. Consequently, they have to initiate and finance certain schemes of labour welfare that involve some expenditure, but which provide many direct and indirect benefits to the worker that place him in a very favourable state of mind. Their needs being fulfilled, they are inclined to respect and obey their employers, to work for their better being in turn. They have confidence in their employers, and thus they are never induced to work contrary to the interests of their employers.
5. **Incentive in Industry.** Motives have an important place in the life of man. In the absence of a motive no individual can either work hard or do anything to better his lot in life or improve his work in any way. Inspiration of this kind is available to the individual in his trade in the form of various kinds of incentives such as increase in wages, praise by authorities, promotion, bonus, etc. Incentives are now an important part of any geared up

industry. In most progressive nations, the workers stand to benefit through bonus if the production, and thus the earning, of their enterprise, goes up. In most professions, an individual is promoted to a senior position if he shows satisfactory or more than satisfactory work. If the people in authority are sensible, they will always praise the extra efforts of their subordinates. Their wages can also be increased so as to form an extra inducement.

All the aforementioned physical and psychological conditions have considerable importance for commerce and industry. And psychologists have now seriously drawn the attention of the industrialists to this aspect. It is necessary not only in regard to economic or fiscal gain, but also with regard to humanity that the workers should have the opportunity to work in beneficial conditions, both physical and psychological. Workers being part and parcel of the fiber of the nation, the government also should take steps to have such conditions created. When such a system is in existence in industry, the conflicts are materially reduced and the production materially increased with the result that the employer, the employee and the state all benefit.

CHANCES OF PROMOTION

Every employee wishes that at various stages of his service he be given chances of promotion and progress. Promotion involves change in status or position of authority within the official structure. In every profession and occupation, the services are graded in one definite order. In administrative services, for example, the deputy collector supersedes the tehsildar while he in his turn is superseded by the collector. Above the collector is the commissioner while he is ruled over by the governor. Similarly, in the army, there are various posts, such as second-lieutenant, captain, major, lieutenant colonel, etc. In every profession, the higher post or status carries greater salary as well as greater authority with a correspondingly greater responsibility. Hence, it is only natural that every individual should wish to occupy as high a post as is within his grasp.

KIND OF PROMOTION

But promotion should not be taken to imply only the gaining of a higher post. Although that precisely is the sense in which it is usually interpreted, yet the term should be more properly used to include all increase in pay increase in leave, improved conditions of work, increases in respect and honour, etc., Walters has described the following eight kinds of promotion:

1. Increase in wages, salary or remuneration
2. Increase in position, authority or responsibility
3. Increase in leave or decrease in hours of work
4. Transfer to a better place or department
5. Improvement in place of residence or of working
6. Opportunities of gaining training and experience becoming available

7. Greater security of position of benefit
8. Increase in the period of service.

In this manner, then if the worker's salary or remuneration is increased, he will be deemed to have been promoted. He will equally be deemed to have benefited in the same manner if he is given a higher position, greater authority or responsibility. He may be compelled to work for fewer hours. Or, in others works, time available for recreation will have been increased, whereby he stands promoted. As an indication of promotion, an individual may be transferred to a better place or to another department considered better. Services or employments that involve transfer of employees from one place to another make use of this device to promote their personnel. Seeing that a particular person is good at his work, he can be shown signs of favour by improving his working conditions or by improving his place of residence. Employees who work well are given chances of gaining further training and obtaining additional experience. In almost all services, if the employee continues to show satisfactory progress and work for a certain pre-determined period after his appointment thereto, his post is made permanent and secure. Security of employment is another form in which promotion may be indicated. When individuals show a consistently good record of work, their period of work of service is increased. In many cases, People are re-employed after having been officially retired from service, when they complete their tenure.

From among the various forms or kinds of promotion described above, different individuals favour different kinds, relative to the various professions. Some people place the highest premium upon economic gain while others find more value in increased respect and honour. Improvement in the conditions of work is another mode of promotion that is dear to some individuals. And it is equally inessential that in some specific context only one form of promotion may be awarded. In vary many cases, promotion leads to increased wages, authority and responsibility as well as better conditions in more forms than one.

BASES OF PROMOTION

In every profession there are some definite laws governing, just as there are definite ways of selection and appointment. One of the commonest methods of promotion is that of seniority in which every employee is promoted after he has put in a definite period of work in one situation. But, equally, in almost all services, attention is paid to the individual's ability when he is being considered for promotion, over and above the extent of his service. It sometimes occurs that an individual's ability and efficiency is so great that he is given promotion by superseding other senior officials. Private business lays much stress on work as well as on ability. The employer stands to gain something if his employees work better and more, so that he is easily enabled to enhance their wages or to give them a greater share in the profits. But in certain occupations, inside and outside the government structure, where the employer himself does not superintend the work, or where there is no objective of the employer himself, or where the employer is of the ingratiating type, promotion depends more on pleasing authority than upon seniority, ability or results obtained. In professions in which there are no definite laws and rules governing promotion of workers, promotion takes place through the pleasure of those in authority.

From the above description, it is evident that promotion depends upon the following factors:

1. Seniority
2. Ability
3. Better and more work
4. Kindness of the authorities.

1. **Promotion of the Basis of Seniority.** In most occupations and services, wages of the employee increase somewhat every year, and thus seniority is a basis of promotion common to almost all occupations. Seniority as a basis of promotion has psychological sanction, as every worker wishes that in view of his greater period of service rendered, he should be given a post above the newcomers. Absence of any definite rules regarding promotion on the grounds of seniority leads to discontent and people lose interest in work. At the same time, they show no inclination to stick to any one profession. Naturally, the profession as a whole tends to suffer through such vagrancy as every new entrant takes his time in learning the ropes, and if the old ones keep running away, there is much efficiency and effort lost. It is for this reason that in every service, wages improve with seniority, and in most cases promotion also takes place on the same basis. But it is incorrect to consider seniority the sole basis of promotion. Just as the senior individual desires promotion, the more able and efficient also desires promotion and better prospects. If his talent is allowed to lie dormant, and if he has to wait a number of years before he comes into authority, or if he is required to constantly serve under a less efficient man, he is inclined to lose patience and become dissatisfied. His mind wanders out of the periphery of his work, and he feels imposed upon if asked to obey the less able individual who is in authority. And this insubordination leads to defective administration. Hence, where actuality is concerned, ability should be taken into consideration along with seniority when the questions come up.
2. **Promotion on the Basis of Ability.** The Second major basis of promotion is individual ability in very short periods of time. And if seniority be the basis, then an individual starting at the lowest rung can never reach the top. For this, ability, and consideration of ability, is very essential. Yet, for this reason alone, it is not safe to completely discount seniority, as many occupations place the premium upon experience. Secondly, having put in years of hard and honest service, the employee desires that he be given some token of appreciation for his selfless service, so that if he is not promoted the becomes dissatisfied. And, there can be no general rule regarding the alternate propriety of seniority or ability as the basis of promotion in any individual case, or any single profession. Generally speaking, wages or salary should be commensurate with the years of service put in. But before a key post, or a position that wields very wide authority can be handed over to a person, it is essential to inquire into his antecedents and evaluate his abilities.

3. **Promotion on the Basis of Results.** Those in authority everywhere, whatever the profession, whatever the service, desire that their subordinates should give off their best. Where private business is concerned, the employer is interested in one thing exclusively, that it results in terms of work, both as regards quantity and as regards quality. Hence, in such cases, promotion also is dispensed on the basis of results obtained by the individual under review. This particular method of promotion gives very good result in a large majority of cases since it not only satisfies the instincts and interests of those interested in efficiency and ability, but also appears in the form of added inducement to those not so inclined. In leads most people to emulating others, with the result that very good result are achieved all round.
4. **Promotion on the Basis of Kindness of Recommendation.** Recommendation of kindness of authorities is perhaps the worst method of promotion. Yet, it is very much in vogue in this enlightened age. In government and semi-government organizations, it is the ingratiating type of individual who figures the highest on lists of promotions as he makes his making judicious presents to them and to members of their families or by benefiting them in other respects. Lacking this effusive sociability, even the most efficient, honest without any hope of progress. Cases of this nature also present very bad examples to other workers, with the result that the best part of their energies are wasted in pleasing the authorities in working.

MODES OF PROMOTION

The above description of the bases of promotions also reveals the modes of promotion. In fact, an individual has to be selected for promotion in much the same manner in which he is to be selected for appointment. In both cases, much care and understanding should be used in making the selection. What more usually happens is that the care taken in selecting an individual for appointment is far greater than the attention paid to his promotion. And in most cases promotion is done on this basis of seniority, one of the most prevalent methods. Promoting an individual on the basis of his ability is none the worse. Another good, and fairly reliable, method of promotion is the one based upon efficiency and results obtained in previous position. But to promote an individual on one's whim, on recommendation, on one's pleasure, is not at all a good method, instead a thoroughly undesirable one. It is unscientific, unethical and harmful also.

Chapter 10 FATIGUE

What is fatigue? Starch has written that fatigue is the condition of reduced interest and desire. This a psychological definition of fatigue. According to Freeman, fatigue is a condition in which the organs of the body do not function, and the mind becomes lax. Evidently, fatigue is exclusively neither physical nor mental. This state of laxity, tiredness is a psycho-physical condition. It implies the reduced efficiency and capacity of mind or body, or both. A fatigued individual will either not work at all or workless efficiently than otherwise, and is most likely to lie in a recumbent position, in a hapless mood. In the words of Offner, "Fatigue is the reduced capacity of our organism to work properly, that capacity is accompanied with some feeling also which is known as feeling of fatigue." Having worked for many hours, it is natural for the individual to feel fatigued. The time that a particular individual will take in working before encountering the phenomenon of fatigue or exhaustion is another question, but any individual working to his maximum capacity is certain to get tired, because his capacity to work is reduced. As capacity to work is reduced, fatigue increases. Briefly, than fatigue means the decrease in capacity or efficiency.

CHARACTERISTICS OF FATIGUE

Fatigue influences both mind and body. As far as the mind is concerned, in a state of fatigue the individual lacks his usual power of thinking, and finds it difficult to concentrate on whatever he has in hand. Sometimes fatigue and exhaustion reach such a stage that even emotions cannot burst forth. From the physiological viewpoint, fatigue involves loss of physical efficiency and physical coordination. In a state of fatigue, the poisonous element called lactic acid is produced in large quantities in the muscles and nerves. This element is so poisonous and dangerous that very great excess of it can even lead to paralysis, but in the normal course if it increases in quantity in someone part of the body, that part becomes fatigued. Besides lactic acid, carbon dioxide and ammonia are also produced in the body as a result of exhaustion. They, too are toxic in nature and cause change in the chemical the observation and study of the various parts of the body when in a state of exhaustion and fatigue. Of them, the most important work has been done by Miller and Helmholtz, besides Wundt. Miller restricted his research and study to the condition of nerves during exhaustion. Six years after his effort, in 1850, Helmholtz made a study of the speed of sensation-nerve and motor-nerve, and observed that when the physique is exhausted, it takes longer for the sensation to travel from organ to the mind and for the motor nerve to take the brain's response to the organ concerned. In the process of his study, Helmholtz evolved an instrument used for measuring ontraction of muscles, which was used in 1858 by Wundt. Nowadays the ergpgraph is used to neasure fatigue.

Kind of Fatigue

Fatigue is of more than one kinds, just as efficiency is of more than one kinds. Generally, atigue is believed to take the following four forms:

1. Mental fatigue
2. Physical fatigue
3. Nervous fatigue
4. Boredom.

1. *Mental Fatigue*: Due to persistent mental work or due to excessive strains on the brain, the mind loses its capacity or efficiency. This is mental fatigue. In this manner, in mental fatigue the mind becomes tired or its minute cells and nerves lose their efficiency.
2. *Physical Fatigue*: Physical work leads to decrease in the efficiency of muscles, and this leads to a feeling of fatigue or exhaustion. In this way, physical fatigue is the result of bodily exertion. Mental work in excess of normal capacity leads to an impression of physical ineptitude but in fact this is only mental fatigue. But, as the mind and body are intimately related, exhaustion in the case of either must inevitably influence the other.
3. *Nervous Fatigue*: Man's unconscious mind is very active, but its functioning also involves the expenditure of energy. This too, leads to an experience of fatigue. In cases of mental conflict the unconscious mind becomes exhausted, and this causes nervous fatigue.
4. *Boredom*: Boredom and fatigue are not synonymous. In fatigue the exhaustion is due to the expenditure of energy, but in the case of boredom the exhaustion is caused when the existing energy in the body is not properly consumed. Causes of fatigue have been an important study for psychologists in the field of psychology. Generally there are many causes of fatigue, one of them being, in some cases, the absence of work. But where it is a question of the worker's or labourer's fatigue, it is normally the result of improper method of working or working for long hours without intervening periods of rest. Hollingworth blames long periods of work without rest as the main cause of fatigue. Long work tires the mind as well as the body. But persistent work over a long period of time without any rest cannot be considered to be the sole cause of fatigue. One cause of fatigue is boredom. As has been pointed out before, in much the same manner dis-interest, lack of motivation of inspiration, absence of recreation, mental ill-health, physical ailment etc, can be causes of fatigue. Important among the causes that result in fatigue where industry is concerned are excessive work, interminable work, working without rest, working in wrong manner, and absence of sufficient motivation.

Hence, in order to eliminate fatigue, the above causes should be remedied. Industrial psychology nakes a study of ways and means of eliminating fatigue also, and such study has resulted in many hysical and psychological tools coming to light.

Ways of Eliminating Fatigue

It has been the function of psychology to discover the ways of removing fatigue and exhaustio and if possible, of preventing it. The following methods have come to light:

1. *Sleep*: By far the best method of ending fatigue is sleep. Sleep or repose brings calm an rest to brain cells and body tissues, while all waste matter is excreted. This restor efficiency and freshness of the body.
2. *Relaxation*: Fatigue can also be reduced by relaxing in a sitting or lying position becaus the mind and body are freed of tension. Efficiency is thereby regained.
3. *Balance of Work and Rest*: As has been mentioned often, excessive work leads t exhaustion of mind and body, but complete lack of work and too much of rest also induc fatigue. This fatigue is the result of boredom. Hence, if fatigue is to be avoided, work is a important as rest. Hence, the best things is to strike some kind of balance between wor and rest.
4. *Change in Work*: In specific physical work, certain distinct parts of the body are straine much more than others. But if the work is changed periodically it is possible to wor continuously for longer periods. Similarly, continuous application to the same kind of ment work does not give our faculties a change of expression, and we tend to become bore Hence, change in the nature of work is essential to remove and even to prevent physic as well as nervous fatigue.
5. *Recreation*: Recreation provides an opportunity for our unexpressed capacities to com forward and find manifestation, while at the same time it reduces mental and physic tension. Hence, recreation is necessary for reducing or preventing fatigue.
6. *Change in Experiences*: Fatigue can also come in because people maintain a very inflexib attitude towards life, and always steep themselves in work. Hence, change in experienc can also sometimes remove fatigue.
7. *Creating Interest and Motivation in Work*: Even more important than rest as a cure fc fatigue and mental physical, is the creating of interest and motivation in work. And for thi good work can be rewarded with promotions and bonuses. Such methods prove ver efficacious.

The above methods of ending fatigue will prove useful to the large generality of individual but every individual can pick a method to suit himself. There can be other methods of removin fatigue, according to interest and nature.

KINDS OF FATIGUE

Fatigue can the both mental and physical, but to understand their difference it is necessar first to understand their nature.

1. **Physical Fatigue.** In physical fatigue, as is evident from the name itself, one finds physic characteristics of fatigue. Physical efficiency and capacity fall down and physic

coordination becomes difficult. A poisonous fluid known as lactic acid is produced in the muscles and the nervous system, and when this increases beyond a certain level the entire body becomes lax. If it is confined to any one part of the body, then that particular part becomes tired but when exhaustion increases it is introduced into the blood stream and steadily spreads over the entire body. In addition to lactic acid, the body also produces ammonia and carbon dioxide during fatigue. Both these elements are poisonous and by their influence the energizing elements in the body steadily decreases while the poisonous matter increases. Many psychologists have examined the condition of fatigue, the most valuable work having been done by Miller, Helmholtz and Wundt. Miller confined his study to the state of the nerves in a condition of fatigue. Later on Helmholtz made a study of the functions of the sensory nerves and motor nerves and discovered that, in a condition of fatigue the experience of anything is conveyed to the brain in greater time while the motor nerves take a longer time to react than under normal conditions. Helmholtz invented the Myograph, an instrument used to measure the contraction of muscles. It was later used in 1858 by Wundt in his experiments. This instrument is now used to measure fatigue.

2. **Mental Fatigue.** Fatigue is not merely physical because it is sometimes manifested even when one has no physical work. This is mental fatigue. Mental fatigue is normally apparent after excessive physical fatigue. The symptoms of mental fatigue are an absence of desire to work, emotional condition, lack of interest and concentration, lack of normal efficiency in work, desire to rest etc. At time one's efficiency does not suffer despite some mental fatigue. It is boredom in which one experiences mental fatigue because one's energy has not been properly consumed. One important cause of mental fatigue is the absence of motivation and of a proper aptitude. In such a case an individual loses interest in his work even though he is not physically exhausted. People complain of fatigue despite good working conditions if their aptitude is not correct and if there is absence of sufficient motivation.

Difference between Physical and Mental Fatigue

The difference between physical and mental fatigue is evident from the foregoing description of their respective natures. When a person complains that he is fatigued, in fact he is suffering from both mental and physical fatigue. The symptoms of the two conditions are different. Physical fatigue is recognized by the conditions of the muscles, chemical changes, nervous fatigue, change in the blood chemistry and in the mental condition. On the other hand, mental fatigue is diagnosed from the absence of motivation, a contrary aptitude and primarily a feeling of exhaustion. While physical fatigue can be corrected by rest or by taking rich food, mental fatigue cannot be got rid of in this way. It needs the creation of elements which provide the correct motivation and the correct aptitude.

Relation between Physical and Mental Fatigue

Despite the differences between physical and mental fatigue mentioned above, the two should not be taken to be entirely different, for they are intimately related to each other. A person who complains of fatigue is in fact suffering both from mental as well as physical fatigue. Sometimes a person does not notice physical fatigue if a strong motivation is coupled with absence of mental fatigue. In most forms of fatigue one finds both physical and mental symptoms. According to Watson, mental fatigue is caused by the contraction of the vocal cord. In is also caused by damage to the nerve centres in the higher regions of the brain. Mental work cannot be done efficiently in a condition of physical fatigue, nor can physical work he done well in a condition of mental fatigue. For this reason it is better to define fatigue as a psychosomatic or psychophysical condition rather than a physical or mental condition. In fact it is a physical and psychological condition in which the individual's mental and physical efficiency is reduced. The truth of the matter is that the physical and mental aspects of fatigue can be distinguished only verbally, because in actual fact they are not independent of each other.

OCCUPATIONAL CONDITIONS OF FATIGUE

In different professions, there are different conditions which lead to fatigue which itself leads to a deterioration in the mental and physical health of the workers and ultimately to a fall in production. Such conditions can be briefly summarized as under:

1. **Long Hours of Work.** In some industries the hours of work are so long that the workers become exhausted while in fact these longer hours of work do not result in a proportionate increase in production. Many researches have thrown light on this fact. Musico has mentioned the case of one lady worker who worked only six hours instead of the conventional twelve-hour day observed by the other workers and still showed a higher level of production than any other workers. In this factory the working hours were from 6 to 8 in the morning, eight thirty to twelve thirty, one thirty to five thirty and from eight thirty to twelve thirty. This particular lady refused to work before breakfast and late at night, explaining that by working for such a long time she could not maintain her efficiency. Over a period of one month it was seen that she worked for 150 hours as compared to the other workers who worked for 237 hours, despite which she showed more output than the others. It is evident from the research conducted in various countries on the methods of work that production is higher in shorter working weeks than in longer working weeks. In the second world war the working hours were increased in England. In the first world war of Dunkirk the work done each week was 35 hours but after Dunkirk, in all factories connected with war production increased, the time was increased to 69.5 hours. In the beginning the production increased by about 10 per cent but later on the absentees bean in increase. In a few months it was noticed that the actual working hours fell to 51 hours although the stated working time was 68.5 hours. Before the change the number of working hours averaged 53 out of a stipulated 56 hours. And, in fact, although the working time wad increased the actual production fell by 12 percent. After six months the working hours were again reduced, and it was noticed that production again increased. One explanation of this is that fatigue caused a fall in production when the working hours were increased. It is obvious that long hours of fatigue result in exhaustion. Myers made a study of ladies working in a London factory. Their job was to reverse fuses. When their working hours were reduced from 66 hours to 48.5 the production went up by 15 percent.

2. **Absence of Rest Periods.** A person works for a long time continuously then he feels fatigued. If he does not take rest and continues to work, then his fatigue increases even more rapidly because he is working in an exhausted condition. If he is allowed to rest as soon as he begins to feel exhausted, then he returns to his work refreshed and his fatigue does not increase. Hence it is seen that fatigue is eliminated in all working methods where the workers are allowed to rest for short periods during their working hours because during the period of rest they can regain their energy. Absence of rest period is an occupational condition which promotes fatigue. Even if some workers steal a few minutes of rest where it is not officially provided for, they do not feel relaxed and rested because during that period their aptitude is not correct. In fact, relaxation of this kind results in greater fatigue. Gilbreth's experiment successfully established that production can be increased by providing periods of rest for the workers instead of keeping them at work continuously.
3. **Incorrect Temperature.** Incorrect room temperature is another occupational condition which results in fatigue because in such cases the room is either too hot or too cold. In both cases the mental and physical condition of the worker deteriorated and he soon feels exhausted.
4. **Absence of Proper Ventilation.** If a person does not get clear air while he is working he soon gets tires. In an office or factory in which the air is polluted the incidence of fatigue will he far greater than in any other factory where there is adequate ventilation.
5. **Improper Illumination.** Fatigue also increase if the illumination in the working area is not adequate and proper because the eyes begin to feel exhausted and dry if the light is not enough or too bright. Hence, it is desirable that there should be proper arrangements for illumination in factories and offices. Proper lighting implies that there should be sufficient, and just sufficient, light coming from the right direction. For example, in reading or writing, it is desirable that the light source should be placed behind and to left of the worker. If this is not done, then the eyes suffer great strain. In working on a machine it is desirable that those instruments should be lighted up which are to be seen constantly by the operator. Hence the light provided should neither be to little nor too much, for in both these conditions the strain on the eyes leads to fatigue.
6. **Design of the Machinery.** Certain machines are so designed that they tend to exhaust and tire the operator working on them. Hence modern psychologists give suggestions even in the construction of machines so that they may be designed to minimize fatigue and increase production. This branch of industrial psychology is called engineering psychology. To-day, the aim is to design machinery which involves the least possible amount of movement while maintaining the highest level of production. When the workers become used to operating such machines their fatigue is reduced and their work improves.
7. **Absence of an Adequate Seat.** It is a well known fact that a person feels exhausted much earlier if he has to operate a machine while standing. That is why the absence of an adequate seat is one occupational condition which causes fatigue. Another important feature

of the seat is that it should not offer too much comfort because in that case the operator feels sleepy. On the other hand it should not be so hard that the operator may feel discomfort. Arrangement for a proper seat can help in reducing fatigue.

8. **Excessive Noise.** Another occupational condition which increases fatigue is the presence of excessive noise at the place of work. An individual can work for a long time in an atmosphere which is peaceful and free of noise. Some degree of noise can be tolerated, for it has no appreciable effect on work but when noise rises above a certain level is creates fatigue. Now experiments are made to find out if the noise produced by the machinery is of high enough a pitch to induce fatigue. If this happens, then efforts are made to reduce the pitch of the sound produced and so reduce the level of noise. Kornhauseer conducted an experiment on four typists who worked in a noisy environment for four days. The psychologist came to the conclusion that their work went down by 3.2 days percent while the incidence of errors went up by 23 percent. In an experiment conducted by Western workers engaged in stitching showed 7.5 percent more production when working in peaceful surroundings than while when working in a noisy environment.
9. **Unhealthy conditions.** Fatigue is intimately connected with health. If the occupational conditions are such that they do not promote good health then they are also conductive to fatigue. Unhealthy conditions include such factors as incorrect room temperature, improper ventilation, excessive noise, etc. In addition to these certain other occupational conditions like excessive humidity, absence of rest, presence of some disturbing smell, inadequate arrangements for medicine and medical attendance or the total lack of such facilities also have a bad influence upon the health of the workers with the result that they soon become tired.
10. **Absence of Proper Training.** In every profession there are certain functions which require some training before they can be properly performed. If such functions are entrusted to untrained employees then these workers become exhausted very rapidly. Hence the employees should be trained by the best methods about the easiest and least tiring way of handling certain instruments. They should also be guided in adjusting the hours of work and the periods of rest according to their individual differences. Hence, the absence of proper training is also an occupational condition which results in fatigue.
11. **Lack of Sleep.** In factories in which the workers have to work at night and cannot get adequate rest during the day, lack of sleep is another factor which results in fatigue. To eliminate this, facilities for sleep should be provided for the workers so that they can sleep during their periods of rest. Absence of sleep is invariably an exhausting factor, irrespective of the condition which leads to it.
12. **Low Morale.** Conditions which are conductive to low morale are also conductive to fatigue. Conditions which result in low morale are harmful attitudes towards the management, hatred, suspicion and jealousy, dissatisfaction with work and absence of any hope, mental unrest and dissatisfaction, uninteresting work, improper rules governing promotions, absence of a proper wage increase, improper methods of distribution of wages, lack of adjustment

on the part of management etc. In all such conditions fatigue also increases rapidly and leads to physical fatigue. Conditions in which high morale can be generated also lead to energetic work.

13. **Defects of the Social Environment.** The defects of the social environment of an occupation in which many people work also lead to fatigue. A worker cannot maintain high morale in a condition in which the relations between the employers and employers are not good or in which the atmosphere is one of hate or suspicion. The result is that in such conditions the workers feel exhausted very quickly. Since people have now understood the significance of maintaining a healthy social atmosphere in the place of work, efforts are made to make the social atmosphere cooperative and refreshing or encouraging. This must be done so that the worker can work for a long time without feeling exhausted.

In fact, all occupational conditions which have an adverse influence upon the worker's mental and physical condition are conductive to fatigue because in such conditions mental and physical fatigue is very rapid. But for this all workers and the managers and the government will have to work cooperatively.

MEANS OF REDUCING FATIGUE

Roughly speaking the chief method of reducing fatigue is to eliminate all occupational conditions which increase it. Hence, mention will here be made of those means by which fatigue can be reduced. It should always be kept in mind that work invariably results in some degree of exhaustion and that there can be no ways of eliminating fatigue completely. One can only hope to devise means by which fatigue can be reduced or controlled before it becomes excessive. Briefly, this can be done in the following ways:

1. **Reducing the Hours of Work.** One way of reducing fatigue is to reduce the hours of work. It has been seen in many experiments that fatigue is reduced when working hours are reduced, whereas the production does not fall proportionately but in many cases actually increases. In 1928 Sheppard pointed out that for the previous thirty years workers were made to work ten hours a day for six days a week in all American industries. On the other hand, the workers are now made to work eight hours, besides which on Saturdays they are required to work only four hours, while Sunday decrease in the hours of work. Many other experiments have substantiated Sheppard's conclusions. Hence, one way of reducing fatigue is to reduce the hours of work. But at the same time care should be taken to avoid reducing working hours to such an extent that the worker's energy is not fully utilized. The most appropriate method is to have sufficient working hours in which the worker can continue to work without feeling totally exhausted. Evidently, the working hours will differ from industry to industry, according to the nature of the work.
2. **Provision of Rest Periods.** Another way of reducing fatigue is to introduce appropriate and properly time periods of rest. An appropriate period of rest involves calculation of the total rest period allowed in proportion to the work expected from the workers. And a

properly timed rest period implies the time at which this rest should be allowed and the frequency with which it should be allowed. Many experiments on this subject have yielded a fund of valuable facts. According to Vernon the worker should be allowed rest after every hour while according to Sheppard the worker who works for eight hours a day should be allowed to rest for 16.6 percent of the total working time. It is evident that in providing rest periods, one must consider the total rest period in proportion to the working hours one must consider the total rest period in proportion to the working hours as well as the frequency and duration for which it should be given.

3. **Arrangement for Maintaining the Correct Temperature.** In order to reduce fatigue it is necessary to maintain the correct room temperature in the place of work. Arrangements should be made to raise the temperature in winters and to lower it in summers. If the temperature is adequate then the workers can work longer hours without experiencing fatigue. For this reason many modern factories have air - conditioned rooms or others means of reducing the heat during the summers while heaters and other contrivances are used to increase the temperature in the winter months.
4. **Proper Ventilation.** Fatigue can also be reduced by improving the ventilation so that the polluted air is eliminated and fresh air admitted into the factory. Most factories make use of exhaust fans designed to suck the polluted air out of a room or a hall.
5. **Arrangement for Proper Lighting.** Fatigue can also be reduced to some extent if proper provision is made for lighting up the area in which the workers work. For this it is necessary that the light should come from the right direction and it should be of a particular intensity. The advantage in this is that the eyes do not suffer strain and hence the workers do not become tired quickly.
6. **Improvements in the Design of Machines.** The shape and the size of the machine operated by the worker also influence fatigue. If the machine is so designed that it can be run efficiently by making the minimum possible movements the workers will not feel exhausted.
7. **Proper Seating Arrangement.** A proper seating arrangement for the worker also helps to reduce fatigue. As far as possible the workers should be allowed to work while sitting. The seat should provide normal comfort to avoid fatigue but it should not be too comfortable, for in that case it will induce sleep. But it should also not be too hard.
8. **Control Over the Noise.** Since excessive noise also induces fatigue, it is desirable to have some control over the amount of noise in or near the working place, if fatigue is to be avoided. This can be done in many ways. It is more difficult to reduce the noise made by the machines installed in the factories but efforts should be made to control the noise produced. If the noise in the factory or office is less, the workers' fatigue will also be less.
9. **Healthy Working Conditions.** If the working conditions are conductive to health then fatigue always remains at a law level because the worker's health and his fatigue are directly related to each other. In order to create healthy conditions it is necessary to pay

attention to the ventilation, sufficient light absence of noise, proper room temperature, control over the humidity, medical facilities, adequate arrangement for rest and food, etc. All these things help to refresh the worker.

10. **Arrangements for Industrial or Professional Training.** The worker feels less fatigued in manipulating a machine for which he has been trained because he does not make any unnecessary movements. Hence professional training can also help to reduce fatigue.
11. **Proper Arrangement for Sleep.** In many kinds of work it is necessary to provide some arrangement for sleep. Even if the worker is given a change to sleep on a comfortable bed for only half an hour out of the total working time, much of his fatigue disappears. Such an arrangement is particularly useful for the workers working in shifts.
12. **High Morale.** High morale can also help to reduce fatigue among the workers. Maintenance of high morale requires an attitude favourable to the management, generated discipline, group confidence in the management, etc. If these factors are present, the incidence of fatigue is much lower.
13. **Proper Social Atmosphere.** Even the social atmosphere plays an important role in reducing the worker's fatigue. The worker's enthusiasm can be easily maintained and fatigue kept at a low level if good relations with the management can be created and if the general atmosphere is one of cooperation.
14. **Special Means of Reducing Fatigue.** In addition to the factors explained above many other means are now being adopted to reduce the worker's fatigue. For example, in many factories arrangements have been made to play music to the workers while they are engaged in their work because the workers feel less tired if they sing as they work. Many new experiments are being conducted on this aspect these days. Besides, change in the nature of work also helps to keep the workers' interest alive. Hence efforts are made to make the work interesting in many different ways. As industrial psychology progresses many new ways of reducing fatigue will definitely be discovered.

CRITERIA OF FATIGUE

The criteria of fatigue implies the symptoms by which its presence can be diagnosed and recognized. In order to understand this it is essential to keep in mind the various aspects of fatigue. Since fatigue is a psycho-physical condition its symptoms are both mental and physical. It can be recognized by the following factors:

1. **Feeling of Exhaustion.** The chief symptom of fatigue is the feeling of fatigue even if the individual is not feeling physically exhausted. In a state of exhaustion the desire to work is noticeably reduced and the desire to rest is clearly heightened. Generally, it also leads to a fall in the individual's production, though this is not universally true. In the state of exhaustion the individual's feelings about work change and he evinces no desire to do any kind of work.

2. **Muscular Condition.** In a state of fatigue the muscles lose their power to contract and expand. Hence, physiologically, fatigue is a muscular condition and the failure of the muscles to contract and expand is one criterion of fatigue.
3. **Chemical Changes.** As a person works the proportion of acetic acid and other poisonous chemicals in his body increases. In a healthy body the oxygen is properly distributed through the blood stream with the result that poisonous matter is eliminated from the body. When the muscles become tired, this process of elimination does not work efficiently. This leads to a fall in the quantity of glycogen in the body along with an increase in the quantity of poisonous matter. In this matter many chemical changes occur in the body fatigue, and it can be recognized by these chemical changes.
4. **Nervous Slackness.** One criterion of mental exhaustion is nervous slackness. Sometimes it is caused by muscular fatigue but it also has many other causes. In a state of nervous exhaustion the nerves lose their power to react with the result that the individual cannot work efficiently. Many experiments have established that, in a condition of exhaustion, the nerves and muscles do not have the power to react properly or to achieve the normal state of excitation. As a result of this slackness the sense organs do not react properly. The sense of smell is particularly influenced while the powers of seeing, hearing and touching are also adversely influenced.
5. **Change in the Blood Chemistry.** Some symptoms of exhaustion can also be found in the tired person's blood. If some of this blood is introduced into the blood of some healthy person, one will find the symptoms there too. The same is true of the muscles also. On the one hand the blood stream helps to eliminate poisonous matter from the body but on the other hand it also helps to distribute the fatigue even when the only one part of the body is bearing all the strain. If any one part of the body is put to excessive use then that part shows signs of fatigue earliest but soon these symptoms can be seen all over the body because exhaustion is communicated by the blood.
6. **Change in the Mental Condition.** One criterion of fatigue is the change in the mental condition because in an exhausted condition the individual experiences deterioration of his mental powers and a loss of interest. He cannot concentrate upon anything for a long time and becomes bored with work. Because of this influence upon the mind, fatigue is considered a psychological phenomenon.
7. **Increase in the Number of Accidents.** An analysis of accidents in industry has revealed that majority of accidents occur either in the morning or late in the evening. This fact has been generally substantiated by studies in Germany, England and America. A study of fatigue has also shown that it is maximum early in the morning and late in the evening. Hence one can estimate the extent of industrial fatigue from the number of accidents. For this reason now provisions are made for introducing rest periods in the early hours and in the late evenings. The pattern of accidents can be seen in almost any industry but while the morning accidents are uniformly present, the late evening accidents follow various patterns in different industries. Accidents in the late evening take place more rapidly but

the total numbers is not much more than that of the accidents in the morning. One can see a difference in more than that of the accidents in the morning. One can see a difference in the number of accidents that take place during the morning and the night shifts. Hence, the relationships between fatigue and accidents is obvious.

In should be kept in mind that despite the clear relationship between fatigue and accident, fatigue is not the sole cause of accidents and for this reason an increase in accidents is not a criterion of increasing fatigue. Many other factors apart from fatigue often prove far more important in causing accidents. For example, women are more accident prone than men because women tend to tire easily and more rapidly. It cannot be denied that in a state of exhaustion the individual becomes restless, he cannot control his movements properly, he may even go to sleep, he lacks concentration. Despite this, fatigue cannot be accepted as the sole cause of accidents.

8. **Fall in Production.** Sometimes fatigue is defined in terms of the fall in production. As has already been mentioned in connection with accidents the early morning shift and the late evening shifts results in accidents and also in a fall in production. The cause of this fall in production is believed to be fatigue because as fatigue increases the efficiency of the worker decreases. During the first hours in the morning the production rate rises steeply because this is the warming up period. This warming up can be due to numerous mental and physical causes. And the period consumed in warming upto one's work will depend as much upon the work as upon the individual differences one worker and another. Two factors which are responsible for the rate of worker's output are health and the nature of the conditions under which he has to work. When the work is restarted in the third quarter of the day the phenomenon of warming up is not seen at all for the work starts at high speed. But this rate of work declines steadily till it reaches the lowest level of production in the last hour of the day. Apart from fatigue, many other factors may also account for this. Sometimes the workers begin to put away their tools quite sometime before the closing hour, which is one reason why production during the last hour is much lower. It is evident from the above explanation that the fall in production after the first two hours and again in the afternoon can be accepted as a criterion of fatigue.

   In addition to the above factors all other symptoms of physical and mental fatigue can be accepted as the criteria of fatigue. Fatigue can be recognized by such mental and physical conditions as change in the respiration, blood circulation, blood pressure, disinterest, lack of concentration, slackness, etc. Nowadays many scientific instruments are employed to measure fatigue.

DIFFERENT ASPECTS OF FATIGUE

In order to fully understand the nature of fatigue it is important to consider its objective, physical and mental aspects.

1. **Objective Aspect.** In its objective aspect fatigue can be defined as a fall in the efficiency to perform some function. This occurs when some work has been done for a long time. Fatigue does not occur if the worker intersperses his working periods with short rest periods. In the laboratory the decline in the ability to work is measured by the ergograph while the decline in the mental ability to work is measured by the word elimination method. Fall in efficiency is evinced not only through the fall in production but also through the deterioration in the quality of the work because the worker begins to make more mistakes when he is exhausted.
2. **Physical Aspect.** The physiological aspect of fatigue is concerned with its influence upon the body. Many experiments in this connection have revealed that in a state of fatigue the poisonous substances in the body increase in quantity while the energizing elements fall in number. From the physiological point of view, in a condition of fatigue one can observe an increase in the rate of respiration, blood circulation, blood pressure, etc. Many other chemical changes also occur within the day.
3. **Mental Aspect.** The mental symptoms of fatigue are exhaustion, lack of a desire to work, emotional instability, lack of concentration slackness, etc. All of these are expressed through lack of interest in work and a desire to rest.

A complete definition of fatigue cannot be produced by placing stress on any one of the above aspects of fatigue. The objective aspect is not the best method of recognizing fatigue because fairly often people do not show any deterioration in the performance of work despite some mental fatigue. Despite fatigue the production does not fall nor do the number of mistakes go up. Poffenberger conducted an experiment on twelve college students. In this experiment the student were required to make sentences, and the scientist showed that over a period of five and a half hours, the ability to make sentences did not deteriorate despite increasing fatigue. On the other Robers' subjects showed a decline in the quality of work despite an absence of any feeling of fatigue. Hence the objective definition of fatigue is incomplete.

Separate explanations of the mental and physical symptoms of fatigue may lead one to the conclusion that they are completely disconnected, but this is not true. Hence it is incorrect to believe that fatigue can be exclusively mental or exclusively physical. Fatigue of all kinds is manifested by physical as well as mental symptoms, a fact which has been established by experiments. Watson has proved that the contraction of the vocal muscles leads to mental fatigue. In the same way any damage to the nerve cells in the higher parts of the brain leads to mental fatigue. It is a matter of common experience that one cannot efficiently perform physical work in a condition of mental fatigue, or mental work in a state of physical exhaustion.

Briefly stated, fatigue can be defined as a psychological condition in which the individual's mental and physical ability to work deteriorates. It is apparent from this definition that the mental and physical symptoms or aspects of fatigue are verbally differentiated only for convenience because in actual fact they are not independent of each other. And while on the subject of ways and means of removing fatigue, it is necessary to remember that only unnecessary fatigue can be eliminated by these means, there is cannot be eliminated completely. To put it differently, it is not possible to create conditions in which fatigue can be eliminated completely. It is, on the other hand, possible to reduce it.

MEASUREMENT OF A FATIGUE

As far as the measurement of fatigue is concerned it is essential to remember that the measurement can be definite only if all the other factors and their influence is shown. For example, fall in the production curve is an incontrovertible proof of exhaustion because it can also be caused by changes in aptitude, excitement or interest, etc. At present we have no means of knowing whether fatigue is the cause of fall in production or whether it is caused by any of these other factors. For this reason the psychologist Musico believes that the measurement of fatigue is unscientific. Dhers say, "Fatigue can neither be scientifically isolated nor measured." Despite this, fatigue has been measured with varying degrees of accuracy, and most of the methods employed have proved of some practical value. Mosso, Greff, Kraeplin and other psychologists have discovered some valuable scientific facts by the measurement of fatigue. Hence it would be in keeping with the context to give a brief account of the methods of measuring fatigue. Generally, the methods of measuring fatigue are divided into three parts according to the three aspects of fatigue. They are objective methods, physical methods and mental methods.

1. **Objective Methods.** These include mainly those methods which measure variation in the quality and quantity of production. Such tests as word elimination method may be included in this category. But it should be kept in mind that these tests do not determine whether fatigue is present or not because the fall in production may even be caused by such other factors as opposite motivation, lack of enthusiasm or excitement through habit, despite the presence of fatigue.
2. **Physical Methods.** These include the methods which measure the physical symptoms of fatigue. Methods involving the chemical analysis of urine and saliva, the measurement of pulse, heart beat and blood pressure are included in this category. The ergograph, hand dynameter and Martin's spring balance can also be included in this group. But the symptoms measured by them may have some source other than fatigue.
3. **Mental Methods.** This group includes the methods which measure the mental symptoms of exhaustion. Such symptoms are the deterioration in attention, memory, imagination, mental decision, emotional analysis and power of reasoning. As in all the other methods, these methods too cannot determine the true source of the change, because it may be caused by something other than fatigue.

It is evident from the above brief account of the methods of measuring fatigue that results arrived at may not be valid. Even eminent scientists have their doubts about the validity of such measurements. But it cannot be denied that these method have helped in practical situations and it is possible that the future may bring more accurate methods of determining fatigue.

ERGOGRAPHIC STUDIES

The ergograph is used in the measurement of fatigue. The instrument was invented by Angelo Mosso, a famous Italian psychologist. With the help of ergograph he studied the relation between fatigue and the functioning of any particular part of the body. He studied the working of a particular muscle and induced fatigue in it. In this manner he eliminated the influence of such complex psychological phenomena as boredom and monotony, and studied fatigue in its more simple manifestation.

Ergograph is a simple instrument in which the hand is placed on a frame in such a way that it is not exerted or pressed in any way, but it cannot move. All the fingers except the middle one are tied in such a way that they cannot be used. Then a string with some weight on the other end of it is tied to the middle finger. This weight is lifted by the middle finger. In the ergograph this string passes over a pulley and has a weight attached to it. In the more modern adaption of this instrument, arrangement is made to expand and contract the finger without lifting the weight. The finger is made to perform various functions according to the pattern determined by Metronome, and then these movements are studied. The most important thing to be noted is the frequency of the contraction and expansion of the muscles. For this reason only this contraction and expansion is controlled. The graph of the fatigue is prepared by a moving sting attached to a needle which moves on a revolving drum and draws straight lines. The frequency of contraction and expansion in the muscle is shown by the irregularity in these lines drawn by the needle.

Conclusions Reached Through Ergograph Studies

Ergograph studies provided many results which have proved useful for application in industries. Mosso reached the following nine conclusions about fatigue on the basis of ergographic studies:

1. If the frequency of muscular contraction, in lifting any weight is once every two seconds, then the rate of contraction gradually falls, till in the end there is no contraction. With a weight of six kilos this state is reached in approximately one minute. If the weight is then reduced, the contraction of the muscle can be started again but even then fatigue will be induced soon.
2. If the muscular contraction is induced after a long time period, such as ten seconds, for the same weight, then there is no external manifestation of exhaustion. In such conditions even the weight of six kilograms can be lifted for an indefinite number of times.
3. If work done is measured in terms of the quantity of weight, then the work done for smaller weights is definitely much more than for heavier weights. Hence a weight of three kilograms can be lifted more than twice the number of times than a weight of six kilograms can be raised.
4. If the given weight is raised rapidly a number of times, then the fatigue induced is greater than in lifting it once. But if the weight is lifted slowly, then fatigue is less.
5. Time taken to regain energy increases with an increase in the intervals between periods of work. For example, if the time required to regain energy for sixty contractions may even

be 30 minutes. When a situation is reached that the finger cannot be moved at all, then the fatigue which has been induced by the attempts to lift weight cannot be easily eliminated. It requires a very great time to regain energy, and this cannot be done by providing the normal intervals of rest. Putting it another way, as fatigue accumulates the effect of fatigue in contracting the muscle also increases rapidly and cannot be overcome easily.

6. If other muscles of the body also function at the same time as the finger, then the finger loses its ability to lift weight to some extent. If the individual has performed some strenuous exercise before the ergograph experiments, then the state of total inactivity is arrived at much sooner than under normal circumstances. In this way the ergograph exercises indicate that fatigue is communicated to those parts of the body, through the blood stream, which are not being used at that time.
7. Such factors as lack of sleep, mental causes, hunger and the shortage of blood in the muscle reduces the efficiency of the muscle. In fact any factor which is an obstacle to nourishment or tends to reduce it will also tend to increase fatigue.
8. The efficiency of the muscle can be increased by massaging it, by increasing the quantity of sugar in the blood, by giving nourishment to the body and by improving the general health.
9. Different people get exhausted at different rates but the principles governing fatigue which have been mentioned above hold true despite all individual differences.

INDUSTRIAL APPLICATION OF ERGOGRAPH STUDIES

Psychologists applied the findings of the ergograph studies to industrial situations, although some objected that this should not be done because the conditions prevailing in an industry and in the psychological laboratory differ to a very great extent. Besides, in ergograph studies only the finger is made to work, in a factory the worker has to exert his entire body. For this reason the laws governing fatigue in the two cases may not be the same. But these objections against the conclusions obtained through ergographic studies were not found to be valid because the conditions in the psychological laboratory and an industry have some common features., although there are many differences. The application of these conclusions to industry has provided many beneficial results. Despite this it should be kept in mind that ergographic studies have been conducted in the laboratory and the results obtained should not be applied exactly as they are without testing their validity in the industrial situation, because in a factory the worker has to exert his whole body, not only his finger. Besides, the production of some worker may suffer or change not only because of the work done or the number of hours of work but also as a result of his attitudes and motives. If the worker wants an interval in his work, it is not only because he wants rest but also because he may wish to have a chat with his colleagues over a cup of coffee. Sometimes workers ask for an interval soon after arriving in the factory, or soon after the lunch interval. It also happens that some workers utilize the lunch interval to do some personal work and then use the interval to take lunch, in which case the purpose of the rest interval is defeated.

ATTITUDE OF TRADE UNIONS

One difficulty in applying the results of ergographic studies to industry is created by the attitudes of the industrial trade unions. It has been seen that once the working hours are reduced and the rest periods increased, the workers do not easily agree to an increase in working hours and a reduction in the rest periods. Many industrial organizations are not prepared to increase the rest intervals for the simple reason that despite all such increases, the workers always demand for a further reduction in the working time and an extension of the rest hours. If some company reduces the working hours from nine to eight, the workers immediately demand that it should be reduced to seven. Even if the company accedes this, the workers do not stop but go further and demand that the working hours should be further reduced to six. For this reason and industrialist prefers to control the workers from the very beginning. In addition to this, it is a generally known fact that, according to their individual qualities, each worker becomes tired after different time and he required a different time in which to recoup his energies. Hence it is apparently unscientific to give the same time of test to each worker and also to provide it at the same fixed time. On the other hand, if differing periods of rest are given to the workers according to their individual differences, then the workers immediately voice a protest against the apparent injustice and inequality in treatment. No trade union is prepared to accept the fact that the workers doing the same work and obtaining the same wages should be allowed to have varying amounts of working time and rest time. All these factors greatly hinder the application of ergographic conclusions in industries, but this does not imply that it is impossible to benefit by their application. At many places the workers and the management have cooperated with each other and thus introduced many reforms in the conditions of work and rest.

EXTENT OF APPLICATION

Now we must turn out attention to the extent to which ergographic conclusions can be applied to industries. One general fact which can be derived from the first five conclusion of the geographic studies is that more work can be done if the limited energy of the muscle is consumed slowly, rather than rapidly. In fact, the principle governing the expenditure of muscular energy can be applied to the use of energy in any form. If, for example, a car is run at high speed it consumes more fuel than when it is run at low speeds. Hence, if one wants to travel the greatest possible distance by using the least possible fuel, then one must run the car at a low and steady speed. Another example of this kind is the long distance runner, because such an athlete must learn to control his energy. If he runs fast in the earlier stages of the race, then he consumes most of his energy very early and fails to complete the race. The long distance runner must begin the race at low speed, increasing it gradually, till he attains the highest speed near the end of the race. He can run fastest near the end of the race because he then loses nothing by becoming exhausted at this stage. But if he becomes fatigued in the beginning, he cannot hope to complete the race, let alone to win it. Here one must keep it in mind that the general tendency is against such a careful utilization of one's energy. Generally, a person likes to work quickly when he is fresh, without realizing that although he is working faster he is in fact wasting a good amount of energy. If a person has to complete some big project he must learn how to husband his strength and to complete his energy project he must learn how to husband his strength and to expend his energy in finishing half the work, he will never be able to complete it. Another difficulty in keeping one's work at a steady pace is the human tendency to retire for rest only when one has become tired and restless, although actually the period of rest should come much earlier. As has been pointed out earlier, a person can do much more work by interspersing the working hours with short periods of rest in which he can recoup his energies. This happens because once a man is completely exhausted he needs much more time to regain his energy. For this reason it is believed that the worker should be allowed a short period of rest after some period of work, if one is to put the worker's energy to the best use.

MUSCIO'S EXPERIMENT

Muscio has proved the validity of the above ergographic principle by giving another example of its application to industrial conditions. In this experiment one individual was made to lift six kilograms of weight three time on the ergograph under different conditions.

1. In the first condition he was made to contact his muscles every two seconds till he could not lift the weight at all. Then he was allowed to rest till he could regain all his energy. In working by his method the individual contracted his muscle thirty times and then rested for two hours. In this way he could sit for the experiment four times in an eight hour period and in each session he contracted his muscles thirty times, a total of 120 times in the entire period.
2. In the second condition, the individual was allowed to rest for half an hour after every fifteen muscular convulsions. The result was that he could put in 16 sessions of muscular exercise, in each of which he lifted the weight 15 times. Consequently, he convulsed his muscles a total of 240 times. It is therefore evident that the individual doubled the quantity of his work because he was given rest at more frequent intervals.
3. In the third condition the individual was allowed a rest of tem seconds before each muscular exertion. This speed of working was so slow that he did not experience fatigue at all. He took two seconds to convulse his muscle and ten seconds to rest it, with the result that he performed one unit of work in twelve seconds. Consequently, he could contract his muscles three hundred times in one hour and twenty four hundred times in eight hours. The quantity of work thus achieved was twenty times the work done in the first condition.

By comparing the first and second conditions of work we come to the conclusion that in the first condition the individual took half an hour to regain the energy he had spent in contracting his muscles. But it took 90 minutes to regain the energy spent in other fifteen contractions an average of six minutes for each contraction. Under the third condition, it only took ten seconds to regain the energy spent in each contracion. It is evident from this that more time is taken to regain energy after work if the periods of rest are far apart. And the most expensive movement is that in which the individual tries to lift some weight when he is almost completely exhausted.

Application in Industry

An experiment of this kind cannot be applied to industrial conditions in precisely the same way because in this experiment only some particular muscles were called into play and were used till they were completely exhausted. In an industrial situation neither of these two conditions holds goods because neither is it necessary to use any one particular muscle nor is it used to such an extent that it becomes completely exhausted. Despite this, the experiment provides a guideline that the intervals of rest should be distributed in such a manner among the working hours that energy spent can be regained as rapidly as possible. And if the intervals of rest can be increased and they do lead to even a fifteen percent increase in production, the change should be considered significant. As is evident from the other ergographich principles explained earlier, if the intervals of rest are distributed between small units of work, it is possible to work for longer periods without becoming exhausted.

Experiments by Gilbreth: This fact has also been substantiated by the experiments of Gilbreth. He made a study of time and motion, and concluded that fatigue can be reduced by reducing the load, increasing the intervals of rest and balancing the movement in the work. But it depends upon the nature of the work as to which load should be reduced, where the interval of rest should be increased and which movement should be controlled.

Experiments by Taylor: Concerning the use of a spade, the experiments of F.W. Taylor revealed that more work can be done by using smaller spades than by using larger spades. But in fact the size of the spade will depend upon the nature of the work and the individual using it. A large spade is needed to lift a light weight and a smaller spade to lift a heavier weight. Yet, it is possible to decide the size of the implements to be used by workers in some particular industry. Large spades induce fatigue, which smaller spades do not. But less weight can be transported by a smaller spade, and if the weight transported is less than the weight of the spade itself then the amount of work done declined sharply. And since the quantity of work done is measured by the total weight carried by the spade, not by weight of the spade itself, it is perfectly possible to have a spade so small that the work done by it is negligible. Still, between the extreme limits of a very big and a very small spade, it is possible to decide upon some practicable size of spade which can be used efficiently in some particular industry. By making experiments of this kind, it is possible to decide the best possible size and weight of the tools used by different artisans.

Certain function can be performed by two people working together, and in all such work it is seen that the result of the combined effort is always better than the sum total of the work done by each individual separately. Whenever it is impossible to reduce the load to be lifted or to allow them to work together, efforts should be made to reduce their fatigue by giving them more periods of rest. In certain industries, instead of lifting heavy loads, the workers have to make some movements rapidly. In such industries the speed of the movement should be regulated or the work should be divided into small units so that intervals of rest can be given between each unit of work. Although it is difficult to determine the speed of work in any kind of performance, it can generally be said that the speed of work should be slow in the first half hour or work, normal in the later hours and the fastest near the end. Maintaining slow speed in the beginning is necessary because it gives the worker time to warm up, after which the speed of work can be increased to the normal level. This normal level should be maintained. The purpose behind increasing the working speed near the end is to finish the work which has been left over and this avoid the adverse effects of fatigue on production. Certain people begin the day by working as hard as they can with the result that their speed falls as time passes. This method is supported by the argument that the worker tries to achieve as much as he can while he feels fresh. But in fact the worker tires very rapidly if he begins working fast too early in the day, and then he continues to work in a state of exhaustion with the result that the working speed declined steadily. This always results in lower production.

Fatigue Covers the Entire Body

Among all the conclusions drawn from the ergographic studies, the sixth is that fatigue is general although only one part of the body is employed. Fatigue is communicated from one part of the body to all the body by the blood stream. It is evident from this that fatigue can be eliminated by giving rest to the whole body, not only to one part. Hence, it is not enough only to stop work, if one wants to rest. The worker must get complete rest during his interval for rest. Arrangements should be made to provide comfortable beds and easy chairs for the workers' use during the lunch and rest intervals. It is essential to have proper arrangements for drinking water. Briefly, fatigue cannot be eliminated merely by stopping work. Arrangement for complete rest should be made.

IMPORTANCE OF HEALTH AND NOURISHMENT

Nearness of Working Place

The seventh and eighth conclusions drawn form the ergographic studies of work fatigue indicate the value and importance of bodily health and proper nourishment for reducing fatigue and increasing output. Hence it is desirable that the condition even outside the factory should be such that they promote healthy living and proper nourishment. In this connection H. Gartner, a German scientist, has suggested that attention should also be paid to the distance a worker has to travel from his house to the place of work. If this distance is so great that the worker becomes exhausted in traveling, be will be working for the entire day in a condition of exhaustion. It has been suggested that the residential districts of the workers should be within the vicinity of the working place. Nowadays there is a great demand that factories should be located outside the city to avoid pollution of air. It therefore becomes even more necessary to pay attention to the aspect of distance from home to factory. Visualizing the problem one can see that the worker should be provided a house near the factory, and in addition arrangements should be made for the schooling of his children and for his purchases which he requires from day to day. The importance of this factor has been realized by many industrialists, and consequently they recruit only such people who live within a reasonable distance from the factory. In Gartner's opinion, the worker should live at such a distance from his place of work that he can reach it within thirty minutes.

Rest in the Factory

Arrangements for the worker's rest should be made within the factory so that his health can be maintained. But the time that should be given for rest is a controversial subject. Two factors that should be kept in mind are that the period of rest should not be so long as to induce lethargy and not so short as not to provide adequate rest. Gartner has suggested that the worker should sleep for thirty minutes in order to get adequate rest. If the workers are allowed to sleep for more than thirty minutes, it is possible that their sleep at night may be distributed.

Arrangement for Food

Food plays an important part in removing fatigue, and hence arrangements should be made to provide cheap, wholesome and appetizing food for the workers. Even if the organization had to spend some money to provide this facility, it stands to lose nothing and to gain much by maintaining the health of its employees. If has been seen that the food brought by the workers themselves for their lunch is more often than not either nutritious nor adequate. The place provided for lunch should not be too far from the place of work, because if the worker becomes tires in traveling to the place reserved for eating, the organization will lose because the production will fall. If, on the other hand, restaurants are attached to the factory premises, the workers enjoy taking their food, with the result that their health does not suffer. Their fatigue is reduced both by the nourishment and by the pleasure they derive in taking good food. The organization benefits by the consequent increase in production. Food can be provided both in the morning and in the afternoon.

Money and Medical Facilities

The health and nourishment of the worker depends not only on the rest and food which are provided for him. Certain other factors also play an important role in it. For example, economic worries have a detrimental effect on health. For this reason it is desirable that the employer should provide facilities for small short term loan so that the worker can tide over a difficult period. Medical facilities provided at low cost also help the worker to a great extent.

Recreation

Healthy recreation is another factor that helps to build up the mental and physical health of the worker. For this reason, most modern industrial organizations provide healthy recreation by opening clubs, cinema halls and other forms of entertainment near the industrial complex.

IMPORTANCE OF INDIVIDUAL DIFFERENCES IN FATIGUE

The last conclusion drawn from the ergographic studies places stress upon the importance of individual differences insolar as they have some influence upon fatigue. It is generally known that some people become tires quicker than other people and also take a longer time in recovering their strength and energy. Other people tire less easily and also regain their energy more quickly. This fact of individual differences has special importance with respect to work in which more than one person work together. If, for example, all the people deputed to perform a single task tire easily, the task will be completed only with great difficulty. For this reason, the fact of individual differences should be kept in mind while selecting people to perform different functions in a factory. Difficult work should be assigned to people who do not tire easily. Certain kinds of work require a lot of hard work in the beginning, but in the end they can be performed without too much effort. For such work it is better that it should be started by a person who is capable of great effort. It can then be completed by another person who is weaker.

The importance of ergographic studies has been made clear by the application of their conclusions to actual industrial conditions, an account of which is given above. Many industrial organizations have benefited by introducing lunch and rest intervals. Whether some difficulty has been experienced as a result of introducing these intervals, it has been caused by those workers who return of introducing, these intervals, it has been caused by those workers who return late to their work, or collect in great numbers in the coffee shops, factories and offices or even in the elevators. As a result organization do experience some difficulty, but nobody complains that the introduction of such intervals is harmful or that it is not beneficial.

Important Researches

Some of the important researches and studies conducted on these subjects are outlined here.

1. *Haggard's Research*: According to W.W. Haggard, a ten percent increase in production resulted when the workers were provided two additional lunches. The workers also reported that they are helped in recovering their energy and that despite the increased work they experienced less fatigue. The provision of comfortable chairs and beds in some other industrial organizations also resulted in an increase in production. The truth of the matter is that if the management does not make provision for rest, the workers themselves take time out for rest, illegally or without permission. In some offices the clerks are seen sleeping in their chairs while in others the workers leave their desks by inventing some or the other excuse. Sometimes the worker seeks relief only in reducing the tempo of his work. If the worker can think of no other excuse he goes and stands in the queue outside the lavatory. It is therefore better that the management should itself provide a rest interval for the workers. Not every worker can think up excuses to get rest and neither can one actually feel relaxed by stealing rest in this way.

2. *Mezerik's Research*: On the basis of his studies Mezerik has written that in one particular case a thirty two percent increase in production was seen employed in many modern industries to perform the lighter functions. The management's attention has been drawn towards providing rest for the female worker because it realizes that the feminine body is naturally softer. Wherever female workers are employed in modern industries, provisions are made for rest intervals, beautiful and comfortably furnished rooms for resting, reasonably a feeling of dissatisfaction which in the long run, harms the employer. The expense incurred in providing such basic amenities is recovered manifold through the increased production.

Chapter 11 BOREDOM

MEANING OF BOREDOM AND MONOTONY

In the context of psychological fatigue, insofar as it pertains to industry, the words boredom and monotony are used in addition to fatigue. Monotony is a mental condition which is produced by the constant repetition of some function over a long period of time. On the other hand, boredom is a mental condition in which the individual evinces negative attitudes and aptitude for a particular work. In other words he does not want to do that work. Both boredom and monotony contribute to fatigue but neither is the result of physical fatigue. Both of them are caused by mental attitudes. Boredom is caused more by the personality of the worker, his aptitude, his emotional condition and the apparent importance of the function he is performing. When these factors are varied one person will feel no boredom in some particular function which bores another person. Some people become bored rapidly with some work requiring repetition but many other people adapt themselves very quickly to such work. For these reasons the workers have completely divergent opinions about work which is boring and other work which is not.

1. **Study by Wyatt, Langdon and Stock.** Some important facts connected with this subject were revealed in the study of S. Wyatt, J.H. Langdon and F.G.L. Stock. This study was conducted on ten individuals and five kinds of work. Each individual was required to do each kind of work for one month, and at the end of the period each individuals was required to point out the extent of boredom experienced in each kind of work. The worker was to award zero points to the work which contained no boredom and five points to the work in which he felt consistently bored. When this evaluation was analyzed it was seen that all the workers considered two kinds of work consistently boring, although some awarded five points to one work and some awarded them to the other. Apart from this the ten individuals showed no unanimity of opinion. The average evaluation for the five kinds of work was 4.2, 2.4, 2.3, 1.7 and 1.7. It is evident that different individual made a separate evaluation of boredom according to their individual differences. The scientists conducting the study pointed out the boredom was evinced by workers with a higher intelligence quotient and an extrovert tendency. But this fact has not been substantiated by other studies.

CAUSES OF BOREDOM AND MONOTONY

Factors which cause boredom and monotony have been revealed through many studies. Some of the factors leading to boredom and monotony, briefly stated, are :

1. **Individuality of the Worker.** As has already been demonstrated and monotony are closely connected with the individual traits of the individual workers. It is commonly seen that particular kind of work will strike some people as boring while others will find no boredom in doing it. In an experiment on 400 students of Munsterberg's college, it was seen that boredom depends upon the individual's particular personality traits, not upon the nature of the work. Different individuals take interest in different kinds of work, and that is why the pattern of boredom in each case is different.
2. **Intelligence of the Worker.** Among the different qualities that make up individual differences, intelligence is important and it as a close relation with boredom and monotony. As has been pointed out earlier, the more intelligent individual is inclined to be bored by mechanical repetition of some activity. On the other hand, the less intelligent individual makes a better adjustment with his work. But in this connection it would be better to give a brief review of some of the studies conducted on this subject. The more important studies are the following:
   (i) *Thomson's Study*: Thomson experimented upon 32 people and came to the conclusion that boredom has nothing to do with intelligence.
   (ii) *Viteles' Study*: Viteles conducted an experiment on girls working in the salary section and concluded that the more intelligent girls working more boredom with the result that majority of such girls are among those who leave this kind of job.
   (iii) *Komhauser's Research*: A.W. Kornhauser conducted an experiment on office workers and supported the contention of Viteles. He also found that the more intelligent people soon become bored with the work and run away. The less intelligent continue to retain their interest in their work.
   (iv) *Burnett's Study*: Burnett came to the same conclusion when he conducted an experiment on four girls. He also concluded that the less intelligent girls achieved higher production than the more intelligent girls.
   (v) *Studies by Wyatt, Fraser and Stock*: These psychologists also came to the same conclusion. It was observed by them that the less intelligent girls take more interest in their work than the average or exceptionally intelligent girls.
   (vi) *Study by a Pound*: In this book 'The Iron Man in Industry' A. Pound has remarked, "A morone trained in habits of doing regularly and obedience, is for many practical purposes, more valuable to his boss for good production than one in higher mental state."
3. **Attitude to the Work.** Many studies have established that workers with a negative attitude to their work experience boredom and monotony much sooner than those with a

positive attitude. People with a positive attitude can maintain their concentration in their work for a much longer time.

4. **Satiation.** Some people soon become fed up with doing work that needs recall, and they do not want to continue doing it. Their attention in the work gradually decreases as their mind becomes more and more satiated. As a result the quantity and quality of the production also declines. Satiation is a psychological condition in which physical fatigue is at a very low level. A. Karsten conducted an experiment in this connection with some college students. When they had become completely bored with the work of writing they were asked to write names on a sheet of paper, in which they experienced no difficulty at all. In an experiment with poetry it was seen that some individuals who did not want to utter one more line of poetry were willing to continue talking for a long time when the subject was changed. They, too, did not experience and fatigue, it is evident from both these experiments that only those muscles were being exercised which already appeared to be fatigued. But this apparent fatigue was due to boredom and when the subject was changed they again began to function normally because the boredom was removed. Obviously, the difficulty in working was not due to muscular fatigue but due to satiation, a psychological condition. Satiation is caused by doing the same kind of work. It does not imply fatigue. This was also proved by the fact that some workers complaining of fatigue. This was also proved by the fact that some workers complaining of fatigue resumed their work when they were allowed to change their position.
5. **Feeling of Progress.** Many experiments have also yielded the fact that if the worker is aware of the progress he has made in his work, he does not experience boredom or monotony. In fact, as the work progresses the worker becomes excited at the prospect of achieving his target and works with renewed energy. An individual becomes bored very quickly with some work the need of which he cannot see or which leads to no tangible result. For this reason it is always better to have recognizable targets at short intervals in any work. The desire to finish the day's work can itself be an aim. In such a case one can observe, the increase in the speed of working. But the feeling of having achieved some target or of being near the end also depends upon the individual's attitude. If the attitude is negative this feeling of achievement is weak. Fairly often the boredom of the individual can be reduced if he can be convinced of the value and importance of his work for others.
6. **Other Qualities.** In addition to the above, individual qualities of the worker also influence boredom. The more important ones are leaning of attention, emotional condition, peculiarities of nature. If these are in favour of the work, the work will produce less boredom. But is these are negative the individual will soon become bored with his work.
7. **Feeling of Leaving Something Incomplete.** One particular worker was lying on his death bed. He was asked to mention the last wish he would like to have fulfilled. He said that he would like to have a board on which the screws were only half tightened. He wanted to complete the work of tightening those screws. This individual had spent all his life fixing screws on a board and half tightening them. But he was always filled with the

desire to tighten these screws fully. Similar phenomena have been observed in many studies. A worker feels dissatisfied and deprived if he is not allowed to complete his task. In another example, it was seen that one foreman ordered a worker to leave the work in hand and go on to something else. The worker did not want to leave his work incomplete, so he refused to obey the foreman. Using his position the foreman ordered him to leave it. This led to an exchange of words and a scuffle in which the worker pushed the foreman who fell against a machine and was killed. The only thing at the root of this incident was that the foreman wanted to take the worker away from his work, which the worker wanted to complete. It is also seen that many workers do not want to start some fresh assignment near the end of the day. They know that they will not be able to complete it, and it is against human psychology to leave some work incomplete. A refusal in such conditions does not amount to disobedience, disrespect or obstinacy, and should not be interpreted as such. Man has a natural desire to finish anything that he has begun, and if he is prevented from doing so, he loses his balance, a fact which has been established by many psychological experiments. When the worker enters the factory, he first of all wants to complete the previous days work before going on to something fresh. While working, an individual enters a psychological state in which he wants to leave some work only after he has completed it. This motivation can differ in degree from person to person and from work to work. And providing an opportunity to complete the work is an important element in job satisfaction. This tendency of completing unfinished work is seen more particularly in those kinds of work which influence the emotions, irrespective of their inherent interest or the lack of it. If the worker is indifferent towards his work, he will show no desire to complete it. A worker is seen working rapidly only because he is pressed by the desire to finish it. For this reason the desire to finish some work has an important influence upon boredom or monotony. If this desire is present the individual does not become bored. In this way this tendency is directed against boredom because it creates motivation. In industrial conditions it is desirable that the work should be derived in such a way among the workers that they get an opportunity to complete their part of the work. This increases motivation and reduces boredom.

8. **Conditions of Work.** From the above account of the causes of boredom and monotony if should not be taken for granted that only individual and personal factors are responsible while the external environment plays no part at all. In fact, the truth of the matter is that the manager or the employer can do more to remove boredom and monotony by changing the external conditions of work than he can by trying to condition the worker's mind or to control his attitudes. Monotony can be reduced and production increased by making adequate changes in the working conditions. This can be done by making the following changes:

   (*i*) *Provision for Rest*: Boredom or monotony increase in the absence of any rest period. In a study conducted by Mayo it was seen that the workers in a cloth mill suffered from boredom because they did not have any rest interval in their working hours. When provision was made for rest, an immediate decline in the level of boredom was soon noticed. This has also been substantiated by the research of other psychologists.

(ii) *Arrangements for Wages*: The salary system plays an important part in creating interest among the workers. They feel dissatisfied and bored if the wages are not paid at the correct time or at the correct rates. Shaaz saw in his studies that the worker experiences less boredom and achieves a higher level of production if he gets proper wages.

(iii) *Working Method*: Wyatt, Frazer and Stock studied the work technique of three girls working in a factory making cigarette boxes. One of these girls had to work three times as much as the third girl, with the result that they regularly exchanged their positions. The scientist, instead of allowing one girl to work at one position for the whole day, made the girls interchange their respective positions six times a single day. It was noticed that their boredom grew less and they produced an extra ten per cent of work.

9. **Nature of Work.** One cause of boredom is the nature of the work because if a particular function does not vary at all the worker becomes bored very soon and experiences monotony. If the work is varied and changed frequently the worker's interest in it is maintained. Many experimental results have confirmed this view. Wyatt and Frazer conducted experiments in which six girls were asked to pack soap, fold handkerchiefs, gather cycle chains and to do a variety of other kinds of work. It was noticed that production went up and monotony declined.

10. **Social Factors.** Boredom and monotony also depend to a large extent upon some social factors because the worker works in a social environment which has a decided influence upon his mental condition. If the mutual exchange upon the management and the worker is entertaining and cooperative then the boredom is quickly done away with. Then the worker takes an interest in his work. As long as conversation and laughter do not interfere with the performance of work, the workers should be allowed to indulge in conversation. This helps to maintain the worker's interest in his work. It has also been noticed that less boredom occurs if men and women work together. On the contrary if the atmosphere is one of mutual suspicion and district in which the management goes out of the way to scold the worker, the worker soon loses his interest in the work, thus adversely affecting production.

REMEDIES TO BOREDOM AND MONOTONY

Many psychological means have now been evolved in industrial psychology to relieve boredom and monotony. Since monotony depends upon the nature of the work and upon the individual differences of each worker, different means are adopted to remove monotony from different kinds of work. But even then the following general measures can be useful in eliminating boredom :

1. **Exchanging Job.** The most important single measure in removing boredom is to exchange the jobs of the workers among them. Since different kinds of work exhaust different muscles of the body, a change of job helps to maintain the novelty of the work and thus monotony is avoided. Again, the worker also gets an opportunity to gain experience about

different kinds of work, while repetition of the same work does not provide any variety of experience. In addition to an exchange of jobs, the worker should be allowed to do the same job in many different ways since this helps to reduce mental and physical fatigue and maintain interest in the work. In the case of girls working in a telephone exchange it was seen that they took more interest in their work and complained of boredom less frequently when they were allowed to exchange their jobs. By hi studies J.R.P. French has shown that job exchange has a positive and beneficial influence upon morale. In his study the working girls were allowed to change the rate and method of working.

2. **Relating the Job to the Large Picture.** Some people become bored with their jobs only because their function is not connected with a comprehensive picture of the job. If a woman who cleans dishes treats each dish as nothing more than another dish, she will soon become bored and will experience monotony. Norman R. F. Maier has described the case of a subnormal boy who cleaned all the dishes in the house, irrespective of the number of guests. And as there were already fifteen members in the household, he should ordinarily have become bored and tired very soon. But he never required any help in this task because, for him each dish had individual characteristics and he could identify each dish by some mark on it. He treated each dish as a friend and found pleasure in cleaning the face of each friend. Some of them he liked more than others and therefore he had reserved special places for them. He found interest in this work because he experienced the feeling that he was rapidly meeting one friend after another.

3. **Knowledge of Work.** It has been seen that working girls soon become bored in their office work if they do not have interest in it. On the other hand, a typist will not experience monotony if he finds the official correspondence interesting or if the office's functions interest him. For this reason it is desirable that all the workers should have sufficient knowledge of the work of their organization. As long as they are ignorant of this they cannot gauge the importance of their own contribution to it. Once they realize this importance of their own job can be seen in the right perspective as part of the larger picture. Then the sense of responsibility increases and better work is done. Sometimes the worker is told instead to mind his own business and to carry out orders as they are given to him, without taking interest in the working of the organization. The consequence of this kind of management is that the worker is not interested in the quality of his own work and neither does he make any effort to improve his method of working.

4. **Use of Sub-Goals.** In order to reduce monotony it is desirable to create sub-goals within the work which can be achieved quickly. One such goal is the completion of the day's work with the result that the worker feels he is making progress as the day wears on. If the goal is too far away or can be achieved only after a long time, it does not serve to inspire the worker in this way. In addition to this goal of completing the day's work, the rest intervals can also be made sub-goals. The worker is inspired to complete his work because he feels that soon he will get the chance to rest. It is often seen that the speed of working

increases as the time of rest comes nearer. In this way the rest period provides relaxation and removes monotony.

5. **Division of Work into Large Units.** Another way of creating goals is to divide the work into large units. For example, if we start reading book with the intention of finishing it chapter by chapter, then the book can be completed without loss of interest or creation of boredom. Besides, the reader experiences a feeling of progress as he moves from one chapter to the next.
6. **Distribution of Units.** In order to enhance this sense of achievement in industry, the various units of production should be distributed among the workers and each one should be encouraged to complete his own unit. Production can thus be increased by making production itself a goal. The unit of production is between two periods of rest, and the desire and enthusiasm to complete the unit tends to reduce monotony.
7. **Use of Pacing Method and Automatic Work Habits.** Psychological analyses have revealed that monotony is repeated activity. It is not caused by recall but by repeating the work. Nowadays efforts are made to turn all repetitive functions into automatic activities, as far as is possible. When this is done the work becomes natural and continues to be done without any attention being paid to it so that the worker can allow his mind to wander here and there. Work of this kind does not cause monotony. For example, people do not notice the distance they walked if they are talking to another person at the same time. But if the individual concentrates his attention on the activity of walking he will soon find it monotonous. Hence, if the work is of the same nature as walking, then the worker should have the liberty to talk to others or to day dream, if he so desires. Many studies have shown that, given the liberty to day dream, monotony can be kept at a low level.
8. **Rhythmic Activity.** Improvement in performance can be seen when some repeated activity is made rhythmic. It has been seen that when many workers are performing the same function they tend to follow a rhythm. Men who carry heavy loads can be seen working in this way. Similarly, less boredom is experienced when walking in step rather than in walking without any rhythm.
9. **Provision of Industrial Music.** Another means of reducing boredom is to provide music to the workers in industry. This measure has proved of great value in all work which does not require the constant attention of the worker. And it should be noted that instrumental music proves more useful than vocal music.
10. **Increase of Experience of Completion.** The awareness of having completed some work provides natural motivation and stimulation. For this reason boredom can be reduced by allowing the worker to have a greater sense of having completed his work. The managers should try to avoid interruption of the worker at his work and in particular not to interfere with him before he has completed his task. The consciousness of completion is created when the worker is aware of the progress he has made. Leaving the work in hand as soon as ordered is not a sign of effective administration or obedience in industry. No intelligent manager will stress that the worker should suspend his work as soon as he is ordered. The

manager will allow the worker to complete the work in hand and then ask him to report. By doing this the manager can help to maintain the motivation of the worker and avoid boredom. In addition to this the work can be divided into small units so that it gives more frequent experience of completion and achievement. These smaller units themselves become the goals for the worker and he gets a feeling of completion and the satisfaction when he achieves even this smaller goal. The total work and the working hours should be divided in such a manner that there should be the satisfying experience of completing each unit. The job of preparing records and maintaining accounts can be made more satisfying by dividing the work into separate files so that the worker can feel relieved after finishing work on one file. Job satisfaction increases as the work is seen coming to an end.

11. **Attending to Individual Differences.** In dividing the work among the workers attention should be paid to their individual differences. If this is done the incidence of disinterest and boredom will be less. As far as possible a worker should be given a task which suits his intelligence, attitudes, spheres of attention, nature and emotional condition.
12. **Improvement of Working Conditions.** Generally, boredom and monotony can be kept in control by providing a properly timed and sufficiently long period of rest, payment of wages at the correct time, by introducing the proper method of working, permitting freedom to laugh and enjoy, and generally improving the working conditions.
13. **Proper Social Environment.** Finally, the most important method of reducing boredom is to maintain an atmosphere of love and confidence, cooperation and faith among the workers and the management. If the social environment is encouraging and pleasant, boredom normally does not occur.

Chapter **12**

ACCIDENTS AND SAFETY

INTRODUCTION

Accidents are mishappening which result in loss of life and property. In our day-to-day life accidents are very common. Transport accidents *i.e.*, air, railway, road accidents are sometimes very severe. Accidents can be reduced but can not be eliminated. Accidents effect the individual and his family life.

Different job situations have different accident rates. A bus driver who drives through busy streets is more likely to have accidents than a driver driving a crowed free roads. The accidents occur more commonly in mines than clerical work.

Every three minutes a worker dies somewhere in the world due to occupational injury and every second at least four workers are hurt, all because of the failure to control effectively the occupational hazards, according to the International Labour Organization (ILO).

As the nation observed its 21st National Safety Day on 4th March 1991 the Bhopal gas tragedy, which took a toll more than 2,000 lives and left behind several hundred crippled, still haunts people's memory.

According to safety experts, the unorganized or semi-organized industries employing over 261 million workforce in India have no proper legislation to provide for safety, particularly in the agriculture and construction sectors.

Despite significant progress in recent years, the safety awareness at the national level was still far from satisfactory, this awareness in a number of important sectors like road transportation, construction industry and agriculture had been grossly neglected.

India has the dubious distinction of having one of the highest rates of road accidents in which more than 50,000 people are killed every year. In the construction industry, more than 3.5 lakh workers suffer injuries annually of which over 2,000 lose their lives.

Many agricultural workers get permanently disabled while using agricultural machinery. Even in the manufacturing sector, the small scale and tiny units are particularly indifferent to the basic statutory responsibilities regarding safety and health of their workers.

The impact of National Safety Day campaign, aimed at generating safety awareness, is yet to be felt by the general public and other sectors of industries.

According to the latest report of the National Crime Records Bureau, 1,52,314 people died in various accidents in 1987, recording an increase of 3.7 percent over the preceding year. The figures for later years, which are yet to be compiled, indicate a staggering increase in accidental deaths.

Haphazard industrialization also causes hundreds of fatal accidents. Maharashtra, a highly industrialized state in the country, leads in industrial accidents, which went up from 61,342 in 1986 to 68,951 in 1990.

ARE ACCIDENTS ACCIDENTAL?

When the scientific attitude had not been adopted by the industry, it was believed that accidents were accidental. But when scientific research began in the sphere of industry, it was soon learnt that if there were provision for safety the number of accidents fell. Where safety methods were introduced a downward trend in the number of accidents was soon noticed. When people were trained to avoid accidents, a marked improvement was observed. Hence, it is no longer believed that accidents are accidental. The Workmen's Compensation Laws have played an important role in this change because once this legislation was introduced, the industrialists in England and America had to pay very compensation to any worker injured or incapacitated in an accident. The consequence was that accidents became very undesirable as far as the management was concerned and they tried to prevent them as far as possible. With the passing of time it was noticed that the sum spent on introducing safety devices proved to be far less than the total compensation paid out in case of accident. Hence safety devices proved to be more economic, and the industrialists stood to gain by introducing them and increasing them. Finding these safety measures a paying proposition the industrialists in every sphere sought to introduce them and also trained their employees to avoid accidents and become more safety-conscious. Another advantage of introducing safety measures was that the loss of working hours through accidents decreased and led to a further increase in production. Besides, the workers now developed a more trusting and confident attitude towards their employers and thus worked harder, again benefiting the industrialist. Many subsequent researches and studies have established beyond doubt that the introduction of safety measures led to the saving of millions of dollars. And the production everywhere went up in proportion to the security measures introduced, besides the improvement in human relations between the workers and the management. For this reason great attention is now paid in all industries to the prevention of accidents. This proves that accidents are not really accidental.

INDUSTRIAL ACCIDENTS

Accidents occurring in the industries are called industrial accidents. These are generally due to faculty equipment and machinery or negligence on the part of the workers. Proper precautions can reduce the accidents. There are always some causes for occurring of accidents.

There are always some chances of accidents while working on machinery and equipment. All industrial operations increase the change of accidents. Proper training and knowledge should be given about the dangers of accidents. Accidents also occur in industries due to faults of the workers. They can be negligent dis-interested in jobs and under the influence of intoxicants resulting in a higher number of accidents.

DEFINITION OF ACCIDENTS

An event or mishappening that occurs unexpectedly is called an accident.

Characteristics of Accidents

1. Accidents are unfortunate sudden happenings about which nothing is known in advance.
2. Life and property are effected by accidents.
3. Due to accidents, work is stopped for a certain length of time.

CLASSIFICATION OF ACCIDENTS

There are several methods of classifying the accidents. Some of the methods are as follows:

1. According to length of recovery from injury
2. According to cause of events
3. According to nature of events
4. According to damage caused
5. According to nature of injury.

1. According to Length of Recovery

This is an important method of classifying the industrial accidents. This is further divided into three categories.

(*a*) First Aid cases

(*b*) Home case accidents

(*c*) Lost Time accidents.

(*a*) *First Aid Cases*: The injuries due to minor accidents are not serious. The workers are given first aid at the factory hospital. After getting the medical treatment at factory hospital. The worker can again start the work. In this type of accidents no time is lost except when the worker is receiving first aid treatment. No compensation is to be paid to the injured worker.

(*b*) *Home Case Accidents*: The injured worker is given preliminary treatment at the factory hospital and is allowed to go home. The worker may not attend his duties for a maximum of 3 days. The worker recovers in this period and is ready to resume his duties. So the workers loses the day, shift or turn of work in which the accident has taken place.

(c) *Lost Time Accidents*: For these accidents, the factory has to pay compensation. The worker has to leave the work on account of accidents for more days in addition to the day, shift or turn in which the mishappening has taken place. The worker is generally admitted to the hospital. In this case temporary or permanent type of disablement may result. The accident may lead to enquiry and investigation if difference of opinion is found regarding the causes of the accidents.

For example, the hand, arm, leg or any other part of the body is injured seriously or cut by the machine.

2. Cause of Events

(a) Machine accidents.

(b) Non-Machine accidents.

(a) *Machine Accidents:* Some example of Machine accidents are given below:

(i) Catching of fingers, arms, clothing etc. in machines.

(ii) Catching of tools, guides etc. in machine.

(iii) Catching of flying objects or particles.

(b) *Non-Machine Accidents:* These are common but generally less serious type accidents. Some examples are given below:

(i) Falling objects

(ii) Objects on floor

(iii) Pushes, bumps etc. by other persons, objects.

3. Classification According to Nature of Events

(a) Traffic accidents.

(b) Passenger accidents.

(a) *Traffic Accidents*:

(i) Collisions with pedestrians

(ii) Collisions with cars or buses.

(iii) Collisions with motor vehicles.

(b) *Passenger Accidents*:

(i) Boarding moving car or bus

(ii) Caught or struck by doors

(iii) Trips, slips, stumbles, falls etc.

4. According to Damage Caused

This classification is based on damage caused. Damage can be that of property, material or building. Some examples are given below:

(i) Damage to the store material

(ii) Partial or complete loss of container or contents

(*iii*) Damage to Hand trucks

(*iv*) Damage to Trolleys

(*v*) Damage to Belt conveyors, cranes or machines.

5. Classification According to Nature Injury

This classification is as follows:

(*a*) Fatal accidents

(*b*) Permanent disablement.

(*c*) Temporary disablement.

(*a*) *Fatal Accidents:* In such a accident, one or more persons are killed.

(*b*) *Permanent Accidents:* Due to accident the worker loses earning capacity. The worker is not capable of earning that much money which he was capable to earn before accident. Compensation is to be paid to the injured worker and the amount depends upon the disablement. For example the worker may cut his finger, arm or hand etc.

Permanent disablement is of two types.

(*i*) Total disablement

(*ii*) Partial disablement

(*c*) *Temporary Disablement:* These accidents are less serious than of the previous category. The worker is unfit temporarily and he loses his earning capacity for a short time. Compensation is to be paid according to the workmen's compensation act. Fracture of an arm is an example of temporary disablement.

6. Accidents on Construction Work

Some examples are given below:

(*i*) Falling of person

(*ii*) Slipping results inner strains of the body

(*iii*) Accidents because of flying objects

(*iv*) Accident due to traffic

(*v*) Burning and Fire accidents

(*vi*) Electric shocks

(*vii*) Explosions.

CAUSES OF ACCIDENTS

Accidents to not just happens but there are always some causes. If we want to decrease the number of accidents, then the causes of accidents must be studied in details. The various causes can be divided as follows:

1. Physical causes based upon unsafe conditions of work
2. Physiological causes based upon defects of physical body of the worker
3. Psychological causes based upon mental disturbances of the worker.

1. Physical Causes

These are linked with the machinery and surroundings. These causes are beyond the control of the worker. The conditions are likely to cause accidents. This is further classified as follows:

(*a*) *Physical Causes Related to Machinery and Plant:* The following can cause accidents:

(*i*) unguarded and unfenced moving machine parts

(*ii*) unbalanced, noisy and improper adjusted machine parts

(*iii*) space between the machines is less

(*iv*) old and worn out machines

(*v*) Improper Insulation of electric circuits and machinery

(*vi*) unlubricated moving parts get heated

(*vii*) Improper plant layout.

(*b*) *Causes Related to Tools and Material:* The following will involve more number of accidents:

(*i*) Dull or damaged tools

(*ii*) Tools without handles

(*iii*) Very sharp edged tools

(*iv*) Inflammable and hot materials

(*v*) Poisonous and toxic materials

(*vi*) Breakable materials

(*c*) *Causes Related to Dress:*

(*i*) Loose or Improper dress

(*ii*) Slippary foot wears

(*iii*) Not wearing personal protective equipment *e.g.*, goggles, gloves, screen required during welding.

(*d*) *Causes Related to Working Conditions:*

(*i*) Lighting is not proper

(*ii*) Improper ventilation for the exit of dust and gases

(*iii*) Slippery floors and stairs cases

(*iv*) Severity of work. For example mines, construction of tunnels, building of sky scrapers is quite risky

(*v*) Working hours are too long resulting in tiredness

(*vi*) Bad discipline

(*vii*) Defective building and projected objects.

2. Physiological Causes of Accidents

These causes of accidents are related to physical body of worker *e.g.*, a weak man cannot lift a heavy load. Weak eye sighted person cannot drive vehicle properly. An old man cannot so heavy work. Some of the causes of accidents are due to following physiological defects.

(*i*) Weak eyesight

(*ii*) Poor listening power

(*iii*) Weak health

(*iv*) Any part of the body may be defective

(*v*) Fatness and high blood pressure

(*vi*) Fatigue and exertion of work

(*vii*) Older employees.

3. Psychological Causes of Accidents

These are linked with the mental disturbance of individual worker. This is not some external environment but the internal characteristics of the employees that the accident occurs to him. The worker is regarded as careless and is victim of an accident. He does not give proper attention to safety rules and regulations. The worker may involve himself in the accident on account of following:

(*i*) His habit of ignoring the things that is carelessness

(*ii*) Frustration, worry or depression

(*iii*) Emotional unequilibrium due to mental tension

(*iv*) Improper co-ordination between body and mental faculties

(*v*) Improper placement of employee that is he lacks aptitude for the work. He is not interested in doing the work

(*vi*) Nervousness and impulsiveness

(*vii*) Over confidence

4. Miscellaneous Causes

(*i*) Lack of training and experience

(*ii*) Intoxication—use of wine, opium etc.

EFFECTS OF ACCIDENTS

The accidents are always undesirable. They result in loss of life and property. They produce evil effects on workers, families, employers and on the society. The bad effects of the accidents are as follows:

1. Effects on the Victims and their Family Members

Humanitarian consideration is an important factor. The social and economic life of the injured employee is disturbed. The injury and disability caused the following problems:

(*i*) Physical suffering of the injured

(*ii*) Spending the rest of his life with reduced ability and earnings.

(*iii*) Accident produces the psychological effects upon the injured

(*iv*) It reflects upon the future life of tile dependents of the employees.

2. Effect on Costs and Employer

Accidents are harmful when we take into account the business of the concern. It adds to the costs of production directly as well as indirectly.

The employer has to bear the following costs:

(*i*) Medical expenses to be paid to the victim

(*ii*) Compensation of injury on the basis of disablement

(*iii*) Fines which may be imposed upon the industry for neglecting safety measures

(*iv*) Loss of damaged materials and machinery involved in the accidents.

Indirect Costs: Indirect costs of the accidents has been estimated to be higher than direct costs. Indirect costs include the following:

(*i*) Time lost by the management and other personnel in helping the injured person on the spot.

(*ii*) Investigating the accident

(*iii*) Preparing the reports of the accidents

(*iv*) Time lost by the workers in observing and discussing the accidents

(*v*) Training and placement of new employees

(*vi*) The injured person on return to duty, may work with reduced efficiency

(*vii*) Psychological effects on other workers—they turn out interior products

(*viii*) If the accident is very sever and deliveries are delayed, he customers may be lost.

3. Effects of Colleagues and Society

(*i*) Sometimes colleagues get demoralized on seeing the severity of accidents.

(*ii*) Funds are to be collected for helping the victim.

(*iii*) Material loss of the society and nation.

(*iv*) Prices are increased due to reduction in production.

(*v*) Family members of the injured may become socially–boycotted.

ACCIDENT PRONE WORKER

The worker who involves himself in more of accidents than the average worker is called accident prone worker.

There are two causes of accidents. First cause is the situational factor and the second cause is personal factors due to which a person is victim of an accident. Different persons have different accident rates under similar working conditions.

If the personal factors are responsible for accidents and the number of accidents does not change even under changed conditions, the concept is called accident proneness.

CAUSES OF ACCIDENT PRONENESS

There can be many physiological and psychological causes of accidents which have been already discussed under the heading 'causes of accidents'.

Sometimes a random happening of an accident may create proneness. If a shop boy just happens to fall from the top of a ladder, he loses self confidence. Whenever he will again reach the top of a ladder, he will become nervous and will lose control of himself and repeat the accident. He will become an accident prone worker. In such a case he should safe asked to work on the floor.

MEANS OF PREVENTING ACCIDENTS

The only means of preventing accidents is to remove all the cause of accidents that have been mentioned earlier. Generally speaking, accidents can be avoided or prevented if the following measures are adopted:

1. **Reform of the Working Conditions.** If accidents are to be prevented, then the conditions of work should be improved. The temperature in the working premises should not be so such that it may lead to discomfort. This helps to improve the health of the worker and-thus prevents accidents. The illumination provided should also be only strong enough and not too intense. Besides, the light source should be installed at the correct angle. Only those parts of machine should be well fit which are to be constantly in the eyes of the worker. The light should hot fall directly on the eyes of the operator. Besides, the machines in the factory should be so arranged that the workers should be able to get maximum production by making the minimum possible movements, so that there is no waste of effort. If some particular machine is likely to cause accidents or if it is dangerous to go near some particular machine, then safety devices should be installed to keep the workers away from it.
2. **Provision of Safety Devices.** Nowadays engineers and psychologists cooperate to design safety methods by which even dangerous machines lead to fewer accidents. Engineers have been responsible for designing safety devices, special kinds of gloves, special kinds of spectacles which shield the eyes, and other gadgets by which machine can be operated from a safe distance, without ever being touched by human hand. Methods of keeping the operator away from the machine while working have also been adopted but sometimes operators wish to show that they are not afraid of the machines and they deliberately avoid

using these devices. In such cases devices have been developed to make up use of the safety devices unavoidable, for without them the worker cannot operate the machine efficiently. If it is not possible to install such devices on some particular machines, the workers should be trained and encouraged to use these devices. And if it is not possible to make provisions for training the workers, then they should be paid some compensation in lieu of this training. In short, the workers should be encouraged in every possible way to adopt these safety devices.

One basic condition of a safety device is that it must be one hundred percent safe. If it is not completely safe then accidents will increase because the workers depend on it and in their own way become careless. If the device offers only 50 percent safety factors, it proves actually harmful because accidents increase. On the other hand, if there are no safety devices, the worker naturally pays more attention and tends to be cautious with the result that fewer accidents occur. Actually, the worker makes his own adjustment with every kind of condition. If he is asked to operate a dangerous machine on which there are no safety devices, he operates it with extreme caution. Workers working on the night shift tend to be more cautious than workers on the day shift because they realize that lack of caution will lead to accidents. The result of this is that while more accidents should occur during the night under artificial light, in actual fact more accidents take place during the day. But if the machine is fitted with safety devices, the worker himself does not take so many precautions and if the device fails, an accident occurs immediately. This fact can be seen in the case of car accidents caused by speed. Few accidents take place at slow speed because no driver has the opportunity to speed up, and besides the presence of other cars makes it dangerous. But when the driver finds an empty and clear road he tends to drive much faster, with the result that many accidents take place on rural roads and only 5 percent on urban roads in America, although the rural roads are generally deserted while the urban roads are far more crowded and carry much more traffic. Similar examples can be found in different industrial conditions.

3. **Warning System.** In addition to the adoption of the above measures, every new worker in a factory should be carefully warned about the dangerous machines. In many modern factories such machines have a danger sign printed on them, the workers may be constantly warned. Sometimes a device installed for safety in one particular direction becomes the cause of an accident in some other. For this reason engineers and psychologists should design safety devices in such a way that they do not disturb the normal pattern of working. In fact even safety devices should help the worker in his work. If such machines are designed, then production increases along with safety, while fatigue is reduced. The worker tends to become fatigued if he is aware of danger because then he is always tense. But if safety devices are provided, this mental tension is avoided and fatigue is reduced.
4. **Attention to Individual Differences.** Many accidents take place because the worker is required to perform some work which is beyond his physical capacity. Women, for example, cannot do heavy work, and if they are asked to do it, accidents become inevitable. Hence,

it is desirable that before allocating a particular task to a particular worker, information about his age, experience, mental health, emotional condition, sex, nature, intelligence, physical qualities and defects should be collected. If, after all this information has been collected, he proves to be capable of performing the particular task, he should be entrusted with it. Besides, if the worker has proved a failure at a particular task and is involved in many accidents in doing it, .he should immediately be taken away from it and put to some other work. And before putting a man on some dangerous machines it is better to test his accident proneness.

5. **Training in Right Work Methods.** Many accidents occur because the operators using machines have not been trained in the correct use of them. It is always better, therefore, to train a person in the use of a machine, in its maintenance, before allowing him to handle it. Another reason why accidents occur due to wrong methods of work is that in such a case the worker becomes tired very rapidly. And once a person is exhausted his tendency to commit mistakes and cause accidents increases rapidly.
6. **Means of Removing Fatigue.** It has already been pointed out that one important cause of accidents is fatigue. Hence one important measure of avoiding accidents is to remove fatigue. The most important method in this connection is to provide properly timed rest at frequent intervals so that the worker can regain his energy and avoid reaching a stage of complete exhaustion. Besides, the hours of work should not be too long so that complete exhaustion should not occur at all. Fatigue can also be prevented by providing a worker with a job which suits his mental and physical capacity. Fatigue can also be reduced by allowing the worker have a sense of satisfaction by completing his job, by creating an atmosphere of cooperation and management, by making arrangements for timely payment of salary, etc. In addition to this, arrangements should also be made for providing drinking water, wholesome and cheap food, and comfortable furniture for resting during the working hours.
7. **Proper Speed of Work.** Accidents frequently occur when the work is performed at a speed much greater than what is desirable. Drivers who often drive at high speeds are very frequently involved in accidents. Therefore, the speed of the worker in an office or a factory should be controlled. Accidents can also occur if the workers make a habit of putting in overtime, in addition to their normal working hours. If the worker tries to work rapidly as soon as he starts working, he becomes tired very quickly with the result that he works for the rest of the day in an exhausted condition, thus increasing the chances of accidents. Hence the workers should be encouraged to work at such a speed that they can maintain their efficiency and work throughout the day without unnecessary fatigue.
8. **Organization of Safety Committees.** Another measure for preventing accidents suggested by psychologists is the formation of safety committees. There should be one such committee in each factory, or even in each department of the factory; should the factory be exceptionally large in size. In addition to the workers, even security officers and psychologists may be asked to function on this committee. In this committee the suggestions

and complaints of the workers are recorded and considered so that the possible areas of accidents can be known and measures for preventing them instituted. At the same time such an organization helps to interest every worker in preventing accidents. Such safety committees can also be organized on a national scale, so that representatives from different industries can take part in them. Such committees help to train the worker, make him more safety conscious, and also help to develop or invent new safety techniques. Another benefit which can be derived here is that the worker who is negligent of safety measures or who habitually pays no attention to the possibility of accidents can be criticized and even socially ostracized.

9. **Safety Campaigns and Posters.** Safety can also be promoted in another way, by organizing a campaign, in factories and offices. Posters and slogans can also be used in such a campaign, but normally the slogans should not be negative. For example, a slogan like 'the careless worker is a fool' is not a proper slogan. Instead one can have more positive slogans such as 'beware of danger', 'keep the hat on the head', 'there is danger from poisonous gases here', 'cross the road here', 'smoke, if you must, but in the next room'. These slogans can be printed and hung up in various places within the factory premises. They will help to drive away the worker's fear, awaken his sense of safety, and direct him to act in the correct way. Any poster, concerned with accidents should not contain only a mention of the accidents possible because this will serve only to frighten the worker. Posters should tell him not only that accidents are possible but also how can avoid them.
10. **Habits of Safety.** Despite all the measures adopted, by far the best and the most successful method is the creation of habits of safety. If some worker has made a habit of operating his instruments improperly and of not using the safety devices, he may have an accident despite his efforts to prevent it. Different kinds of safety devices are built into different machines, and it is necessary that the worker should be trained in the use of them. But he must also be in the habit of using them. At times the workers resist the installation of some new safety device. In such a case they should never be forced to use the new device. They should be psychologically convinced that it is to their own advantage to make use of the safety devices. Once they are convinced they rarely have any hesitation in using it. If such habits have been formed, it is no longer necessary to remind the worker to be careful of accidents because caution becomes part of his thinking. That is why training is considered to be so important in all industries. Experience also has importance precisely for the same reason.
11. **Motivating Safety.** Unless the worker is motivated to exercise caution and to make use of the safety devices installed for his benefit, accidents cannot be prevented. Therefore, now-a-days workers are motivated and encouraged to work cautiously. One way of doing it is to increase the salary of those workers who follow the safety regulations. Another way of doing it is to counteract opposite kinds of motivation. For example, if a worker is encouraged to adopt safety measures on the one hand and is also forced to increase production on the other hand, then the work will defeat its purpose. Sometimes safety

devices are not adopted by the workers because they cause discomfort. In that case efforts have to be made to make these devices more conformable and endurable. Sometimes workers are even punished by fines if they do not make use of the safety devices but this method is harmful in as much as it does not encourage the worker to make use of the safety device but only forces him to find ways of concealing his practice. To put it briefly, the best way of encouraging the use of safety devices is to make use of the psychology of motivation. In the first place, contradictory motivations should be removed and then useful safety devices should be sought out. Workers should also be rewarded for making use of them. Even safety committees encourage the use of safety devices.

It is evident from the above description of the means of preventing accidents that the goal can be achieved only by the willing cooperation of the management, the workers and the psychologists. The government too can make a valuable contribution in this effort. Nowada great efforts are being made to avoid industrial accidents in all progressive countries.

ACCIDENT PRONENESS

What is Accident Proneness?

Generally more accidents take place in some industrial circumstances as compared to the others. Most psychologists feel that a particular pattern can be seen in accident. For example, once a person has been involved in one accident, he is inclined to get involved in another because the first accident causes to lose his self-confidence. In other words, his accident proneness increases. Accident proneness is that tendency due to which some particular people get involved in more accidents than some other people. Accident proneness is found in industrial circumstances which lead to more accidents, while there are certain individuals who, because of their psychological and physiological structure, are inclined to be involved in more accidents.

LAWS OF ACCIDENT PRONENESS

Psychologists have made a study of accidents in order to discover the laws governing accident proneness, and in this connection it is possible to make the following remarks:

1. If the accidents are accidental then some people are only rarely involved in them, where some are involved very frequently the majority of people are at a stage somewhere between the two extremes.
2. If the accidents are due to circumstances then it will be seen that people who suffer from many accidents in a particular period, will be comparatively free of accidents in the following period.
3. If accident proneness increases because of accidents, then the particular individuals found involved in accidents in a particular test will also be found to be involved in accidents at any later test.

4. If the accidents are due to some particular qualities of the individuals then people obtaining a particular grade in a particular accident will obtain the same grade in future accidents also.

Psychologists have been able to come to some conclusion about the causes of accidents. Most studies have indicated that some individuals are so constructed that they are involved in more accidents than other, and are also the cause of involving other people in accidents. Individuals of this kind are called accident prone. Normally there is always some scope for more or less accident proneness in every sphere where human beings work. It has therefore, come to be believed that instead of throwing out, the accident prone worker, it is better to analyze his accident proneness. This phenomenon can have many causes, and it may be possible to remove some of them. It has been found, for example, that accident proneness is definitely reduced if the individual is imparted training in some specific job. Then there are certain kinds of work which naturally lead to a greater number of accidents than other kinds of work. Experience also takes care of accident proneness because the individual becomes less prone to accidents once he gets experience. Besides, the basic cause of accident proneness is some fault in the working conditions, such as improper illumination, lighting which is either too strong or too dim or lighting which is directed from the wrong angle, or improper arrangement of machinery, etc.

TESTS OF ACCIDENT PRONENESS

Psychologists have succeeded involving certain tests by which it is possible to discover accident proneness. These tests have been developed after extensive study of accident proneness. It is sometimes noticed that the more skilled workers are more accident prone than the less skilled ones. One cause of this is that they work with such speed that the probability of accident increases rapidly, and for this reason accident proneness cannot be taken as an indication of lack of skill. In the second place, identical characteristics are not found in all individuals who are accident prone. Despite this it has been possible to identify certain characteristic qualities which tend to promote accident proneness. The tests for determining these qualities are the following:

1. **Sensory Motor Tests.** Accident proneness and muscular coordination are intimately related. Individuals whose muscular coordination is not good suffer from more accidents. It has been observed that the relation between accidents and results obtained in sensory motor tests increases with experience. In the second place, skill and accident proneness have been found to have a definite relationship. If the individuals who achieve the lowest scores in tests for accident proneness are selected, there are fewer accidents and the standard of the workers rises. It is a commonly accepted fact that lack of skill, slackness of motor reaction cannot escape form a situation with an accident potential without sustaining some injury and in certain situations they cannot escape accidents. They may just be accident prone without being careless or irresponsible. Hence it is evident that accidents take place due to lack of proper muscular coordination.

2. **Emotional Stability Tests.** Emotionality and accident proneness are also intimately related, and it has found that highly emotional taxi drivers are involved in more accidents than other drivers while people with more stable emotionality have a lower accident proneness. Lower accident proneness is found in those individuals who are capable of controlling their reactions even in situations which distract attention or which disturb the individual. Briefly stated, individuals obtaining high test scores in emotional stability tests have four times the probability of avoiding tests as compared to others with low test scores. Mood also plays an important role in accident proneness. It has been seen that depression was the cause of almost two hundred minor accidents out of four hundred such accidents. On the other hand, production went up by 8 percent in a mood of happiness which proved that this mood not only prevents accidents but actually promotes production. Himler made a list of 28 personality traits which were the causes of accidents, and more than half of them were connected with emotional coordination or stability.
3. **Intelligence Tests.** Tests which indicated a relationship between accidents and muscular coordination or emotional stability did not indicate any relationship between accidents and intelligence. But some other researchers indicated a relationship between accident proneness and mental traits. And in these studies it was found that the test scores of intelligence and emotional stability showed more valuable conclusions about accidents than the test scores of emotional stability alone. In another study the relation between intelligence and accidents was discovered in tests at some professional college. But it was not clearly evident how far the more intelligent individual avoided an accident because of his intelligence rather than as a result of his better skill. In a study concerning motor car drivers it was found that generally individuals with lower intelligence were involved in more accidents than people with more intelligence. But generally it is believed by most people that intelligence is an important factor in avoiding accidents.
4. **Sensory and Perceptual Speed Tests.** In certain tests it was seen that people with greater perceptual speed, meaning people who could rapidly observe even minor differences in perceptible pattern, were less inclined to be involved in accidents. On the other hand, individuals whose perceptual speed was less than their muscular reaction showed a higher degree of accident proneness. In this manner accident proneness is increased if perceptual speed is less than muscular reaction because such people react faster than they can observe.
5. **Tests of Visual Skills.** Since the use of the eye is very important in almost all industries it is natural that defects of vision result in more accidents. In a study of this kind it was seen that 63 percent of people who did not cause accidents passed the eye test while only 33 percent of the people causing accidents could pass them. Nowadays, in many modern industries, efforts are made to find out the minimum level of visual skill which is needed for the successful performance of a particular work. For example, the visual skill of people applying for jobs as signallers in the Indian railways is tested particularly because if they have some visual defect they may endanger the lives of thousands of people. And the truth

of the matter is that as the efficiency of all the sense organs, not only the eyes, increases accidents decrease in number. Accidents increase when such defects increase.

Psychologists nowadays emphasize that the difficulties of the accident prone individual should be examined with great care and measures for eliminating them should be evolved and suggested. With the adoption of such an attitude the rate of accidents of 44 accident prone motor car drivers fell from 1.3 to 0.75 over a distance of one thousand miles within one year. For a study of this kind it is necessary to find out and to isolate the particular individual factor which has been responsible for accidents. For example, in connection with motor car drivers it has been seen that about 64percent of accidents take place due to a defective aptitude, failure to anticipate the possibility of an accident, incorrect judgement of speed and distance, excessive impulsiveness, irresponsibility and failure to keep attention for a long time, or a combination of these factors. Studies of this kind can help to reduce the accidents in many kinds of jobs but it must also be kept in mind that the analysis of accidents often becomes subjective. Besides, mistakes can be made by an error of human judgement. Again, analysis of this kind cannot take the place of the tests described earlier in establishing a relation between accident proneness and individual traits. But as far as one is concerned with the influence of emotional instability on accidents, such an analysis can be useful.

Chapter 13 SAFETY

CONCEPT OF SAFETY

Safety is opposite to accidents. If accidents are harmful, safely is beneficial. Man's greatest desire is security. He wants longer life. Accidents are one of the major causes of deaths. So accidents should be minimized. Safely is beneficial in all respects. Safety has become an essential feature of all walks of life.

The maintenance of safety has become a major programme in the industries. Specially trained persons known as safely engineers are appointed in the industries. The government has also framed rules and regulations towards safety. The Factories Act has special provisions on safety. Violation of these provisions is punishment. Some of the factories conduct special programmes in first aid treatment. The workers are acquainted with the preliminary treatment to be given to the injured. Programmes like extinguishing fire, removing the people from the building on fire are also carried out.

SAFETY CONSCIOUSNESS

"The awareness and carefulness of the workers to prevent the accidents is known as safely consciousness."

While at work, the workers must be always conscious of accidents and must take all the precautions for enhancing the safely. A bus driver while driving is always safety conscious and avoids the accidents.

Safety consciousness should be increased by adopting the following methods:

(*i*) Display of safety posters and boards to remind the workers about safety

(*ii*) Workers should be educated to use safety devices

(*iii*) Organising safety competition and awarding prizes to the winners

(*iv*) Give due respect and recognition to safe workers

(*v*) Send information and literature about the safety at the homes of the employees

(*vi*) Welcome all safety suggestions

(*vii*) Cross mark and identify all accident areas

(*viii*) Conduct safety training lecture periodically.

NECESSITY OF SAFETY

Safety helps the industries and workers in the following ways:

(*i*) Production is increased

(*ii*) It reduces the cost of production

(*iii*) Reduces damage to equipment and machines

(*iv*) Prevents premature death of trained workers

(*v*) Prevents needless pain and sufferings to the employees.

SAFETY PROCEDURE

There are two ways of looking at this problem—one is from, the point of view of an engineer and other from the point of view of a psychologist. The engineer can remove the hazards from the work by introducing the following measures.

(*a*) Designing and formulating of safety devices.

(*b*) Procedure and methods of work on the dangerous machines should be changed.

(*c*) The safety of the factory and machinery should be inspected by a safety engineer and change it from structural and functional point of view, if required.

Simple improvements can be made in this regard which are given below:

(*a*) Moving parts should be enclosed with guards and covers—Such as belts, gears, clutches etc.

(*b*) Moving and stationary parts should be distinguished adopting suitable colours.

(*c*) The rotating saws should be guarded properly to avoid the workers to come in contact with them physically.

(*d*) Safety devices should be reliable.

(*e*) Safety devices should not be easily detachable.

(*f*) Safety dress, protective goggles, gloves, shields should be suitably designed.

(*g*) To reduce chances of falling slipping from stair cases, floors etc.

(*h*) Prevention against receiving electric shock. Every electric installation should be properly insulated.

The psychologist also plays very important role in avoiding the accidents and increasing the safety. It has been observed that many of the accidents are due to psychological problems of the workers. The human factors in case of accidents should be analysed and corrected. The psychologist adopts the following procedure:

1. Making the worker safety conscious
2. To make men aware of hazards
3. To train them to use safety devices
4. Reducing the fatigue and exertion of the worker
5. The attitude of co-operation should be developed among the workers.
6. Proper selection and placement of the worker for the particular work situation.

SAFETY MEASURES

To ensure and enhance the safety in the factories, the various steps are to be taken. The safety Engineer and the shop in charges take the following measures according to their experience and guide lines of the factories Act.

1. **Machine Guarding.** The running parts of the machines should be properly guarded. The machine guard should provide full protection, they should be of permanent nature and it may be difficult to remove them. The rotating parts should not be operated at speeds higher than the recommended speed.

   To reduce accidents of machines, the manufacturing processes should be modified and their operational efficiency is increased. In case of process and sheares, hazards are reduced by using, automatic feeds.

2. **Personal Protective Equipment.** Protective dress should be worn where ever necessary. Gloves are worn by the operator to save his hands from cuts, splinters and chemicals. Aprons protect the trunk of the body. Metallic foot the leg guards are also available. Where falling objects can pose a problem one can safely use the protective helmets. The women workers use hair pin and nets so that their hairs are not caught in the gears, drills and spinning shaft.

   In welding, goggles and face shields are used. If the noise is unbearable, ear plugs should be used. Safety shoes are used where the feet are exposed to heat and pricking substances.

3. **Protection Against Radiation Hazards.** Two types of radiations such as heat produced in steel manufacturing and radiation of radio active particles, cause health and safety problems. The people suffer from exertion and over perspiration and skin irritation. The plant and equipment should be so designed that radiations are minimized. Air conditioning, ventilation system, protective clothing can decrease this problem.

4. **Noise Control.** Excessive noise is not only uncomfortable but also harmful. The measure of noises is decibel. Where conversation producers only 40 decibels, the office work may produce 50 and dangerous if not checked. The working efficiency is decreased. The forging hammer produces high noise.

Fatigue Elimination: Fatigue is also one of the causes of accidents. Fatigue is caused if one is doing hard work continuously or if one feels bored at work. It has been found out that during the end of the working hours, the number of accidents tend to increase, which is due to fatigue. A driver if asked to drive the bus for long hours, he may be fatigued and fall asleep on the steering and cause the accidents.

Fatigue is eliminate by providing rest pauses to the workers, reducing the working hours, and severity of the work.

Proper Lighting: Many accidents are the result of poor lighting. So every working place should have proper light. There are two sources of light–Natural light and light from bulbs and tubes.

Controlled Atmospheric Contaminants: Many industries produce gases, vapours, fumes, dusts, pungent smell etc. The atmosphere is polluted which is harmful to health and many a times accidents are caused due to dirty atmosphere.

The pollution of the atmosphere should be decreased by the safety Engineer. For this some of the suggestions are given below:

(*a*) Substitute a safe material instead of toxic material

(*b*) Personal protective equipment should be used

(*c*) Remote controls should be used

(*d*) Wetting may be done to control dust

(*e*) Exhaust fans to be used to draw out contaminates.

SAFETY PROGRAMME

These programmers try to discover the causes of accidents of accidents and aim at reducing the accidents. This is a continuous process for enhancing safety. These try to minimize the bad effects of accidents. Training about safety devices is given to the workers.

SAFETY COMMITTEES

The participation of employees in the safety programmers is very important. The formations of safety committees makes the workers to resume responsibility. Workers, supervisors from different sections should be selected to be members of the committees. Safety programme should be conducted to train the worker in handling and approaching emergency conditions. Various institutions whereas Red Cross, Civil Hospitals can be approached for health and the conduct of first and classes.

Educational films of safety and safety posters are useful steps to be taken by the committees. The main objects of the safety committees are to make the workers safety conscious and to see that safety measures are adopted.

SAFETY PUBLICITY

Safety publicity is a general programme to bring to the minds of the people, the meaning of safety. The people should realize the necessity of safety.

Safety publicity is the functions of the state and the particular industry.

State and Govt. takes the following steps:

1. Road sign boards having the safety quotations are installed.
2. Advertisement regarding safety in the newspaper, magazines and other journals.
3. Safety programmes on Radio and televisions.

Steps Taken by Industries. The following are some of the steps regarding the safety publicity taken by the industries:

1. Safety posters are installed on the walls of the industry.
2. Every accident prone situation should be well marked as cautions for the safety of the workers.
3. Safety programme should be conducted to educate the worker and make them safety conscious.
4. Safety pamphlets and magazines should be published and distributed free of cost.
5. Documentary films on accidents and safety should be shown to the workers.
6. Safety committees consisting of trade union and management should be set up to promote publicity.
7. Workers should be encouraged to suggest the methods to ensure safety.
8. Safety contest may be held occasionally.

SAFETY QUOTATIONS

1. Make safety a habit.
2. Drive slowly for your own children.
3. Where cautions end's Accidents begin.
4. Better late than never.
5. Accidents do not happen they are caused.
6. If married, divorce speed.
7. Safety is the pride of good workman.
8. Machines are good servants only if handled carefully.
9. Do not overtake.
10. Safety first, speed afterwards.
11. Drive carefully, and reach home safety.

Chapter **14** *JOB ANALYSIS*

AIMS OF JOB ANALYSIS

It has been pointed out before that the main objective of job analysis is selection of personnel. But it can also have other objectives such as improvements in the methods of working, training of employees, promotion of employees, obviating accidents and protection of health, etc. Defining job analysis Blum has remarked, "A job analysis is an accurate study of the various components of a job. It is concerned not only with an analysis of the duties and conditions of work, but also with the individual qualifications of the worker." It is evident that job analysis will reveal the duties of individuals in a particular job or profession, as also the conditions in which they will be required to work. It will also bring out the qualities required of an individual aspiring to perform some definite function or piece of work. According to J.D. Hackett, in the process of job analysis, the fundamental elements of a job are established and clarified, while simultaneously the abilities desirable in the worker are known, the abilities that will help him to perform his function skillfully. Thus, job analysis has two aspects, one the analysis of duties and conditions of work, and the other, the analysis of qualities desired in the worker or employee.

ADVANTAGES OF JOB ANALYSIS

Job analysis concurs many advantages. On the basis of 401 essays concerned with job analysis, Zerga pointed out twenty advantages and utilities of job analysis. One is the increase in efficiency, as well as increase in the mutual feelings of workers since everyone is happy to be employed in the job he cherishes. Job analysis can help to determine the salary or wages accruing to the employee for a particular function performed by him. Job analysis helps in the classification of professions and occupations, it thereby becoming possible to determine the qualities and abilities required for them. Through job analysis it also becomes possible to determine the extent of training necessary for a specific individual to be given a particular job of work. Job analysis determines the duty of everyone in his own job by determining the responsibility inherent in any kind of work.

VARIOUS COMPONENTS OF A JOB

Now, the first thing to be mentioned in connection with job analysis is the presence of various components in a job. Headings of information collected in this connection are the following :

1. Identification of the Job
2. Number employed
3. Statement of duties
4. Machines used
5. Analysis of operations
6. Conditions of work
7. Pay and incentives
8. Relation to other allied jobs
9. Opportunities for transfer and promotion
10. Time and nature of training
11. Personal requirements:
    (*a*) General—Age, sex, nationality, marital status.
    (*b*) Physical
    (*c*) Educational
    (*d*) Previous experience
    (*e*) General and special abilities
    (*f*) Temperamental and character requirements.

As is evident from the above list, there is extensive collection of data regarding job analysis. Of the many methods employed in job analysis, the main are the following :

1. Individual psychographic method
2. Questionnaire method
3. Job psychographic method
4. Job analysis by text
5. Motion study method

These methods will now be described in brief.

1. **Individual Psychographic Method.** In this method, the mental peculiarities of an individual successful in a particular kind of job are examined, a list of these peculiarities prepared and this list transcribed in figure form on graph. This provides some standard of judgment in future recruitments for the same job.
2. **Questionnaire Method.** A list of questions is prepared on the basis of the different qualities of personality concerned with the job. This list is then provided to the individuals doing the job, and they are asked to answer these questions. An analysis of the answers received helps to reveal the special qualities necessary for the job, a list of which can now be prepared. This, too, helps in the future selection of candidates for the job in question.
3. **Job Psychographic Method.** According to Viteles, there are three things essential to job psychographic method :

(*a*) Accurate classification of mental qualities

(*b*) Valid method of evaluation

(*c*) Direct examination or analysis by trained examiners.

In this manner, in this method, some specialist analysts study the work, and they evolve a valid and standard method of evaluation. They prepare a very accurate list in which the various mental qualities required for the job are properly and reliably classified. A graph of these qualities is prepared so that selection of candidates for the job may become easier.

4. **Job Analysis by Test.** In the test method, some reliable and valid tests are performed on the basis of essential qualities and abilities; the candidates are tested for selection and suitability by these tests.
5. **Motion Study Method.** Under this method, the speed of an individual worker in performing some job and time consumed therein are both noted. Similar examinations being performed on other individuals doing the same work, the results obtained are compared. Such a study of speed and time helps in job analysis and classification of the workers.

Job analysis can be done by any one or more of these methods, the choice of method being governed by the situation or circumstances.

ESSENTIAL ELEMENTS IN WORKER'S ANALYSIS

The second step in personnel selection is that of worker's analysis. In worker's analysis, as is apparent from the term used to denote it, detailed information regarding the applicant's qualities, abilities, experience and other factors is obtained. Roughly speaking, worker's analysis requires information under the following heads :

1. Age
2. Caste
3. Sex
4. Nationality
5. Physical health and characteristics
6. Education and training
7. Experience
8. Level of intelligence
9. Mental abilities and their level
10. Interests and aptitudes
11. Personality traits.

Having gathered the above information regarding a particular applicant, it becomes possible to determine the kind of job he is likely to prove proficient in, and the kind of job in which he tends to be failure. Worker's analysis also reveals the extent and nature of training that a particular individual will require before he can successfully enter a particular profession. Worker's analysis can also help to make a rough estimate of the remuneration that can justifiably be paid to the worker, for the job in which he is expected to excel. Worker's analysis prepares a picture of an individual's personal excellence, by virtue of which it is also called individual analysis.

Method of Worker's Analysis

Worker's analysis is now a matter of science, so that it has come to use certain specific methods. Broadly speaking, the following are the various methods used in worker's analysis :-

1. Application Blank,
2. Letters of Recommendation,
3. Academic Record,
4. Psychological Tests,
5. Physical Tests
6. Group Tests
7. Rating,
8. Interview.

It is not essential that all above methods be used to analyse the abilities of any individual worker, a selection of any one of them being required to meet the need in a particular case. It will be in keeping with the context to glance briefly at these methods.

1. *Application Blank*: Nowadays, the first step in the worker's analysis is the filling in of a blank by the applicant. This application blank can be designed to reveal much information of a varied kind, sometimes being so successful as to reveal the individual's entire background. In the application blank, the individual provides information regarding his age, sex, caste, nationality, earlier or past level of education, training, personal experience, history, etc. What kind of information should be provided in the application blanks is determined differently in different professions. Professions that are likely to be influenced by the worker's attitudes, mental inclinations, interest, etc., require that information regarding them should also be provided in the application blank. Many advertisers do not make a detailed report of what the applicant is expected to include in his application; they make a brief mention of a very few things. Application blanks should preferably contain detailed enquiries regarding all important facts and details. Research in this direction can help to form outlines of application blanks for various professions, and according to that outline blanks can be provided to the various applicants and aspirants. Often, evidence is required to substantiate the facts detailed in the application.
2. *Letters of Recommendation*: Letters of recommendation also help in worker's analysis. In this method, the aspirant produces various recommendation, recommendations from his previous employer, the principle of his school or college, or from some respective stalwarts of society, etc. In these letters, in addition to the natural commendation, some degree of ability is also evidenced, but often these letters are seen to contain many confusing and incorrect piece of information regarding the individual. One of the simplest ways of misleading the intended employer is to include mention of many qualities that the aspirant does not possess, or to overemphasize the qualities that he is fortunate enough to possess. As a general rule, such letters of recommendation usually prove to be hindrances rather than helps to the process of job analysis, but if they are valid and justified, reliable and temperate, they can definitely promote job analysis or rather worker's analysis.
3. *Academic Records*: Different professions require different levels of education as an essential qualification. Academic records are evidences of the individual's educational progress and proficiency. These sometimes include cumulative records of the universities.

4. *Psychological Tests*: But the most important and valid method of worker's analysis is that psychological testing in which the applicant's mental ability, interest, personality and particularly attitude is tested. Results of these tests should be employed with exemplary caution since they can also lead to very serious mistakes.
5. *Physical Tests*: There are some jobs that require physical fitness of various kinds as an essential pre-requisite; for example, the eye-sight of a railway guard should be normal and not impaired. And for satisfaction on this point, different physical tests have been devised to suit various professions and their requirements. Nowadays, physical or medical tests have become an essential part of examinations for governmental jobs.
6. *Group Test*: There are some professions in which many workers have to work collectively but even if they work individually they are constantly thrown together in the process of their work. Hence in their case, it is essential for them to possess certain group qualities which are otherwise not taken into consideration. And it is with the intention of evaluating such qualities of collective behaviour in the individual that the employees or applicants are tested in group. In other words, their conduct in the group is judged.
7. *Rating*: One of the many aspects of worker's analysis is the rating given to the individual by his Principal in school or college or by psychologist. This rating is sometimes taken into consideration by the worker analyst.
8. *Interview*: Finally, in most of the industries today, the applicant is personally interviewed by the employer and some other specialists, during which he is questioned by them on various topics so that they can form some estimate of him as an individual. Every examiner or individual of the board of interviewers asks some or the other question, but even while the applicant is engaged in answering it, the rest of the board is very minutely observing his reactions and conduct. Interview as a method of guiding personality has advantages over other methods in that it reveals certain aspects of the individual that cannot be brought to light otherwise. It helps to form an estimate of the individual in respect of his self-confidence, self-control, response to discipline, presence of mind, dynamically, interests, manner of dressing, conduct, behaviour, manners, attraction of personality, if any, etc. besides many other intangible things that make an impression on the mind of a viewer. But for this method to yield valid and desirable results it is essential that the interviewers themselves be educated, trained and unbiased since, otherwise, such an interview can lead to many misunderstandings and misjudgments.

The method of personnel selection is evident from the detailed description of its two aspects, job analysis and worker's analysis. Following job analysis and worker's analysis, all that remains to be done in the way of personnel selection is to provide the individual with work for which he has been found and pronounced most able.

Chapter **15**

RECRUITMENT AND SELECTION

INTRODUCTION

After the process of Manpower Planning is over and finalised, the next step is to hire the personnel according to the requirements. Now various questions arise to he answered where to hire, when to hire, who is to hire hiring should he from within or outside, what should be the media or source and finally how they should be hired? All these questions are responded properly when a company is having suitable and appropriate Personnel Policies and procedures. Recruitment has been regarded as the most important function of Personnel administration, because unless the right type of people are hired. even the best plans, organisational charts and control systems would not do much good: Recruitment makes it possible to acquire the number and type of people necessary to ensure the continued operation of the organisation, Recruiting is discovering of potential applicants for actual or anticipated organisational vacancies. Flippo views Recruitment as both positive and negative factor. Positive because, it is the process of searching for prospective employees and stimulating and encouraging 'them to apply/or jobs in an organisation. Negative because it rejects a good number of those who apply leaving only the best to be hired," Thus, the company must have its policy on Recruitment, Selection and placement. It must also have its policy regarding Interviewing, Induction and psychological tests which form on important base of selection.

"Once the determination of human resources requirements has been made, the recruitment and hiring process can begin. It is the second step in the Procurement function of Personnel Mgt. Recruitment forms the first stage in the process which continues with selection and ceases with placement- of the candidate. Recruiting makes it possible to acquire the number and types of people' necessary to ensure the continued operation of the organisation. Recruitment is the Process of searching for prospective employees and stimulating them to apply for jobs in the organisation. It is a linking activity bringing together those with jobs and those seeking 'jobs.

Dale Yoder has defined, "Recruitment is a process to discover the sources of manpower to meet the requirements of the staffing schedule and to employ effective measures for attracting that manpower in adequate numbers facilitate effective selection of an efficient working force." It is important in the sense that unless the right type of people are hired, even the best plans, organisation charts and control systems would not do much good.

SOURCES OF RECRUITMENT

Before the process of recruiting applicants starts, it should consider the most likely source of the type of employee it needs. Some companies try to develop new sources, while most only try to tackle the existing sources they have. Basically, we may divide the sources as internal and external.

Internal Sources

This is the most important and most obvious source of recruitment, which means the personnel already 'on the pay-role or the working' force of the organisation. Whenever, there arises any vacancy, somebody from the inside of the organisation is upgraded, transferred or promoted or sometimes demoted. This source also includes personnel who were once on the pay roll of the company but who plan to return or whom the company would like to re-hire, such as those leave of absence, those who quit voluntarily or lay-off etc.

Internal source of recruitment has several uses. It improves the morale of the employees for they are assured that they will be preferred over outsiders as and when vacancies arise. The employer will also will be in a better position so as to evaluate the performance over outsiders. It also promotes loyality among employees because they are provided with 'job security' and chances for advancement. It is less costly in the sense that the employees who are already working with the organisation better know the policies and procedures of the Co.

So, it requires lesser training than outsiders.

It has certain demerits also. It discourages new entrants in the organization who are developed in the current environment, thus discourages innovations. If promotion is based on seniority, the employees of best talents may not be chosen discouraging and demoralising the efficient employees.

External Sources

This type of recruitment is done from outside. This may include new entrants, mostly young men experienced potential employees, with a wide range of skill and abilities, retired experienced persons such as operating employees and others may include married women and persons from minority groups.

The external source has many advantages. It provides the requisite type of personnel for an organisation having skill training and education upto the required standards. Recruitment is made out of a large number of applicants selection can be made without any discrimination of caste, creed, sex or colour. It is also economical, as these type of employees don't require further training. The main demerit of external source is of Brain Drain, when experienced persons are there, they are raided or hunted.

There are many sources of external recruitment, they are explained here under:

1. *Advertising*: This is the most popular source of recruitment in India. Private, Public and Govt. sector give their manpower requirements with job description and job specifications. No of vacancies, pay-scale etc., to the local or national newspaper.

They publish the advertisements in the "Appointments columns or Situations Vacant Columns." It is most widely used source of information regarding recruitment. Employment Bulletins, Rozgar Smachar, Employment News are the names of the papers published only for employment purposes. Doordarshan is also giving the advertisement on every Sunday headed by "Rozgar Sarnadhar". When time is limited, the daily news paper, particularly the Sunday edition, will reach the maximum number in the shortest period.

2. *Employment Agencies*: Employment agencies may include private and public agencies. Private agencies are very specific as they help in providing employment in general office. Salesman, technical workers, accountants, computer staff, engineers and executives. They are brokers in the sense that they charge a small fee from an applicant and bring employers and employees together. The State or public employment agencies which are known as employment exchanges, are the main agencies of public employment. They provide a clearing house for jobs and job information. Employers inform them of their personnel requirements, while job seekers get Information for them about the types of jobs are referred to by employers. In India, Each Distt. Sub-Division and sometimes Bocks, are having Employment exchanges, headed by Employment Officer at Distt. Level, Assistant Employment Officer (AEO) at Sub-Division Level. They are helping a lot in providing the employment to the job- seekers.
3. *Recommendations of Present Employers or Employees Refers*: Friends and relatives or present employees are also a good source from which employees may be drawn. When present employees are asked to recommend new hires, particularly, when labour market is tight, a type of preliminary screening takes place. It is a award or Prize of Bonus for existing employees from the employers, there are many companies and public sector which are following the policy of kinship. They provide a job to the kin or one of the dependant of the existing employees. Escorts Ltd. Haryana Electricity Board are the examples. It is useful in the sense that the present employee knows both the company and the acquaintance and presumably would attempt to please both. But this system is defective in the sense that it encourages nepotism-persons of one community of caste are employed, who may or may not be fit for the job.
4. *Schools and Colleges, Universities and Professional Institutes*: The job Descriptions are increasingly become complex and technical in nature, accordingly, job specifications, nowadays are more demanding skill, education, knowledge and experience. There is hardly any job where school or college degrees are not demanded. Only unskilled workers can be placed without proper formal education. The Institutes operate placement cells where complete bio-data and other particulars of the students are available. The Companies that needs employees, contact to the Counsellors of employment Bureaus and teacher of the concerned business and vocational subjects. In the campus or in the employers office, the candidates may be interviewed for

management trainees or Probationers. In India, Indian Institute of Technology, Indian Institute of Management (Bangaluru, Lucknow, Kolkata, Ahemdabad), YMCA Institute of Engineering (Faridabad) X-vier Institute of Management, Jamnalal Institute of Mgt. Regional Engineering Colleges, and all universities. Employers go to the campus and conduct an Interview and select the bests among bests, for their requirements. These institutes provide technical, professional, managerial and white collor personnel.

5. *Labour Unions*: Organised labour unions constitute an important source of Personnel. It saves the cost of recruitment. This condition is only possible with the presence of harmoneous industrial relations. Incase of adverse, relations, it is not possible. Under agreement, the union members may agree as to who is to 'be given preference. In industrial and business sector, trade union are playing important role in employment function.
6. *Casual Applicants or Casual Labour*: Casual applications may be called as unsolicited applications, both at the gate and through the mail, constitutes a much used-source of personnel. These application's may be kept in a separate fill and may be used as and when vacancy arises. Causal labour is also constitutes an important source. Most industrial units rely to some extent on the casual labour which presents itself daily at the factory gate or employment office of the organisation. However, this source is uncertain and the candidates cover a wide range or abilities. Many industrial units make use of casual labour to fill up its casual vacancies.
7. *Voluntary Organisations*: There are certain voluntary organisations who are putting their efforts in providing employment to the needy person. These may be social organisations, private clubs, Lions Club. Rotary Club are, helping the handicaps, widows, old persons, retired hands etc. in providing suitable jobs.
8. *Computer Data Bank*: In case, the Co. desires a particular type of employee with certain job specifications and requirements, are fed into a computer, where they are matched against the resume data stored therein. The output is a set or resumes for individuals who meet the requirements. This method is very, useful for identifying candidates for hard-to-fill positions which call for an unusual combination of skills.
9. *Nepotims*: The hiring of relatives and friends in family owned firms or the firms where one occupies monopoly, is an inevitable component of recruitment. Such policy is always biased and the recruitment is not on the basis of merit but their interests and loyality will be with the firm. This system gives birth to Nepotism which is a social-evil.
10. *Leasing*: In India, Leasing-system has become increasingly popular because the company not only obtains well-trained and selected personnel but also avoids any liability or obligation in pensions, Insurance, Provident Fund and other fringe benefits. Examples of Computer service, Management services and certain other specialized jobs are 'hired to adjust the short-term fluctuations in personnel needs on the basis of leasing.

There are as many more sources of the recruitment. Which particular source is to be tapped will depend on the policy of the firm, Govt. regulations, position of Labour Supply, and agreements with, labour organizations. The personnel manager must have a close link between all the sources of recruitment. The best management policy regarding recruitment is to look first within the organisation. If that source fails, external recruitment must be tackled.

THEORIES REGARDING RECRUITMENT

It is generally said that human beings join the organisation to satisfy his certain needs, like economic, social-psychological and physiological needs. But the second side, why organisations hire the prospective employees? The answer is very simple. Organisation is having its objectives and which can be accomplished by the group efforts of human beings *i.e.*, employees. On the other hands human beings are also having certain needs. So, it is the satisfaction of mutual interest which is called the integration function of Personnel. There are certain statements given and enunciated in this respect which are explained here under:

(*i*) Recruitment is two way communications, one side recruiter, other side recruitee. The recruiter has the choice whom to recruit and whom not, in the same way, the prospective employee has to-make the decision if he should apply for the organisations job.

(*ii*) The second view is objective factor in which a comparison is made between what employment offers like benefits, pay, location, opportunities for advancement, nature of work and the work to be performed and educational opportunities.

(*iii*) The third view is of the choice *i.e.*, personality patterns and the image of the organization. Choices are made on a highly personal and emotional basis.

CONSTRAINTS FOR EMPLOYER TO RECRUIT

It is well-established fact that recruitment is he process of searching for prospective employees and to stimulating them to apply for jobs in the organization. Hiring through selection means to eliminate those applicants not suitable arid to choose the best. But the question is that selection is always of the best candidates? The answer is, not always best. Because there are certain factor's which restrict the freedom of the employer to choose the best one, those are explained here :

(*i*) **Goodwill and Image of the Organization.** There are certain factors which increase goodwill of the organisation like living and working conditions. Nature of job, Wage structures, Profitability, Payment of Dividends, Reserve and Surplus, Attitude of the society towards the Co. etc. A prospective employees may not be interested in getting job in a particular organization where the above cited factors are adverse. One will definitely be interested in getting the job in the organization where these conditions are positive. These factors play an important role in attracting the best personnel role.

(*ii*) **Nature of Job.** The job is considered good where the nature of job is positive *i.e.*, interesting, No Hazards, anxiety creating, potential, learning promotion and career development and the prospective employee will be attracted to join it. If the conditions or job factors, are adverse; people would not be attracted to such an organisation.

(*iii*) **Organizational Policies.** Organizational working, to a large extent depends upon the internal policies of the organisation. For example, promotion and career development, morale Building, incentives schemes industrial relations set the pace of organizational growth and development. If these things are positive will definitely encourage good people who "are ambitious and improving the probability of a good selection.

(*iv*) **Trade Union's Intervention.** Trade Unions can also restrict the recruiting sources. Some union emphasise on recruitment to members of the union only. Where such situation occurs, Management has to recruit from a restricted supply. However, these things depend on the labour-Management and Union-Management relations and their agreements.

(*v*) **Govt. Regulation or Constitutional Rights.** An employer cannot distinguish any individual on the basis of physical appearance, sex or religious background for the purpose of recruitment. In India, the Constitution under the head of Fundamental Rights has very clearly stated that Equal pay, for Equal work. No distinction will be made in respect of caste, creed, sex, religious and, physical appearance.

Therefore, these are the factors which impose certain restrictions on the employers to choose the Best employees. Sometimes the problem is from the prospective employee; sometimes from the employers and sometimes other factors.

In order to initiate the procedure for hiring, we must satisfy the three preliminary requirements. First, there must be authority to hire which comes from the employment requisition, as, developed on the basis of work-load and workforce. Analysis Secondly, we must have a standard of personnel with which we can compare prospective employees. This is represented by the job specification, as developed through job analysis. Finally we must have job applicants from whom we can select the persons to be hired.

The hiring process is essentially a series of steps or stages by which additional information is secured about the applicant At each stage, facts may come to the light which may lead to the rejection or selection of the applicant. A procedure is compared to a series of hurdles which an applicant must cross. These are termed as screens or successive hurdles techniques. The Selection procedure is not an universal process it depends on the complexity of the job. The complexity of the selection process increases with the level and responsibility of the position to be filled. Dale Yoder has defined selection process as "The hiring process is of one or many 'go-no-go' gauge's. Candidates are screened by the application of these tools. Qualified applicants go on to the next hurdle while the unqualified are eliminated," The Selection procedure is essentially designed on the following factors:

As already it has been stated that Selection is the process followed by a series of hurdles and screens. There are several steps in the selection process which we as follow:

1. **Reception; Initial or Preliminary Interview or Screening.** The initial screening is usually conducted by a special interviewer or a high calibre receptionist in the employment office: It is essential for both the company and prospective employee. These interviews

are very short and informal arid may be conducted at a-desk. The main objective of this interview is to screen out, undesirable/unqualified candidates at the very outset, so it is called screening. A, typical selection program tries to fit applicants to particular job, i.e. match jobs and people. This selection philosophy assumes that the requirements of a given job and the characteristics of a given applicant are sufficiently unique and explicit to make an intelligent match possible between them.

2. **Applications Blank or Application Form.** One of the general principles of hiring procedures is to assign to each step information objectives that can be best obtained by the methods of that particular step. An application Blank is a traditional, widely accepted device for getting information from a prospective applicant which will enable a management to make a proper selection. It is a good means of quickly collecting verifiable basic historical data from the candidate which is a convenient device for circulating information about the applicant. Sometimes, application is quite lengthy, sometimes it is very brief and precise. Generally there ate six main blanks to be filled in:
   (*i*) Biographical Data *i.e.,* Name, Father's Name, Date and Place of Birth age, sex, nationality, height, weight, identification marks, physical disability if any, marital status and number of dependants.
   (*ii*) Educational Qualifications *i.e.,* school Ievel, college level, University level, Professional qualification technical qualification, special training gained, subjects studied, marks/division/grade awarded, specialisation in the subjects etc.
   (*iii*) Work Experience. In this blank, previous employment record is to be furnished with the same organisation or other employers. Date of joining, Date of leaving, reason for leaving, nature of duties and responsibilities handled and discharged, grade, designation held, salary received etc. must be furnished.
   (*iv*) Salary. Salary drawn, salary expected, other benefits like conveyance, housing, medical, LTC, demanded.
   (*v*) Personal Traits. This blank deals with extra-curricular activities association with sports, membership of NSS: Nee, hobbies, and any other information supporting a candidate's suitability, for a post.
   (*vi*) Specific Information. Sometimes: in the application-Blank, itself, a candidate has to support his suitability for the post in writing 200 or 250 words like "Why I consider fit for the job." DCM, Shri Ram Group of Companies are following this application Blank. And also a declaration is obtained in the end of application regarding its reliability correctness and truth.

   The questions included in the application blank should be such as are valid and necessary. Superfluous guest ions should be avoided and also they should not encourage dishonest answers.

3. **Psychological Tests.** The next step in selection procedures is to conduct a test. As organisations, their working, duties and responsibilities have become complex in nature, so

hiring 'process gives more importance to test. However, small organisations without complexities generally don't bother about the test. But the larger companies can afford to have a more, detailed and accurate selection procedure do utilise some form of employment testing. Tests are the most misused, the lest understood, yet the most valuable sources of information about applicants. They are the sophisticated tools of measuring human characteristics and individual differences that form the very basis of industrial psychology. "A test is a systematic procedure for comparing the behaviour of two or more persons." Tests are of various types which will he discussed in the next question.

4. **Interviewing.** Interviewing is probably the most widely used single method of selection. It is a most complex selection technique because its scope, includes measuring all the relevant characteristics and integrating .and classifying, all other information about the applicant. In professionally manage companies interviews are used for a variety of purposes including selection performance appraisal disciplinary action, counseling and general problem solving. Interview is most important in the sense that it enables the employer to view the total individual and directly appraise him and his behaviour.

   According to Scott and others, "An interview is a purposeful exchange of ideas, the answering of questions and communications between two or more persons," An Interview is an attempt to secure maximum amount of information from the candidate concerning his-suitability for the job under consideration. The process, technique and types of interview will be discussed in detail in the next question in this chapter only.

5. **References.** The purpose of reference checks are to obtain information about past behaviour of applicants and to verify the accuracy of information give on the application blank. The use of references is common in most selection procedures, for it involves only a little time and money and minimum efforts. This bases its relience on former employees, friends and professional personnel. The may be made over telephone or by mail or on a form made for this purpose. It is vitally important that references should indicate how long and in what capacity the refers had the ton tact with the applicant. Some employers are in the opinion that references are useless as it rarely, gives unfavourable opinion but even then it is used as an integral part of selection process.

6. **Physical Examinations.** The physical examination is an employment step found in most businesses. It can vary from a comprehensive examination and matching of an applicant's physical capabilities to job requirements. The physical examination has basically three objectives, First, it serves to ascertain the applicant's physical capabilities. Second, objective is to protect the company against unwarranted claims under Workmen Compensation Act. The final objective of physical examination is to prevent communicable diseases from entering the organisation.

   Usually, a medical check-upinvolves a quick examination of the eyes, ears, and throat. Pronchial weakness, tuberculosis, nervousness, hernia and lungmay also be thoroughly examined. Stone D. Kendall have outlined the following contents of medical check-up.

(*a*) Applicant's medical History.

(*b*) Physical Measurement *i.e.*, Height, Chest, Weight and abdominal.

(*c*) General examination of skin, joints and musculature.

(*d*) Examination of special senses like audio-visual activity.

(*e*) Colonical examination of eyes, cars, nose, throat arid teeth

(*f*) Examination of Chest and Lungs,

(*g*) Examination of Heart and Blood-Pressures.

(*h*) Laboratory test of blood and urine

(*i*) X-Ray of Chest and other part of the body

(*j*) Any other test depending on the job requirements and the Medical history of the applicant. In some organisations, these tests are taken seriously and comprehensive study of medical reports is done, while in others, it is a farce. A candidate is often approved within a few minutes without having really been examined by a qualified physician.

7. **Induction or Placement.** If all the hurdles or barriers have been passed successfully, the candidate is hired, Medical examination is the last step at which a rejection can be made and thus, it is the end of selection process. The induction function, however, immediately follows and is generally considered to be a part of the hiring procedure.

   Induction is concerned with the problem of introducing or orienting a new employee to the organization. In other words, it is a welcoming process-make him feel at home and generate in him a feeling that his own job is meaningful and has a significant part-of the total organization.

   Induction is the next step to placement. When a candidate is hired, he is assigned with a job according to the job requirements and his fitness, to a particular job. There are three main objectives of Induction programme. First when a new comer joins the organizations he is quite, stranger to the company's policies, environment, work-place, living and working condition's. It enables him to feel case and at home as brief history of the company. Its policies programs, growth and expansion, labour-relations and certain other important aspects are inducted to the new comers, Secondly, the newcomer may, expect more from the organisation regarding promotion, opportunities for advancement responsibilities, social status and so on. Induction programme gives him a real picture and he knows the realities of the company which is called reality shock. Lastly, the purpose of induction is to introduce the new employee and the organisation to each other, to help them become acquainted and to help them accommodate each other.

ELECTION IS SUCCESSIVE HURDLES TECHNIQUE

The hiring procedure is essentially a series of methods of securing pertinent information bout the applicant. At each step we learn more about the prospect. The information obtained can ıen be compared with the jobspecification, the standard of personnel. If the applicant qualifies, he r she advances to the, next step. This technique is known as the successive hurdles technique. As ale Yoder asserts, "the hiring process is one or many 'go-no-go' gauges, Candidates are screened qualified, they go on next test, if disqualified, they are eliminated. So, this is a technique of Selection r rejection which is shown in the diagram.

The diagram is self-explanatory. It is really a series of hurdles. It is a matter of Selection or ejection, decision being taken by the candidate's success or failure in the successive hurdles.

Hugo Munsterbery had been father of Industrial psychology, in this, century, .since then, sychological tests have occupied a prominent place in Personnel Management. He identified his ole as helping to find employees best suited to a job and determining under psychological conditions, ıe great output per person could be achieved, As the organisations, nature of job, have become ıore complicated and complex; the need of something, which can measure one's intelligency and sychology was felt. Psychological tests are the answer to such problem, as selection decisions may e arrived at with the help of tests which are more objective and less biased than others. Tests are ıe most misused, the lest understood, yet the most valuable sources of information about applicants. hey are the sophisticated tools for measuring human traits and characteristics based on the concept f Individual Differences.

Broadly we may define a lest as a "*systematic procedure for 'comparing the behaviour f two or more persons*" In other words, we can say it is a sample of all aspect of an individual's ehaviour, performance or attitude. It. is a, systematic procedure for .sampling human behaviour. n India, these tests are widely used in seeking admissions to engineering colleges, Management ıstitutes, Medical Colleges. Most the organisations are conducting these tests for selection purposes. ngineers India Ltd. Banking Service Recruitment Boards, LIC, GIC, Railway Recruitment Board, ublic Sectors' Recruitment Board NTPC, Indian Oil, ONGC, NRDC, ICSIR are the examples hich are conducting psychological tests for selection purposes.

IATURE OR BASIC CONCEPTS OF TESTING

Psychologists, after a long research, have identified certain standarised tests based on complex uman nature. These tests are very carefully developed and designed to test the individual traits, equired by the job. However, there is no rod or battery of tests that can fully capture the complex ature of humans being. However; efforts have been made to test the prospects on certain grounds:

1. **Individual Differences.** The basis of conducting psychological tests is the prevalence of Individual differences. These tests are used on the assumption that no two Persons are

similar so far as perception, intelligency, learning, skill, aptitude, and personality developme are concerned. These potentials traits and attributes are revealed only when tests a used. People possessing varying traits and attributes, skilled and knowledge perfor differently on a job.

2. **Job-Analysis.** The next basis of these tests is the technique of job analysis. It is th process of aggregating the information of a particular job. Job- descriptions and jol specifications are the output of job analysis. Job description deals with the nature of dutie and responsibilities *i.e.*, summary of a job. What should be the "qualifications and huma characteristics in the prospects (or successful job performance. Tests are designed 0 th basis of these two factors, intelligency, reasoning quantitative aptitude, aptitude test, ski tests, interest tests etc. all or some may be these depending upon the adaptability t measurement by tests.
3. **Reliability.** Reliability and Consistency are the two important factors of psychologic tests, without these two things the tests become useless and worthless, Test reliabilit means, "The Consistency of the scores obtained by the same person when retested wit the identical test." Test Consistency is very important if a person scores say 70 on a intelligence test on Sunday and 110 when retested on Tuesday, tests can not be relied upo in this case. If the consistent scores are obtained we are assured that we are measurin something.

   But, now, the question is of measurement of reliability: The reliability can be measured b maintaining the relationship between test and re-test, the relation can be .shown by th process of correlation which varies between 0 to 1. Regarding tests the reliability shoul be .90 or .85 but in Interviews the degree of coefficients will be lower.
4. **Validity.** Psychological tests designed for employment purposes must possess th characteristics of validity. Validity means, these tests measure for what it is designed t measure. Validity is very typical and highly specific in nature. A test may be valid for on objective but invalid for another objective. So, tests are designed according III job descriptio and job specification.

Validity of tests may be grouped under four categories:

(*a*) *Content Validity*: Tests are designed on the basis of job requirements, in other words we can say test as a sample which represents all the situations that could have bee included. For example; if one has to do the jot-of typing financial statements, writin Business letters, writing menu scripts from a rough note-book, tests must designed t Judge the content viability, the test is said to be reasonably of content validity.

(*b*) *Predictive Validity*: The relationship must be shown between the score of the test an some future behaviour. Because, he has been tested so that the job assigned to hir would be performed successfully. This is most important validity for personnel selectio since predictive validity tells that there is a strong relationship between a test scor and some later outcome.

(c) *Concurrent Validity*: This validity is related with the test scores and the behaviour on a job that is available at the same time. In the organisation there are two types of performers, high performers and low performers. To correlate them, a standardised test may be taken. If it is found that high performer's score is high and those of others is low. These tests can be used for new applicants predicting high performance in the job.

(d) *Construct Validity*: It is most complex type of validity to understand and to prove. It reflects the extent to which the test measures the psychological quality like intelligence and introversion, it is supposed to measure. It is a theoretical type of validity since it aimed at measuring the relationship between a test and intelligence or construct.

5. **Standardisation.** Standardisation is the another basis of these psychological tests. A test must be standardised that administered under standard conditions to a large group of persons who are representative of the individual for whom it is intended. Reliability of the test largely depends on standardisation of the test. If the tests are not standardised, the correlation between the test and score of one to another can not be administered. Standardisation of tests is the primary need to make these tests reliable.
6. **Objectivity.** A test must be reliable, valid and standardised, so it must be constructed in such a fashion that two or more persons can score the responses to items questions or tasks in the same way.

Types of Psychological Tests

It has already been stated that tests are designed on the basis of Job Description and Job-Specification. These two things will decide the behaviour of human being. Because the behaviour of a man is mould according to his aptitude, qualification, experience and knowledge. Ultimately the behaviour of the organisms is going to affect the organisntional behaviour. So, the classification the basis of human behaviour is as follows:

1. ***Aptitude or Potential Test***: Intelligency is a general traits while aptitude is a more specific capacity. Aptitude tests measure whether an individual has the capacity or latent ability to learn a given job if given adequate training. The use of aptitude tests is advisable when an applicant has had little or no experience along the lines of job-opening. We will be naturally interested selecting persons who will show a higher degree of success after training period. Examples of specific capacities of aptitudes are as follow-mechanical, clerical, linguistic, musical and academic. Some psychologists include in this category certain motor capacities such as finger dexterity, hand dexterity and hand-eye coordination.

(a) *Intelligence or Mental Test*: These tests measure the overall intellectual or (I.Q.) Intelligent Quotient of a person and enable us to know whether he has the mental capacity to deal with new problems. These tests play an important role in employment purpose as they determine the future of an employee's word fluency, memory, inductive reasoning, speed of perception and spotial visualisation. The administration of these tests calls for much preparation of the past of an organisation and they are expensive and cumbersome as well.

(*b*) *Mechanical Aptitude Test*: In this test questions are/asked which fall into general area of understanding mechanical relationship. Some questions relate to knowledge of actual shop machines tools and similar equipment. They, also measure specialized knowledge and information of techniques, arithmetical problem solving ability and technical vocabulary. Some are measured by apparatus others are measured by paper and pencil tests. These tests are generally used for the selection of-personnel in lower position, who are entrusted with the jobs of operating machines.

(*c*) *Skill or Psychomotor Test*: These tests measure one's stability to do a specific job, they measure mental dexterity, motor ability and similar attributes involving muscular movement control and coordination. This is useful in the selection of workers, who have to perform semi-skilled and repetitive jobs as packing, testing and inspection.

2. ***Achievement Tests.*** Whereas aptitude is a capacity to learn in the future. Achievement is concerned with what one has accomplished. When applicants claim to know something, an achievement test is given to measure how well they know it. Trade Tests are the common type of achievement tests. These test are also known as Proficiency test which measure the skill of knowledge which is acquired as a result of a training' program and on the job experience. Achievement Tests are of two types:

(*a*) *Test for Measuring Job-Knowledge*: These tests may be oral or written. The administration of these tests to determine proficiency in short-hand and in operating calculators adding machines, dictating and transcribing machines etc. These "tests are practically useful for office, workers, mill supervisors. Inspectors, public utility employee's sales girls etc.

(*b*) *Work Sample Test*: In this test the administration to determine the capability of the employee on the real job. For example, a typing or shorthand test provide the materials to be typed and dictation to be translated, Note the time taken and mistakes committed. The result will give clear picture about the knowledge of the job to particular employees.

3. ***Personality Tests.*** Personality is a psychological phenomenon which is combination of three aspects *i.e.*, physical appearance, personality traits and knowledge and adaptability to the situation—which is called Situational approach.

It is very complex subject and to test one's personality is very difficult. However, psychologists on the basis of research conducted, have designed some personality tests. These tests measure one's value system, judgement, decision-making, emotional reactions and maturity and human characteristics. These tests also determine what is his self-image, self-concept. self-judgement, impulsiveness, inter-personal relationship. These tests also administered to determine his self- confidence, emotional stability, cooperativeness, aggressiveness, reflectiveness, thoughtfulness, self-restraints, obsessions, initiative, motivation, dominance, fear, patience, distracts, sympathy or apathy attached or detached etc. These tests are taken to select supervisor and higher executives. In Industry, these tests have wider applicability because these tests give a well-rounded picture of personality of the applicant. These tests are also of three types which fife pen-and-paper based:

(*a*) *Objective Tests*: These tests are called personality Inventory test, which measure the tendencies of self-sufficiency, dominance-submission; and self-confidence.

(*b*) *Projective Tests*: This test is based on human behaviour which is the result of stimulus. SOBA Model tells us when an organism is given a situation his behaviour will be according to his perception and interpretation to the situation. His response to the situation will be positive or negative will give a picture of his personality. The way he responds to the situation or stimuli, depends on his value system, motives and personality. These tests are called Thematic Appreciation Tests (T.A.T.).

(*c*) *Situation Tests*: It is a group test which -is called Group-Discussions (G.D.) to test the leadership, initiative and demonstration qualities. This test is without a lender. Such tests usually relate to situations in which some problem is posed to a group and its members are asked to reach some conclusion without the help of a leader.

4. ***Interest Test.*** It is a well-established fact that a person who is interested in a job or task will do much better than one who is uninterested. These tests aim at finding out the types of work in which a candidate is interested. They are the inventories of likes and dislikes of the people of some occupations, hobbies and recreational activities: They are useful in vocational guidance and are assessed in the form of answers to a well-prepared questionnaires.

To sum up, these psychological tests have emerged in India to greater extent. In Industrial and Public sector. However, these tests have distinctive utilities. They may be administered as per job requirements. These tests have wide applications in the firms, agencies, educational institutions etc. These tests have been standardised and some firms and companies have developed tests to suit their own requirements, known as tailor-made-tests. Examples of these tests, can be quoted of BSRB, for clerical and officer G.I.C. NIBM and IPBS for Banking internal Promotions, Educational institutes for admission to various courses, Railway Recruitment Boards, etc. they have developed tailor-made-tests according to their requirements.

Psychological tests are based on objectivity, reliability, validity and standardisation and hence less subject to biasness. Specially, these tests are more fruitful when there is a continuing demand for large number of new employees for a single job. The utility of these tests depend upon using the tests appropriately under a well-planned testing programme. Tests can and do lend to a number of positive benefits to the company ill the long run. For example, some of these advantages are explained here:

1. ***Most Appropriate Mode of Selection.*** It will be better to determine the value of tests as a selection device. As selection process is a series of hurdles or screens, and at every step we gel- mere and more information about the candidates. However, before tests, Preliminary Interview, references, Application blanks are over, but these don't give the required

information of the candidates. These are the tests only which determine the candidate's fitness or unfitness for a job according to the requirements of a job. So; nowadays, tests are deemed to be most useful device for employment purposes.

2. ***Minimum Subjective Biasness.*** Because the tests are most standardised and objective, so, there are minimum chances of subjective biasness. Tests are most appropriate, less biased because of reliability and standardisation, and most objective selection device than any other selection device presently available.
3. ***Uniform Basis of Comparing Candidates.*** Test is a systematic procedure for comparing the information of the candidates or sampling human behaviour. They provide uniform basis for comparing candidates from diverse background. It reduces and minimises the chances of nepotism, self-interest, favouratism and biasness.
4. ***Reduces Labour Turnover.*** Through rests hiring is always the best and is reduces, to a greater extent, the rate of labour turnover. Consequently, the training cost will be minimum because lesser workers will have to be trained as a result of reduced turnover.
5. ***Increase in Production and Productivity.*** Tests are the screens through which the bests among bests are selected in the light of job requirements. Because they are placed 011 the job for which they are most interested and competent, consequently production will increase due to increase in Productivity, ultimately increasing the profits of the company. It will also reduce the rate of Absenteeism, accidents and build the morale of workers.
6. ***Minimum Time Consuming.*** Tests consume minimum time in selection process and makes (he selection most judicious. Training for workers programmes can be designed appropriately by determining their training ability on the basis of test score. Tests also help in selecting people with promotional ability discovering the various causes of failure at the job by analysing the personality traits of the individuals.

To sum up, the psychological tests are widely used and most acceptable devices of selection process. It must be admitted that tests are an extremely sophisticated technique for measuring behavioural characteristics.

Criticism: The applicability and administration of the tests has been criticised on certain grounds but when we observe, analyse these criticism deeply we come to know that the criticism has been only for the sake of criticism without having any solid base it is observed about tests, "It must he admitted that though tests are all extremely sophisticated technique for measuring behavioural characteristics, they have their own limitations." Tiffin & McCormick, points out, "It should be recognised that psychological tests are not infellible and that sometimes they reveal results which are not true indication of the potential Job· success of the candidate," Tests are sometimes criticised on the ground that they cannot make prediction of changes of success of an applicant because he was nervous. And research data about their validity are lacking.

It is true that tests are far from perfect but other methods like application blank, interviews, reference checks ate also of limited value. Further tests may be administered by incompetent personnel which give wrong result. Therefore, tests should be cautiously within the organisation to take care of its selection needs. In the last it would not be wrong to say, "Tests are the most misused, the lest understood yet the most valuable sources of information's about the candidates,"

DEVELOPING A TEST PROGRAMME

As, it has already been discussed, that psychological tests arc most difficult, complicated and complex if nature, so its developing and designing is rather more difficult. These tests are the basis, to some extent, of selection or rejection of the applicants, so developing a testing programme calls for a careful planning, experiment and technical knowledge. It is not a lay man's job, for this purpose, the services of extra-ordinary qualified person-who must be well-acquainted with psychology, must be taken. Examples of such persons may be given as Personnel Manager, Industrial psychologist, psychometrics, expert statisticism and psychologist, An example, here may be quoted of Banking industry where recruitment and promotion tests are conducted and designed by the National Institute-of Bank Management (NIBM) and (IPBS) Institute of Banking Personnel Selection where all the designers are perfect arid expert in various fields with doctrate degrees in the field and possessing a lot of experience. Following steps are generally involved in establishing a. sound testing programme:

1. **Selling the Objectives of the Testing Programme.** It is a well-known fact in Management MBO (Managing By Objectives) is the most important tool for getting the things done most successfully. In testing, objectives of the test must be clear, whether it is meant for hiring personnel, or for promotions or transfers. In the beginning, the testing may be set up only for some jobs, it may then he expanded to cover all types of jobs in an organisation.
2. **Analysis of Job.** For successful development of a test the essentials of a job should be thoroughly understood. What are the requirements of a job *i.e.*, social traits intellectual traits, physical demands nature of duties and responsibilities, in other words, it has to be decided as to which human traits and skills lire required for adequate performance of job. Tests must be designed based on two factors; first Production related and second personnel Data.
3. **Choke of the Tests.** The tests may be chosen while keeping in mind the factors like reliability, validity, level of difficulty, ease of administration and the cost involved. Tile best choice is only based on experience, previous research and guesses. For example, Battery Tests are chosen with the purpose of measuring a variety of possible predictors such as impulsiveness, aggressiveness, extroversion and numerical ability.
4. **Preliminary Try Out.** Any policy, prograinme when implemented after trial and error method, will bear fruits over the policy which has been implemented without its checking. In the same way test should be tried out and then revisions and refinements may be made in the light of experience. Tryout can he done on available office and factory personnel

group. The intention is to select item's that are too difficult or too easy item that fail to discriminate between high performers and low performers of the group.

5. **Administration of the Test.** The administration of tests can only be used to determine to those applicants under consideration for jobs. In case of employment purposes, a test is usually administrated after preliminary interview and an application Blank has been examined. But many candidates are rejected for a variety of reasons before tests are administered.
6. **Criteria for Job Success.** While establishing the criteria of success or a job certain factors must be taken into consideration. The relevant factors may be quality and quantity of the product, accident frequency, punctuality and regularity, speed of promotion in an organisation, training aptitude, professional achievement and ratings by the supervisors, these factors must be taken into account while designing at lest.

PRINCIPLES OF EFFECTIVE TESTING

There has been criticism of testing on so re grounds which can be improved and refined. If tests are properly designed and developed, properly conducted and evaluated, the outcome of the tests will be fruitful. There are some rules and principles which should be observed while considering the testing alternatives. The general principles of testing are:

1. **Tests are Used as Supplement and not as Substitute.** Test should not be used as a whole and sole criteria for judging the candidates performance. Tests present small sample or a little information about the applicant which should: be treated as a part of information. Reliance on other procedures like preliminary interview, application blanks, Interview and background checks should be placed.
2. **Tests are Better at Predicting Failure than Success.** Testing mostly determine. Which applicants will not or cannot perform a job satisfactory depending on the scores gained in a test, but they don't necessary can only be a perform the Job in an effective and efficient manner.
3. **Tests Must be Used as Screening Device.** As already discussed, tests are the screening devices and one of the hurdles in selection process. Tests are useful and necessary to pick up a small select group from many applicants. When there are large number of candidates for a few jobs, a test can only be a preliminary selection technique.
4. **Tests Must be Validated in the Organisational Environment.** The validity, reliability of the tests are very important. Every test must be validated in the organisation in which it is used. To make these tests more result-oriented and fruitful, a test must be tested in the same organisation to prove its validity. A person should receive the same score whenever he takes the same, test unless some significant educational development has taken place between testing dates.
5. **Conduct of the Tests.** Tests must be conducted in private, quiet well- lighted ventilated place. All the applicants should take tests under the same test conditions, it means some do

not get high or low score due to change in conditions or different test conditions. Question papers must be in strict confidence and, security so as to avoid leakage of the test.

6. **Privacy in Evaluation.** These tests are personal and hence they must be conducted in strict confidence. Because these are psychological rests, where necessary, must be evaluated by experts. The organisation and administration of the tests should also be in strict confidence. No leafage of results should be there before the declaration of results. Tests administration must be done by trained expert psychologists.

It has been very rightly said that Interviewing is probabty the most widely used single method of selection. It is most pervasive and complex, technique of selection because its scope integrates and classifies all the information about the candidate, it is the process of analysing and interpretating the information about the interviewee thus being more subjective in analysing the stress situation: The interviewer put him on the defensive by trying to annoy, embrass or frustrate him how asking questions rapidly, criticises his answers, interupts him frequently, too many questions are asked by interviewers at a time, puts the interviewee in an awkward situation by dropping something on the floor and asking him to pick it lip, accusing him that he is telling lies or giving wrong answers. This type of interview is a highly dangerous tool if given in the hands of unskilled interviewers. However, it does not give the real picture of human behaviour as it necessarily does not imply that how an employee will behave in real stressful life situations involved on a job. Yet, its judicial application may reveal many characteristics of an interviewee.

PROCESS OF INTERVIEW

The process of interview varies from organisation to organisation and individual to individual according to the objective of the interview. The first point to hold an interview is the selection of candidates to be called for the interview and preparing a schedule for the interview. The pertinent information may be gathered from the application blanks filled in by the candidates and the score in psychological tests by which, decision is made whether or not a particular candidate is worth interviewing and if he is, the interview should be planned in the light of information supplied on the forms. While matching the people to the job, it is necessary that the interviewer must have the detailed knowledge of the requirements of the job and the qualities required to fulfill these specifications. Being interview an objective phenomenon, it must be conducted in strict confidence private and according to the purpose of the interview. The following process or Technique may be used for the conduct of an interview:

1. **Preparation of the Interview.** Before anything takes place there must be preparation of some type for all the interview, scheduled or unscheduled. Obviously a considerable amount of planning is required for interviews that are scheduled in advance such as employment and appraisal interviews. A number of decisions have to be taken and arrangements have to be made before the interview begins. These steps includes:

(a) *Determine the Specific Objectives of the Interview*: In employment interviews, some decisions must be made as to which information objectives are to be accomplished in the interview. There should be little overlap .with other employment steps, the interviewer should not repeat all the basic information given on the application blanks. Employment interviewing objectives are largely intangible, dealing with such traits an character, social adjustment, attitude, oral expression and capacity for growth and advancement. According to American Management Association, the main objectives of the employment interview are:

(i) To afford 'the interviewer an opportunity to judge an applicant's qualification, knowledge and experience.

(ii) To provide the candidates the essential facts about the job & company.

(iii) To, Establish a rapport-a: feeling of mutual understanding and confidence-between the Personnel Deptt. and the applicants.

(iv) To promote goodwill towards the company, whether the interview culminates in employment or not.

In all interview, adequate information can be had in six broad areas:

(a) Personal characteristics-physical, psychological factors, situational, factors and other personality characteristics.

(b) Technical competency-examination passed, subjects studied, specialisation in subjects, extra-curricular activities.

(c) Skill, adaptability, Dependence initiative, ability to, inspire, confidence by subjects efforts without supervision

(d) Characteristics regarding group efforts, family background, hobbies, rationale, behaviour etc.

(e) Potential for growth, learning, motivation etc.

All these factors have already been discussed in detail in psychological tests and application Blanks.

(b) *Determine the Method of Accomplishing the Interviewing Objectives*: This principle involves a decision to utilise either the guided or the unguided, approach. It involves such questions as whether to use a standard rating form of a less systematic evaluation, whether to take-notes or to rely upon the memory. To achieve the objectives of the interview, we have to decide the type of interview, mostly structured, guided, directed or patterned. Interview may be used. Group interviews may also be conducted, where necessary. For Salesman, stress interview is must. But for any type of interview, proper and detailed information about the job description and specification must be retained by the interviewer. Managers or interviewers who retain less information tend to rate the interviewee higher and with less variability, a type of Halo effect. Those with more information allocate lower ratings and recognise the concept of individual differences.

(c) *Inform yourself as Much as Possible Concerning the Known Information About the Interviewee*: For employment interviews, the interviewers must acquaint themselves as much as possible information of the interviewees. This information may be had from application Blanks of the applicants reference checks, past experience of the applicants if any, reason of leaving, testimonials and certificates, his past record in school and college, result of psychological tests etc. It will guard the interviewer against any prejudices.

(d) *Determination of Number of Interviewers*: The number of interviewers depend upon the nature and objective of the interview. For lower posts, two interviewers are considered sufficient whereas for higher posts maximum eight are considered sufficient. But we have to decide the interview is simple or penal or Board or stress interview. Sometimes, the different, interviewers raise questions in their respective fields, according to the pre-planning and assignment of the field in which they will ask questions. Sometimes, it is in a haste, sometimes, they ask questions one by one. All these things have to be decided upon. Selection of the interviewers must be from the specialised fields who are having vast knowledge and experience ill their Gelds. If it is a stress interview, it is in haste, no systematic procedure is to be followed because this type of interview tests the temperament, fear, self-confidence of the applicants. So, the interviewers must be expert in their fields. The interview committee or Selection Committee may be comprising of one personnel Manager, or representative of Personnel Deptt, Chairman, 'Department' head; one psychologists and-one or more experts.

2. **Physical Setting of the Interview.** The proper physical arrangements for the interview are of great importance as planning of anything requires actions. These things enhance the reputation of the company in the eyes of the candidates. The place of interview should be carefully chosen, the physical setting should be both in private and comfortable. This can be classified in two heads-physical and mental setting.

   (a) *Physical Setting Should be Private and Comfortable*: The place of interview should be in private and comfortable. It should have cross ventilation, proper lighting arrangements cooling and heating devices. Such room is generally at the back of the office building where there would be no disturbance, interruptions, frequent telephone calls or noises outside the room, The room should generally have two doors, one for entry and one for exist, Nearby, those should be drinking water facilities and the room should be preferably furnished with sofas and easy chairs. A few magazine and. dailies must be placed on the table for the use of the candidates in the sitting room which will be apart from the place of interview. The seating arrangements are of great value of the interviewers as well as of interviewers. An individual who is sitting in a comfortable padded chair has a tendency to relax and talk more freely, thus providing more and truer information for the interviewers to evaluate.

   (b) *Mental Setting*: The-mental setting should be one of rapport. An initial effort should be made by the interviewer to establish an atmosphere of ease. The candidate should be well-received by receptionist, who is generally a member or representative of Personnel Deptt. The treatment of the applicant before he meets the interviewer is very important. The time set for starting the interview must be adhered strictly. It will be better if the waiting candidates-are offered with a cup of tea or coffee.

Instead of plunging directly into tile business at hand, some seemingly idle conversation should take place first. Interviewers should show pleasing attitude to the interviewees. If one interviewer seldom smiles and always keeps a physical barrier between oneself and the interviewee, very little rapport will be established.

3. **Conduct of the Interview.** This is the step of the interview where most of the action takes place. It is usually aimed at establishing rapport with the candidate, getting a complete and accurate information from him and recording it properly.

(*a*) *The Interviewer Should Possess and Demonstrate a Basic Liking and Respect of People*: The principle is considered by some to be the most fundamental in interviewing. The interviewer who like to talk with people and is truly interested in them will find out the most about them. The interviewer should gain the confidence of the candidate at the very beginning by establishing rapport with him. The interviewer's saying, "Please take your seat and relax and tells us about yourself so that we may get acquainted," this would serve the purpose. The applicant's tense-physical and mental stress will be lessened. The interviewer list create such an environment which leads the interviewee to open up. He must also have respect and liking for people.

(*b*) *Receiving Complete, True and Desired Informations*: The basic purpose of the interview to know and evaluate the personality of a man to be hired in depth and evaluate his suitability for the job-getting complete, true and accurate information from the applicant is an art which calls for experience, skill and technique of the interviewer. The questions must be asked in such away that encourages the interviewee to talk. There are two types of questions close-end no open-end questions. Close-end questions will be responded only 'Yes' or 'No' which can never give desired information about the candidate. There should always be a spirit to ask open-end questions which will provide the interviewer with accurate and desired, information about the applicants. The situational questions must be asked. He must be given with a critical situation and let the interviewer come up with his solution. This will have some light on the behaviour of the human being in the organisation.

(*c*) *Listen Attentively and if Possible Projectively*: The interviewee must have the full attention of the interviewer. Marginal or poor listening not only prevents the obtaining of full information but is insulting to the interviewee. On the part of the interviewer, they must not only listen but projectively listening is required, the interviewer who can listen much faster than the interviewee can talk must utilise that time by attempting to project into the position of the interviewee. This will be revealed by imaginative study with that of the applicant's blanks. The impression's and 'records' and 'observations' gained by the interviewer regarding interviewee must be noted down. Brief notes are taken, own of the correctness or otherwise of his answers, the way he behaves; and overall general impression he creates on the interviewer.

4. **Close of the Interview.** The next step in the interviewing process is its lose which must end in the same pleasantness with which it began without eating any awkward or embarrassing situation for the interviewee. The interview should not end normally without giving the chance to the interviewee speak something, if he likes, on any point concerning the job and the interview. It must be closed diplomatically, so that interviewee may feel satisfied that he was given a full hearing. The interview must be closed which certain signs which is as follow:
   (a) *The Interviewer Should Make Some Sign to Indicate the End of Interview*: The applicants often mentioned the problem that they are never sure when the interview is ended. The close of the interview may be indicated by some over sign such as the interviewer may lay down a pencil, push back a chair, stand up, or do any of a number of things to indicate that the conversation is coming to a close or by saying to the candidate, 'Thanks, that will be all.' Courtesy demands that the close of interview must be very pleasing, relaxed and encouraging the applicant. However, these principles don't apply in case of stress Interview. The stress interview should be used only where the job specifications justifies its use as a technique of selection.
   (b) *The Interviewee Should be Indicated the Future Course of Action*: In Employment interviews, many things may happen, selection or rejection or calling for further employment process. In case' of selection or any future employment process, free to face information has no problem. But in case of rejection of the candidates face to face information is avoided generally, and rely on some impersonal means such as regret letter. Some prefer to speak frankly to interviewees and inform them of the rejection and of the reasons for it. In short, there must be some future course of action regarding the applicants which must be intimated to them, so that they should not be left hanging in the air, wondering what, if anything happens next.

5. **Evaluation of the Interview.** After the close of the interview, as son as the interviewee Ieaves the interview room and door closes, the Interviewer must immediately undertake the task of evaluating the candidate while the details are fresh in mind. Records and notes have already been prepared during the process of Interview, on the basis of that information and analysing the, information, he must be evaluated. If the Interview is Structured or Guided, evaluation sheets are provided entries and supporting information should be entered: At this stage, 'some decision should be taken by the candidate. Some Interviewers give the grades like +A, A, +B. B. +C or C and-so on. These grades are converted into marks as per their pre-planned programme.

After the Interview of all the candidates is over, analyzing and interpreting the candidates takes place. The strengths and weaknesses of the interviewees are balanced, decisions may be taken on the basis of his 'performance in job factors - 'or job requirements and his arrearance and poise. Weightage is also given to test experience, habits, behaviour, attitudes and actual facts that come in the mind of the Interviewers. The marks obtained in the interview must be included with the marks allocated for qualifications division obtained past experience and thus the positioning of the candidates may be-made. The list of the selected candidates must be prepared in order of merit or alphabetically as may be decided by the interview committee.

The process of the interview is a very complex and perhaps the single technique of selection process. The technique of the interview as already, explained, if strictly followed will bear fruits but it is not always there. Each company has its own interview procedure and in the same way because of individual differences, the interviews may apply their own perceptions and technique. Establishing the rapports with the applicants is of vital importance, the interviewers find sometimes, it difficult to maintain and thus losing the factor of basic liking and respect for people. Many deviations may take place during the process of Interview. Sometimes Interviewers may be biased or self-destructive and may favour a wrong candidate, Generally, there are six areas in which interview is sought, as already explained, they are, manners and appearance. Family background, education, work-history, personality and 'Social adjustment' and health. Sometimes, the interviewers may not take the Interview accordingly.

Thus there may be number of reasons of the failure of the Interview:

1. **The Halo Effect.** Halo Effect is an ugly and negative error which makes 'the Interview biased. Halo effect means first impression is the last Impression, "leans, when the interviewer selects or rejects the interviewee on the basis of one trait, leaving all other traits aside. Halo effect works according to his liking or disliking of certain traits and characteristics. On the basis of single trait, the interviewer evaluates the whole personality which is wrong. The characteristics like, physical appearance, his brilliant educational record, his fluency, or lack of communication, experience of living abroad, experience as a sportsman, his manners, his score in the psychological tests, any one of these qualities may crate a 'Halo Error' or 'Halo Effect'. The Interviewers should assess the whole of the candidates personality and should not be led away by anyone, trait or achievement. He should remember that good candidates' come in all snapes, sizes, ages education, religion, caste, rationality etc.
2. **Leniency Vs Strictness.** The concept of human behaviour is dependant of individual difference which has a wider applicability. Some individuals may be strict and others may be lenient in ratings or evaluating others. Specially, when an interviewee is rated-by two different rates, their ratings may be different. One may show considerable leniency by giving him high score, the other may consistently rate him by giving low scores. Leniency is usually associated with the lack of self-confidence lack of interest in rating and lack of expert knowledge, Strictness may be associated, on the other hand, lack of contact with the people, general rigidity in Personality and over-expectations from the interviewees.

3. **Projection.** The concept of self-image is' very important for interviewers. First of all, he should know his' self-concept. Sometimes, he evaluates himself ideally which is called ideal concept of Personality. Error of projection arises when an interviewer expects his own qualities, skills, values in otherwise the objective of the interview cannot be achieved. The interviewer should not take quick-judgement before all the relevant facts have been gathered and evaluated, otherwise it will be a pre-matured evaluation which is dangerous, if an applicant is unable to answer the question or fails to furnish information properly, the interviewer should smoothly move to another topic. Hostility or nervousness may be minimised with the interviewer pleasant behaviour and reception. Employment is the function of two way communication. The feeling must be created among the interviewees that organisation needs a good man just, as much as the applicant wants a good job.
4. **Good Impression About Himself and the Company.** The interviewer should create good impression about himself by his pleasing behaviour and attitude. He must stimulate the candidate to come up with the realies of his life and other related fields. He also should create a good impression about, the organisation, he represents. Interviewees form overall impressions of the goodness or badness of an interviewer-and this in turn may affect their decision to join or not to join the company. Because, as the interviewer assesses the performance of the interviewee, in the same way, interviewee also makes an assessment of the former.

These are the certain principles or a successful interviewee, most of which depend upon the interviewers. In the words of Wendell French, "Good interviewers arc those who take the many needs of the interviewee into account of security, belonging, esteem, wholeness and self-actualisation. Orderly proceedings, cordial 'relationships, avoidance of unnecessary, ego-damaging events and an understanding of the process are ingredients in, the best interviews."

Chapter 16 RELIABILITY AND VALIDITY OF RECRUITMENT TESTS

RELIABILITY OF RECRUITMENT TESTS

Reliability is different from validity. Reliability is another feature that a test should have a high. A test in repeated trails refer to the consistency to reliability. A person responding to the same test on two different occasions is likely to get different test scores. This is the cause of attitude, physical conditions, incentives or distractions present during the second testing occasions.

A reliable measurement does not mean that the device used is accurately measuring what is designed to measure.

For example, if the aptitude test conducted on an individual on two different occasion show the same scores, it shows that the result is consistent but this consistency cannot indicate whether the test actually measured the aptitude of the person correctly. It can be effectively valid. For instances if both tests scores of the same person indicated that the person had aptitude for 'mathematical ability' using this news the person goes in for higher studies in maths. Any selective tests needs to be validated but it can be use for selection. The result of such test are used for the purpose of recruitment and selection. The test should be tried and tested on a group of old employees and a group of new recruitment.

VALIDITY OF RECRUITMENT TESTS

Validity is a main device which is used for the selection of workers and choose their success on the job. Validity is a feature that related from high to low *i.e.,* its predictive power varies from great to little.

When the degree of relationship between workers and job success is expressed as a reliable. It is based the validity. When the coefficient of correlation is 1.00 *i.e.,* validity is perfect. The selective device is the best suitable for the job and the individual who receives the highest appraisal and the second highest is the second best appraisal on the job *i.e.,* an individual's performance on the job can be predicted by the higher validity.

For selection of employees, an applicant's performance on a specific job as measured by particular index of job success. A specific job has given to the employee after a definite amount of training.

Many Types of Psychological Tests

1. *Tests of Achievement*: These tests are used for educational testing of pre primary to post graduation and professional levels as designed for measuring knowledge , understanding in specific subjects.
2. *Special Aptitude Test*: These are special tests which was designed to fulfil the needs of vocational selection designed for a variety of aptitudes, they measure speed and dexterity in motor movement and help to discover individuals interest in law, music, medicine, painting, sports and other fields.
3. *Intelligence Test*: These were used for measuring the general intelligence simon and binet.
4. *Personality Test*: These tests means those characteristics of personality which are non intellectual in nature, behavior like emotional adjustment, aggressiveness, honesty, perseverance etc. They also measure motivation, attitudes and interests etc., of individuals.

Different types of tests, intelligence tests have been used most frequently for every kind of job, intelligence tests are primarily intended to give a general idea. They can also indicate the employee's ability to contain on a job and his for promotion. Recruitment and selection aided by psychological testing can help to select the employees best qualified for a job.

Moreover sometime there is chance of disqualification of some eligible applicants merely because of failing in the test there is certain chance that there applicants might have been very successful they have selected.

Selection by Interview

Interview is one of the methods for the purpose of industrial selection. An interview should succeed in:

1. Providing information about the organization, the specific job in question and the personal policies of the company.
2. Providing an employee personality by describing the information. The prospective employee regarding his background work, history, education, interests and training etc.
3. A satisfactory applicant creating in him a desire to join the Organization for his motive.

There are many personality features that are known by the course of an interview. The interview method has a few limits, for instance personality traits such as honesty. Some time two or special feature may overpower the traits and give the bad impression to interviewee.

If the interview is obtained by untrained interview, an objective attitude are very important for the right selection choose of an employee is give to an interviewer helpful aid it guicles the interviewer during questioning in applicant. For applicant evaluation have many aspect as work experience, training and finally personal history helps the choose employee.

APPLICATION BLANK

Application blank is another technique of employee's selection which is used in combine with the interview method. Application blanks range in size form a single page and many pages for the information of applicant like name, address, age, marital status educational experience etc. There are many features that is essential for one job another.

Application blanks shows the information to the employee and it is help him in the interview for discussion. Interview needs to be trained to read the body language of an applicant.

An application blank has a very high margin of error. It is very useful as a tool for reaching an application. It is an interview's duty to create a favourable impression of the company.

Research and training is necessary to increase the impression of employee.

Unit IV

Chapter 17 TRAINING AND DEVELOPMENT

The main objective of Personnel Deptt. is to put the right man at the right place. This purpose can only be achieved and fulfilled when the human resources are fully developed and trained. Training and development is the most important activity of Personnel Deptt. Growth, expansion, and modernization cannot take place without trained manpower. No one is a perfect fit at the time of hiring and some training and education must take place. No organization has a choice of whether to develop employees or not, the only choice is that of the method. If no organized programme exists, the development will be largely self-development while learning on the job by hit and trial method which an industrial and modern organization cannot afford. Training and development cannot be segregated from each other. Development is the end and training is the means. Development, thus, would include both training to increase skill in performing a specific job and education to increase general knowledge and understanding of our total environment. Planned training and development programme will return values to the organization in terms of increased productivity, heightened morale, reduced costs, greater organizational stability and flexibility to adapt to changing, external requirements. So, training must be systematic and organized on the basis of organizational and individual needs. As from the definition it is very clear. It is an organized procedure for increasing the knowledge and skill of people for a definite purpose. Training is also an important and required factor for maintaining and improving inter-personal and inter-group collaboration.

Human resources, for any organization are the life-blood which is very much required for the success, survival and existence of the organization. But it needs to have well-trained and experienced people to perform the activities that have to be done. Moreover, in adequate job performance or decline in productivity or changes out of job redesigning or a technological break-through require some type of training and development efforts. As the jobs become more complex, the importance of training to the employees also increases. In a rapidly changing situation, "employee training and development is not only an activity that is desirable but also an activity that an organization must commit resources to if it to maintain a viable and knowledge work-force."

Training may be defined, "Training is an organized procedure for increasing the knowledge and skill of people for a definite purpose." The purpose of training is to achieve a change in the behaviour of those being trained. In the industrial situations, it means that trainees will acquire new skills, technical-knowledge, problem solving attitude and general behaviour of the well-being. Training, development and education are three terms frequently used. For a lay man, all there three seem to be the same but when we analyse and interpret the concepts, these appears some differences between them. Training is a process of learning a sequence of programmed behaviour. It is the application of knowledge which gives people an awareness of the rules and procedures to guide their behaviour. It tries to attempt to increase and improve the performance on the current job.

Development is a somewhat related concept. It not only improves the performance of current job but also bring about growth of personality, help individuals in the progress towards maturity and actualization of their potential capacities. Training a person for a bigger and higher job is development. Training is for imparting technical and mechanical knowledge whereas the process of development takes place in top or middle level management which imparts not only skill and knowledge but also certain personality and mental attitudes. There are four basic differences Training and Development:

(*i*) Training is for non-managerial personnel while development is for managerial personnel.

(*ii*) Training is designed to impart technical and mechanical knowledge while Development is for theoretical and conceptual ideas.

(*iii*) Training is related with specific job while as Development relates with acquiring of general knowledge.

(*iv*) Training is short-period concept while Development is related with long period.

Education is the analyzing understanding and interpretation of knowledge. It does not provide definite answers but rather it develops a logical and rational mind that can determine the relationship among pertinent variables and thereby understand phenomena. Education must impart qualities of mind and character and understanding of basic principles and develop the capacities of analysis and objectivity. It can only be provided by educational institutes. Organisations take help of these institutes in order to support and supplement its internal training and development efforts. So, education supports the both training as well as development.

NEED FOR BASIC PURPOSES OF TRAINING

Training is most helpful in imparting the technical and mechanical knowledge to the personnel involved in operative jobs. It enables the employees to get acquainted with jobs and increase their aptitudes skills and knowledge, adaptability and thus increases the reliability and validity of training programme. Training is a continuous process, it will never be finished as long as the organization remains in business. The need for the training of employees would be clear from the observations made by different authorities, they are:

1. **To Increase Productivity And Profitability.** It has been very rightly said by some management expert. "Training increases the skill, knowledge and operative competence of the employees with help to increase the level of increased operative performance and profitability of the company." It is more fruitful on new employees who are not yet fully aware of the most efficient and effective ways of performance.
2. **To Go for Better Quality.** Training gives the knowledge and technical skills to the workers. Well informed or well instructed workers commit minimum mistakes and minimum wastage of raw materials. Quality makes the reputation and creditability of the product and the product becomes of merchantable quality. Increased quality will definitely create healthy environment of the company. Quality circles may be created to achieve this end.

3. **To Help in Replacement Planning and Promotion-within.** The process of manpower planning can be only fruitful when its employees are being imparted with upto date knowledge with the help of continuous training. There are two sources of filling up manpower requirements, internal and external. When the need arises, organizational vacancies can more easily be staffed from internal sources, especially in case of sudden personnel alternations. This is only possible when a company initiates and maintains an adequate training programme both for workers and managers.
4. **To Improve the Culture of the Organisation.** The reactions of training are always positive and hence it requires a systematic and well-planned training programme. As already stated, training helps to increase productivity and consequent increase in production, increase in quality and increased profitability, as a result the financial rewards and incentives may be increased. The training programme reduces the degree of supervision, becoming or making the workers more independent. Thus the degree of dependence may decrease making the workers more responsible and establishing the principle of Industrial democracy.
5. **To Improve the Organisational Environment.** The environment of the organization attracts the outsiders or prospective employees to join the organization. To a greater extent, training helps to generate an improved organizational environment. Proper training helps in preventing industrial accidents. Proper and safer living and working environment leads to more stable mental attitudes on the part of employees. The mental state of supervisors can also be improved with the help of well-planned training programme. It reduces the rate of absenteeism and labour turnover.
6. **To Prevent Obsolescence.** Better and Sound training and development programmes increases the motivational approach, initiative, creativity and learning and this helps in preventing manpower obsolescence. With the increase of age, temperament, the learning may be down and productivity may also decrease. A stage in learning process comes which is called 'Plateou' which means stagnation and is very dangerous for the growth and development of the company. Training is the only motivator to fight against age factor, inability of a person to adapt himself to technological changes and temperament.
7. **To Initiate Personal Growth And Development.** It is a well established fact that knowledge is a power, money, pest and respect. One learns from own experience as well as training programmes organized in a company. Knowledge is an indivisible asset. "Employees on a personal basis gain individually from their exposure to educational experiences." These programmed provide participants with a wider awareness, an enlarged skill and enlightened philosophy which tend to enhance personal growth and development.

It must be remembered that the need of training arises for more than one reason:

IMPORTANCE OF TRAINING PROGRAMMES

Training is potentially one of the most useful tools available to management. A manager can make use of training to help him to get things done through other in a formal organization most effectively and most effectively. Any food manager should have goals in his mind for his operation in the organization. If these goals are to be translated into action, those working under him in the organization must share the responsibility for their fulfillment. Training helps the management in its obligation to communicate its purpose and policies to all levels of personnel so that they may cooperate in the attainment of organizational objectives. The most important task of management is to improve the competency of the personnel. Training focus on interaction problem-solving and information sharing and as a means of expeditiously pooling knowledge. Training is a corner-store of sound management, for it makes employees more productive and effective. The importance of training programme may be expressed in the following heads:

1. **Training is a Service to Management.** It is a service to management in the sense that under the umbrella of training, several useful functions of management can be performed. It reduces the need for constant and close supervision, thus it helps in management by exception. The manager would like to share authority and responsibility to his sub-ordinates, who will be reluctant to accept until and unless they have been given proper training.
2. **Manhour Economy of the Organization.** The training may be of two types. On the job and off the job, both are equally important. If the employees are systematically well-trained theoretically and practically, they will take minimum time in understanding the things. It helps to reduce the learning time to reach at the acceptable level of performance. Instead of wasting the time in learning by hit and trial method or observing others, it can be imparted through well planned training programme with a short span of time. Thus, it saves manhours of the organization by helping it to go at higher heights.
3. **Better Performance with Increase in Quantity and Quality.** As already stated in the need of training programme, "the objective of training programme to increase quantity and quality, better performance, less supervision, intitiating and motivating the employees." When the objectives of some programme are achieved, they become the uses and advantages of that programme. In the same way, by training the employees, quantity and quality may be decreased. But the training programmes must be designed according to job-requirements.
4. **Establishment of Industrial Democracy.** The concept of Industrial Democracy is to vital importance in an business or industrial based economy. It means the degree of supervision may lesson and degree of self-reliant and independence may be increased. Training is the tool used to achieve this objective. Training does not eliminate the need for supervision. A well-trained employee is self-reliant in his work because he knows how to do and when to do, what to do etc.
5. **Proper utilization of 5 M's.** "Management is the proper utilization of Men, Machines, Money, Materials and Methods." This definition applies not only on operative level employees but also on managerial level. Trained employees as well as managers can achieve this target by doing everything with proper planning and by using other managerial and operative traits as and when are required. When employees are given proper instructions, they will commit minimum mistakes and less wastage of raw-materials. Rate of accidents will be minimum, the rate of absenteeism and Labour turnover will be minimum. All these things

will lead to lesser cost of production. Training, this helps to make the economical use of the resources of the organization.

6. **Standardisation.** With the help of proper and pre-planned training programme, the best available methods of performing the work can be made available to all the employees. Standardisation, will thus paves way for high level performance and minimizing the scope of management by exception. The employees will understand the nature of their jobs, inter-dependence of one job on another. A sense, of coordination and cooperation is developed.
7. **Building an Efficient and Cooperative Work-Force.** Proper and adequate training, helps to achieve the performance standards, quality and quantity, increased productivity and ultimately increased profitability. Consequently, the basic pay and other benefits will be increased which will bring forth the welfare of the employees. It will motivate the employees, as a result, the morale-building of the employees will take place. There will be better cooperation, change in the attitudes, greater loyality and sincerity, which will build an efficient and cooperative work-force in an organization with the help of training.
8. **Promotion Policy And Career Development.** The concept of manpower Planning gives the idea of internal sources and external source of hiring man power. There is a hyeirchy of jobs and each job is followed by career routes or career paths, accordingly the employees are trained and promoted to higher grade. This is only possible in case of high performance employees who can be given advanced training programmes. The positions or jobs requiring high-technical competency or conceptual knowledge or any skilful qualification, may be selected from outside with the help of selection techniques.
9. **Organizational Stability and Flexibility.** Training increases the stability and flexibility of the organization which are most required factors. The creation of trained employees will increase the stability in the sense that it will be able to sustain its effectiveness despite the loss of key-personnel. Training is also helpful to the employees to gain multiple skills to enable their transfer to jobs where demand is highest. It will bring forth the flexibility in the sense that organization will be in a position to adjust a short-run variation.

Training is a widely accepted problem-solving device. Indeed, out national superiority in manpower productivity can be attributed in no small measure to the success of our educational and industrial training programmes. It is almost traditional in America, to believe that if something is good, more of thing is even better. Hence, we take more vitamin pills of solve personal health problems and more training to solve our manpower problems. The responsibility of training is vested into two levels. First the training Deptt. should assume the primary responsibility for the instructions of trainers in methods of teaching—primary responsibility for the instructions of trainers in methods of teaching. Secondly, line supervisors and employees should carry the bulk of teaching load.

Training is a very useful device to increase the skill, knowledge and aptitude among the workers. Training is related with a repeated cycles and it never comes to an end. It is a continuous process which is aimed at increasing technical, human and concepted competence of new as well old employees to enable them to perform their job well. Training involved learning and imparts knowledge in the different areas of the job. But, sometimes management thinks to start training programme because it is a popular thing to do and because other organizations are doing it. Such a tendency is not objective and fruitful because it is not good in the long run. Training programme must be set up in the light of (MBO) Managing By Objectives. Training, without having a clear cut objective in mind is useless and sheer wastage of time and money. Training programmes are costly affair, and a time consuming process. Therefore, they need to be drafted very carefully. Generally, in organizations, the following steps are taken in devising a training programme.

1. **Identifying the Training Needs.** Training programme is helpful in finding out the solutions of specific problems. Training programme must be designed after thorough analysis of operational problem in an organization, manpower resources available and their viability and the study of the organization, it goals and objectives. This analysis will given an idea of the "Trouble spots," where the training is required. Training may be helpful to should, however be noted that a training is not a cure-all. For example, if the productivity of certain employees is low because of certain faulty job factors, first these factors should be rectified. While identifying the training needs three types of analysis is to be conducted:

First, Organizational analysis which is primarily concerned with the organizational goals and objectives. The goals establishes the framework in analysis which deals with job requirements. The nature of duties and responsibilities *i.e.*, job descriptions and specific human behaviour required *i.e.*, the job specifications. So, training is designed on the basis of job description and job specifications, aggregating the process of job analysis. Third is the main analysis which reviews knowledge, attitudes and skills of the incumbent in each position and also determines what knowledge, skill and attitudes are required to contribute satisfactorily to attain the organizational objectives. This task may be summarized, as given by Willam Besliner into five categories:

(*i*) List of duties and responsibilities or task of the job under consideration using the job description as a guide.

(*ii*) List of Standards of work performance on the job.

(*iii*) Compare Actual performance against the standards.

(*iv*) Determine what parts of the job are giving the employee trouble.

(*v*) Determine what kind of training is needed to overcast the specific difficulty or difficulties.

These five steps may be classified into two categories (*i*) Task Description Analysis which is nothing but job analysis comprising of job description and job specifications. (*ii*) Determining the training needs which covers the last three points. Comparing the actual performance with that of requirements and finding out where the employee is lagging behind, what is the season, what type of training is required to rectify it. The assessment of training needs may be identified from the following steps:

(*a*) *Identifying Specific Problems*: There are number of problems which an organization has. These problems may be relating with quantity and quality, subordination, behavioural, raw-materials waste, Accidents, fatigue, Labour, Turnover, Absenteeism, violation of code of conduct etc. To evaluate the need, the task and the workers should be closely observed and the difficulties found out.

(*b*) *Forecasting*: Forecasting and anticipating future requirements of manpower in relation to business expansion, introduction of new product, new services and new designs. Because of the changed technology, organizational change is required, training may be designed according to the need.

(*c*) *Recommendations*: Sometimes, management may request to training Deptt. to conduct specific training programmes for certain employees. Although this method is very simple and based on the correct evaluation of the employees yet, it suffers with certain defects. However, it is also a source of fixing training needs.

(*d*) *Interview and Personnel's Observations*: Training needs are determined by interviewing the personnel directly to know their interests aptitudes, morale, skill and knowledge. Observation of employees by their immediate superiors, is also a factor of determining the training needs.

(*e*) *Performance Evaluation*: Performance appraisal is the most important tool of determining the training needs. Standards are fixed for each job, and his actual performance is measured and compared with standards. Deviations or merits may be found. His past experience and performance appraisal record is also helpful in determining the training needs. Performance Appraisal provide clues for specific inter-personal skills that may need development.

(*f*) *Questionnaires*: Questionnaire is the other tool for determining the training needs. In this certain questions are designed on the basis of job analysis morale motivation, communication, skills and attitudes to get the opinion of the employees. This will reveal much information about where an employee's skills and knowledge are deficient.

(*g*) *Checklist*: The use of checklists supports the information obtained from interviewing and observations. Through it, more reliable information can be obtained and the data got are quantifiable. This facilities evaluating the training programme's effectiveness.

(*h*) *Morale Survey*: Personnel audit it the most important tool of forecasting future promotions, skill requirements and merit rating to initial informal discussions and on examinations of records and statistics of personnel to reveal the potentials problems to be tackled through training programme.

2. **Test of Interpersonal Skills.** Role playing, case study, group task and discussion, critical incident. Method etc., may reveal the training needs.

   The information, thus got, may be tailored according to the needs and programmes of improvements can be developed. This will give the trainees are opportunity to learn and develop his skills and abilities.

3. **Organising Training Programmes.** This step involves four stages. Preparation of Trainees, Preparation of Trainer, fixing the period of each training and methods of training are also important steps of organizing the training programme.

(*a*) *Preparation of Trainees*: Under this step, it is to be decided who is to be trained, the new corner or the older employees or the supervisory staff or all of them selected from different departments. Selection of trainees should be according to the needs as specified in relation to job descriptions and job specifications. Careful screening of candidates for training raises the effectiveness of the training work, After careful Screening, lists should be prepared of trainees according to the needs of training. Incase of supervisory training. It is better to include all supervisors and other employees considered suitable for promotion to such posts. Even outstanding employees persons benefits from well managed training programmes and their presence helps the less competent persons.

(*b*) *Preparations of Trainers*: The trainer has to be prepared for the job for he is the key-figure in the entire programme. Qualified Instructors may be obtained from inside or outside the organization. He must be able to divide the job into logical parts and teaching or instructing the trainees accordingly. He must be able to appreciate the value of training work in relation to the enterprise and an understanding of what the employees are in order to impart the skill and knowledge for which the programme is designed. He must have the skill and knowledge for which the programme is designed. He must have the skill to communicate and must be patient and tolerant. As training is based on the training requirements and organizational goals. Trainers must have clear cut idea of training courses which seem to them to be interesting or an agenda its developed in terms of some preconceived notion of what constitutes a body of useful information. The trainer needs professional expertise in order to fulfill his responsibility. His incompetency with the training needs, knowledge, methods of instructing etc., will make the training programme a fun and wastage. In short, we can say that the trainer must be well qualified, professional, expertise, and well acquantited with training aids, methods and potentials. To make training more effective selection of the expert trainer is most important.

(*c*) *Contents of Training Programme*: This study materials or the courses of study during training period is fixed whether the training is on the job or off the job. The contents of the study is developed by the experts, psychologists, experts in human behaviour, material Management, Production, Finance, Personnel, according to needs of training programmes. The most important consideration while designing the contents, must he kept in mind, the need of training programme. Training in general areas is given in such subjects as report and commercial latter writing, reading using gauges, the operation of machines, fire-fighting and safety-devices, shop practices and secretarial practices, industrial psychology, motivational traits, time and motion study, public speaking and public relations, selling and communicating with people.

(*d*) *Training Period*: There is no hard and fast rule regarding the period of training. It depends on the skills and knowledge to be required, the capacity of the learner and the methods and media of training used. To make training more interesting and goal-oriented; one session should not be longer than two hours and a break should be given in between the two sessions. Now the question arises, the training should be given during the working hours which may affect production and the organization will have to compensate for this time. Other alternative is to organize training programme after working hours. If convenient, employees may be trained for a week or fortnight for an hour or two after the working hours. The training period for a weeks to six months or more depending upon the job requirements. The physical location of the programme should be in a pleasant surroundings away from the noise and tension of the work place.

(*e*) *Preparation of Supporting Materials*: During the training programme, the trainer may use the methods and media according to the needs of training and job requirements and sometimes he may use certain audio-visuals and aids as he thinks fit. He may use the method of delivering a lecture, role playing, case study or problem-solving, pamplets, charts, booklets, brouchers, handbooks, manuals, graphs, pictures, slides, projectors, tape-records, posters, display, reading rooms and Liabries, under-study, etc. Accordingly these materials may be made ready before conducting a training programme.

4. **Conduct of Training Programme.** White conducting the programme the trainer must try at his best level to make them understood or impart the knowledge and skills for which the training programme has been designed. First step in conducting the programme, the trainee should be made at ease so that he does not feel nervous because of the fact he is on a new job. The next step is to state the importance and ingredients of the job and its relationship to work flow. Third, he must tell the trainees why they are being taught, the objective of training, fourthly, the trainer must motivate and encourage questions finding out what the learner already knows about the job and thus, making training programme more interesting. Fifthly, to put the learner as close to his normal working position as possible and thus creation of practical environment. Lastly, the trainer must try at his level best to familiarize the learner with machines, tools, materials, equipments and trade terms used. Training is a two way communication, one side, the trainer is communicating the required skill and knowledge to the trainees, the trainees must listen carefully, attentively and projectively on the other hand. Training will bear fruits if both are actively involved in the process of learning.

5. **Presentation of Operations and Knowledge.** This is most important step in training programme. The responsibility of trainer is to make trainees satisfied and he must not leave any efforts untouch to make the trainees understand and learned. The trainer should clearly show, tell illustrate and question in order to put over the new knowledge and operations. The learned should be taught in a logical order of the job requirements and also the relative importance of each step to the job. Instructions must be given clearly, completely and patiently, emphasis should be laid down on the key-points and explained in detail one by one. For this purpose, the trainer may use slides, projectors, audio-visuals, and for feedback, ask the trainee to repeat the operations. Encouraging questions is most important to know, what the learner knows about the job.

6. **Evaluation of Training Programme.** As it is very clear from the above-cited points, trainee is asked to go through the job several times slowly, explaining him each step. Mistakes are corrected is some complication is there, with the repeated actions of the learners it is removed. Then, the trainee is asked to do the job gradually, building up skill

and speed. The trainee is thus tested and the evaluation of training programme is done to judge its effectiveness. This is usually done by:

(*a*) Giving a written or oral test to the trainee and to evaluate his performance by his score obtained in the test.

(*b*) Performance test-observing the trainees on the job.

(*c*) Evaluation sheets—Finding out individual's or group reaction to the training programme.

(*d*) Structured interviews and questionnaires.

(*e*) Comparing the results of the trainees before training and after training to find out the relevance of training programme.

Thus, one or a combination of these devices may be used to ascertain the validity of training programme. If these are certain weaknesses or errors they may be corrected and instruction must be repeated if necessary, till the trainee has learnt whatever has been imparted to him.

7. **Follow-up.** This is step used after the training is over and the employee is put to his own, it is also called post training performance evaluation. After an employee or trainee is put to his own, frequent checking is required to be sure that he has followed instructions. Until and unless, he is qualified to work with normal supervision, extra and close supervision is to be tapped with. This step is called re-enforcement which is an essential and ingredient part of learning.

The process of training programme is not universal. The different steps taken by the training Deptt. to establish a training programme differ from one organization to other. It is because the organization set up, policies, procedures, manufacturing process, nature and type of product, nature and classification of jobs, job-requirements, training needs etc. vary from one organization to other. Armed with the knowledge of each trainee's specific training needs, programmes of improvements can be developed that are tailored to these needs. This training programme then follows a general sequence aimed at supplying the trainee with the opportunity to develop his skills and abilities. The process of training programme can be shown with the help of diagram:

Training and development would include both training to increase skill in performing a specific job and education to increase general knowledge and understanding of our total environment. Planned development programmes will return values to organisation in terms of increased productivity, high morale, reduced cost and greater organizational stability and flexibility to adapt to changing external requirements. Such programmes will-also -help to meet-the needs of the individuals in their search for work assignment that can add-up to life, long careers.

There are many methods or techniques for imparting training among trainees. It is difficult, if not impossible, to say which of the methods or combination of methods is more useful than the other. In fact; methods are rnultifaced and inter-related in scope and dimension and each method is suitable; for a particular situation. The best technique or method for one situation may not be best for group or, all situations. Care must be taken while adapting the technique or method to the learner or to the job. Training methods basically are divided into two head-(*i*) on the Job-training (*ii*) off the Job-training. There is one vestibule training which attempts to duplicate on the job situations in a company and classroom. It is a classroom training which is often imparted with the help of the equipment and machines which ate' identical with those in use in the place of work. So, this type of training, sometimes included in on the job while other classify it as the off-the job, training technique. To be more se, it is a technique of on the job training.

ON THE JOB TRAINING

It is a well established, fact that every one from the bottom to top position in, an organization gets some on the job training (O.J.T.). "On the Job Training is the most. widely used and accepted; and the most necessary method of training, employees in the skills essential jar acceptable for job performance." Under this, method the worker is trained on the job and his work-place. This enables him to get, training under the same working conditions and with the same process, materials, equipment that he will be using ultimately. Trainees earn as they learn under the watchful eyes of a master, mechanic or craftsman; receives immediate feedback and associate with the same people they with the same people they will with after training.

It is mostly given for unskilled and semi-skilled jobs-clerical and sales jobs. Employees are coached and instructed by skilled co-workers by supervisor, by the special training instructors. It is learning by doing and it is the most useful for jobs that are either difficult to simulate or can be learned quickly by watching and doing. The following are the on the job techniques:

1. **Job-Instruction Training.** This is method is popularly known as JIT and "Training through step by step learning", in which supervisors are prepared to train operatives. It requires skilled trainers extensive job analysis, training schedules and prior assessment of the trainee's job knowledge. The workers are told systematically with each step of the job which show what is to be done, how process. The preparation of trainee's instructions, presenting the instructions clear cut, try out of training programme and finally encouraging questions. It provides immediate feed back on results, quick correction of errors and provision of extra practice when required. However, it demands a skilled trainer and can interfere with production and quality.
2. **Vestibule Training.** A vestibule school is operated as a specialized endeavor by the Personnel Deptt. It usually trains for the same type of jobs as on the job-training, work of semi-skilled machine operator or tender. Then, what is the need of vestibule school? The reason lies in the law of functional growth. When the amount of training that has to be done exceeds the capacity of the line, supervisor, a portion of this training is evolved from the line and assigned to a staff through a vestibule training.

   The advantages of using vestibule schools system are the advantages of specialization. It is a classroom training which is often imparted with the help of the equipment and machines which are identical with those in use in place of work. It is often used to train clerks, bank tellers, inspectors, machine operators, tester, typist etc. It is most useful when philosophic concepts, attitudes, theories and problem solving abilities have to be learnt. This type of training is generally given in the form of lectures, conferences, case studies, role playing and discussion.

3. **Training by Supervisors.** This type of training is also on-the-job training imparted by immediate supervisors. It is useful for both the workers and supervisors. For the workers, they get the opportunities for getting acquainted with their bosses. For the supervisors, they get the opportunities to judge the skill, future prospects and possibilities of the trainees. The success of this method depends upon the expertise of the supervisor. They must also be good teachers and should have incentives and sufficient time for carrying out training programme as per needs.
4. **Learning by Seeing or Demonstrations and Examples.** In this method, the trainer displays something while describing the job-task step by step. He himself actually performs the activity and explains step by step 'why' and 'what' he is doing? Demonstrations are very effective in teaching because it is much easier to show a person how to do a job than to tell him or ask him to gather instructions from the reading material. Teaching by examples is effective in mechanical operations or interpersonal relationship for job duties and responsibilities. Demonstration is particularly useful for the acquisition of skills but their utility is limited when it is a question of training management personnel.
5. **Simulation.** Simulation is a training technique in which the actual conditions encountered on a job. The business games and vestibule training are the examples of simulation training. This type of technique is most widely used in aeronautical industry. The employee's interests and trainer's motivation should be of high degree because the actions of trainee closely duplicate real job conditions. This training involves high cost, if used with error, these will be destruction of valuable materials and resources.
6. **Apprenticeship.** Apprenticeship training is the oldest and most commonly used method especially when a proficiency in a job is the result of a relatively long training period of 2 to 3 years for persons of superior ability and from 4–5 years for others. This method is used to train crafts, trades, technical areas, draughtsman, a machinist, a printer, tool-maker, a pattern designer, a mechanic, carpenters, weavers, jewelers, die-sinkers, engravers and electricians. A major time is spent on productive work which provides him efficient training in trade skills. This training is very useful as a skilled work-force is maintained & immediate returns can be expected from training. The training cost is lower and loyalty and sincerity is increased.
7. **Training by Experienced Workmen.** This type of training is very simple as training is imparted by experienced senior fellow-workers. It is particular adaptable where workers advance through successive jobs to perform a series of operations and they are in need of some helper or helpers. The senior experienced fellow workers gives them instructions how to do, what to do, etc.

There is not best system of on the job training. In any firm, it is not unusual to find all on the job techniques simultaneously. As already stated, on the job system is by far the most commonly used. With the advent of automation and the consequent upgrading of skill-level, it may be that special courses and class room instructions will receive a much greater degree of emphasis in the future but the value of on the job training will never come to an end.

OFF THE JOB TRAINING

Off the job training means the training which is imparted away from the work place. This training's principle is based on the fact that training is a continuous but not everyday activity. The training may be imparted at the location, may be the company class room or places which are owned by the company, school, colleges, universities or associations which have no connection with the company's real work place. Off the job training means classroom training, which are classified as under:

1. **Lectures.** Lectures are the most commonly used method and most simple ways of imparting knowledge to the trainees. Lectures are to vital importance when specialized knowledge especially when facts, principles theories, concepts attitudes and problem solving abilities are to be taught. Lectures are being delivered by specialized trainers or formal superior on the specific topics. The Lecture method is very useful for the organization, in the sense that it decreases or reduces the cost of training and development. It is a especially when a very complicated topic, technical or special of complex knowledge is to be imparted. The method can be used when very large groups are to be trained within a short time. Lectures are usually enlivened with discussions, case studies, film-shows, role playing and demonstration. Audio-visual play more important role and enhance their value. The lecture method is not dead as some would believe. Its success depends on the able and specialized lectures, interests of participants and purpose of training which may turn out to be more interesting and effective than any other method.
2. **Conferences.** In this training system the individuals confer to discuss the issues of common interest to each other. It is most group centred method of development. It is a formal and participative meeting, conducted according to organized plan, in which leader seeks to develop knowledge and understanding by obtaining considerable amount of oral participation of the trainees. It lays emphasis on active participation of the members involved. Through this method, learning is facilitated by building up the ideas contributed by confesses.

   Conference is of three types (*i*) Directed Discussions in which trainer guides the discussion in such a way that the facts, principles, or concepts are explained. (*ii*) Second is training conference, the instructor gets the group to pool its knowledge and past experience and brings different opinions for a particular problems. (*iii*) It is as seminar in which the trainer or leader defines the problem encourages and ensures full participation of the conferees.
3. **Group Discussion.** Group Discussion is based on a paper prepared by one or more trainees on a particular subject in consultation the person in charge of the Group Discussion. The subject matter may be theoretical studies or practical problems and their solution on the basis of knowledge. The trainees read statement given by an expert who is invited to participate in the discussion. The person in charge supplies required materials in advance to be analysed in the form of required readings to the trainees or participants. The seminar thus compares the reactions of the participants, encourages, encourages discussion and defines the general trend and guides the participants.

4. **Case Studies.** This method is also called learning by doing. It was first developed by Christopher Langdell and Harvard Law School in 1880 to help the students to learn for themselves. It is a practical method based on independent thinking, personal efforts and by discovering human affairs, principles and ideas which have lasting validity and general applicability. The purpose of the case study is to develop skills and analytical ability using their own knowledge. It also helps to develop decision making skills.

   In the case study method, certain cases with data and other situational information are given to the participants. There is certain problem in the case which is to be solved by the participants giving their decision and the decision which is most appropriate is arrived at 'consensus'. In this method, the person in charge, makes out a case written or oral and provides necessary explanations, initiates discussions and encourages the candidates come out with an appropriate solution. This type of training is imparted to supervisors and valuable especially as a technique of developing the art of decision marking.

5. **Role Playing.** This method is most useful in developing the skills and poising proper learning. It was developed by Moreno, a Venetian Psychiatrist. He gave the different names to this term as role playing, role-reversal, socio-drama and psycho-drama. The emphasis of this method is laid down on learning human relation skills through practice and insight into one's own behaviour and its effect on others. It has been defined as, "a method of human interaction which involves realistic behaviour in the imaginary situations." It immediately demonstrates the gap between thinking and doing. The idea of role-playing involves actions, doing and practice and again practice by reinforcement. Two or more trainees are assigned a given role to stage a play before the rest of the class. It doesn't require any memorization but the role players are simply informed the situation and the respective role has to play. It involves employee-employer relationship, hiring, firing, discussing a grievance procedure, conducting a post-appraisal interview or disciplinary proceedings or a salesmen etc are the practical problems in which the participants have to learn by role-playing.

6. **T-Group Training.** It is called popularly as T-Group where T. Stands for technical. This method is usually comprised of association, audio-visual aids, and planned reading programmes. Members of this type of training programmes are interested to receive new techniques and ideas pertaining to their own vocations. This can only be possible when there is regular supply professional journals and informal social contacts or gathering and members are kept informed of the latest development in their particular field. To make this type of training a success, audio-video aids, records, tapes and films are generally used in conjunction with other conventional teaching methods. Two things are most required things *i.e.,* planned and supervised reading and technical publications and the latest journals kept in the library for the use of trainees.

   The training programmes are designed for the attainment of specific objectives *i.e.,* skills, knowledge, aptitude, attitude development, personality development, development of decision skills, and improving the efficiency and overall personality development. The failure of success of any training programme depend upon its effectiveness and attainment of training objectives. There is no one generally best method of developing effective training evaluation. Training officers may use of method to evaluate the effectiveness of training programme. The one most frequently found and least effective is measurement of the group after the training has been completed. But a sounder approach it that of measurement both before and after the training. Comparisons can be made to determine if organizational behaviour has improved within the group. A still better method is measuring the group both before and after training experience. To get a valid measure of training effectiveness, the Personnel Manager should accurately assess trainee's job performance two to six months after completion of training.

Questionnaires or structured interview with immediate supervisor of the trainees are acceptable methods for obtaining feedback on training. The supervisor is asked to rate the former trainee on job proficiency directly related to the training objectives. Another method is involved in time series analysis. A series of measurements are taken before the programme begins and continues during and after the programme is completed. The results obtained are plotted on a graph to determine whether changes have occurred and remain as a result of the training effort.

Some writers have suggested that four basic categories of the outcomes can be measured.

(*i*) *Reaction.* Evaluate the trainee's reaction to the programme. Did he like the programme? Did he think it worthwhile?

(*ii*) *Learning.* Did the trainee learn the principles skills and fact that the supervisor or the trainer wanted them to learn.

(*iii*) *Behaviour.* Whether the results of training have finally been achieved? Did he learn how to work on machine? Did scrap page cost decrease? Was turnover reduced? Are production Quotas now being met? Etc.

In evaluating the effectiveness of any programme whatever may be the method used, the following criteria should always be kept in mind:

(*a*) Objectives of Training Programme, (*b*) Cost-benefit analysis

(*c*) Flexibility, (*d*) Results obtained

(*e*) Staff required (*f*) Improvement possible.

The training and development managers must remain alert to the changing trends. A better way of measuring the effectiveness of training is to use various indices of performance. The output and quality of work of employees can be used for evaluation purpose. Before and after training figures on accidents may show an improvements as a result of training but it will take a longer period of time to produce sufficient evidence in this area. Analysis of Absenteeism, employee turnover rates etc. may also reflect the benefits of training.

WHY TRAINING FAILS?

As discussed in the evaluation programme, there are various methods to measure the effectiveness and rationale of training programme. But it is not possible that everytime, training will achieve the objectives for which it has been designed. Sometimes it is fruitful to the extent that it achieves the objectives, it improves the behaviour, brings out improvement changes in the accident rates and absenteeism and Labour turnover. But unfortunately, training fails to achieve the objectives because of lack of interests of the trainees, incompetency of trainer, defective designing of training programme, faulty methods of imparting training, incomplete or irrelevant contents of study or training, lack of incentives by management and certain other problems like poor communication.

The following factors have been regarded as the main reasons for failure of training programme:

1. **Lack of Incentives by Management.** Any policy, programme or strategy cannot be successful until and unless it is backed up, appreciated and rewarded by top management. The benefits of training are not clear to top management. As top Mgt. is only concerned with the factual data of production, sales, income, expenditure etc. They don't know the share of increase in production due to training programmes. The top management hardly rewards supervisors for carrying out effective training.
2. **Insufficiency of Planning and Budgets for Training Programme.** Anything done without proper planning, rarely bear fruits. Planning requires systematic and organized steps of training programmes and for making it successful, planned and directed actions are most important. There things are prevalent only when proper planning is there. Because of absence of adequate planning, training fails. Top management rarely plants budgets systematically for training. Training needs and objectives cannot be accomplished without sufficiency of funds.
3. **No Adjustment of Training in Production Scheduling.** The middle management, without proper incentives from top management, does not account for training in production scheduling. With proper scheduling from above, first line supervisors have difficulty in production norms, if employees are attending training programmes. Because of both the factors, training gets little significance by top management, middle management and even by first line supervisors. Training is termed as a wastage of time and money in some traditional organizations.
4. **Training By External Institutes.** In organizations, where there are no staff training centres or having the tradition of sponsoring the candidates to some other organizations, external training may be less fruitful in the sense that it does not provide the same environment of the participants organization. The teaching methods may also be contrary to the practices of the participant's organization. It is also difficult that the trainers are unaware of the policies, procedures, living and working conditions, plant location and lay out nature of product etc. So, the purpose of training is deviated. Moreover, timely information about external programmes may be difficult to obtain.
5. **Incompetency of Trainers.** It is well-established fact that the success of the training programme largely depends on the competency and skills of trainers. While organizing training programme, the selection of trainer is most important. He must be professionally qualified, experienced, must have liking and respect for people, having teaching tactics, analytical ability and effective communication skills. But proper attention is not paid while selecting trainers. Consequently, he may posses insufficient knowledge, lack of

communications, professionalisation is qualifications and experience may give birth to various training deficiencies.

6. **Lack of Trainee's Interests.** It is not only trainer's defficiency that makes training ineffective but when the trainer is perfect and having sufficiency in his field, training may prove a failure because of lack of interest by the trainees. It is called by some othername,' Disinterested Training,' Training needs proper and careful listening to what trainer is teaching. But when the things are going bye-pass, the objective of training is defeated. Active participation by trainees, projectively thinking, raising questions and ensuring explanation to certain situations must be the tasks of trainees but it is rarely accomplished by the trainees. Consequently training fails.
7. **Defective Designing of Training Programme.** The success of training, to some extent, depends upon the designing of training programme. Physical setting of training programme, subject matter or courses or contents of study, timing of training programme, period of training, method of imparting training etc. are certain steps to be decided and taken carefully. Any deviation, will make training a failure.
8. **Minimum Use of Communication Aids.** The basic purpose of training is to communicate ideas, skills, methods and to develop motivational and perceptual skills of the trainees. The trainer is the sender and the trainees are the receiver of the knowledge. But, when trainee ask certain questions, position is reversed. Communication, in training may be of various types. Sometimes actions speak more than words, symbols, audio, video, tape records, projectors, film etc. may also be used as and when required. Training becomes uninteresting and boredom when not supported by aids to communication.
9. **Inadequate Re-Enforcement and Feedback.** As already stated training evaluation is done by various methods. One of the methods is pre-training and post- training comparison and results may be found out. Other is the behavioural, improved learning, and result-oriented approach. Without Feed back, training effectiveness will be dark and dismal. Re-enforcement is also most desirable. But, the poor feedback system makes training an unsuccessful phenomena.

There are certain other reasons which make training unsuccessful and fruitless, insufficient and ineffective. But the things cannot be allowed to go astray, certain suggestions and right directions are given to make training an effective and efficient tool of skill and talent development. Here, certain suggestions are given if implemented in the right spirit will bear fruits.

IMPROVING EFFECTIVENESS OF TRAINING OR ESSENTIALS OF TRAINING

The training programme can be made effective and successful if the following points are considered:

1. **Knowledge and Attitudes.** The first essential is that every person should be adequately knowledgeable about the man and materials of the organization concerned. However, it is

not an end in itself but it must be directed to create right attitudes towards management policies. In many training programmes, the creation of the right attitudes is very essential for the development of people. Attempt should be made to determine if the trainee has the intelligence, maturity and motivation to successfully complete the training programme. If deficiencies are noted in this respect, the training may be postponed or cancelled till the improvement are visible.

2. **Conformity with Objectives.** Training must be based on the requirement of a particular department. It must be in line with policy and aims of the department which it servers. On the basis of job-requirements, an audit of personal needs compared with operational requirements will help to determine the specific training needs of individual employees. This evaluation should form a well-defined set of performance standards towards which each trainee should be directed.
3. **Rewards and Incentives.** Rewards and incentives act as a stimulus for the trainee to satisfy his need for social approval. The management should give sufficient information about the reward whether monetary or non-monetary to the trainees. The trainee should be helpful to see the need for training by making him aware of the personal benefits he can achieve through better performance. He should be helped to discover the rewards and satisfactions that might be available to him through changes in behaviour. As the trainee acquires new knowledge and skill and applies them in job situations, he should be significantly rewarded for his efforts.
4. **Continuous Participation.** The training programme should be planned so that it is related to trainee's previous experience and background. This background should be used as a foundation for new developments and new behaviour. This is only possible when training is considered as never ending process which never ceases in an organization. The continual process of direction correction and improvement in performance, at every level of employment is one of the chief characteristics of training. Training must arouse active interest and willingness to cooperate.
5. **Support of Top Management.** The favourable attitude of the top management to the day to day process for growth of the mangerail cadres as well operative level of employees, is of paramount importance for the success of a training programme. Attempts should be made to create organizational conditions that are conductive to a good learning environment. It should be made clearly why changes are needed. Any distractions, in the way of training programme's environment should be removed. So, the support of upper level management should be obtained before applying training at lower levels.
6. **Combination of Training Methods.** The various methods of training have their relative merits and demerits. Nobody can claim one method as a best method. According to the suitability of the method and the training needs, it must be decided which is the appropriate method for a specific training programme. If necessary, a combination of training methods should be selected so that variety is permitted and as many of the senses as possible are utilized. Training methods must be ornamented with certain audio-visual aids as they make a training programme more interesting and reduce boredom.

7. **Flexibility.** The trainer must observe the responses of the trainees as a result of his stimuli. The responses of the trainees can be observed by asking questions or allowing him to do the job according to his direction. It should be well-recognised that all the trainees don't show their progress at the same level. It is because of the 'Individual Differences' the foundation stone of industrial psychology. Therefore, flexibility should be allowed in judging the rates of progress in the training programme.
8. **Trainees Involvement.** Training programme is directed to fulfil certain basic needs of individuals in an organization so that they can turn out to be better suited for the discharge of their present or future responsibilities. So, the personal involvement or active participation of the trainees should be got in the training programme. He should be provided with opportunity to practice the newly needed behaviour norms. It is only possible when involvement, proper listening, participation and re-enforcement of training principles, of the trainees is of utmost importance.
9. **Other Factors.** There are some other factors which make training most fruitful, effective, efficient and result-oriented:
   (*i*) The trainee should be provided with regular, constructive feed back concerning his progress in training and implementation of the newly acquired abilities. Abilities and skills so acquired may be permanent and retained with the help of re-enforcement.
   (*ii*) The period of training must be designed according to the job requirements. The session should be maximum of 2 Hours so as to avoid boredom. The contents of study of the subject matter of training programme must be in accordance with the training needs.
   (*iii*) The trainee should be provided with personal assistance when he encounters learning obstacles.
   (*iv*) The choice of trainers must be carefully done, taking into consideration all the factors. He must be well-qualified, professionally skilled and experience, exposure capabilities, communication skills and having respect and liking for people. Above all, he must be a democratic leader. He must also be a good listener. As the trainer is the central point of training programme. He must have practical knowledge of how a job is to be done, and plan to each the steps one by one systematically.

There are the certain points, if implemented and followed sincerely and honestly, will prove training programme a fruitful job. In short, we may summarise that sincerity and loyalty of efforts is required of trainees, trainers and Training Deptt.

AUDIO-VISUAL AIDS IN TRAINING

Audio-visual education is comparatively a new concept but it has a very valuable contribution to make in developing good training techniques. In recent years, its scope has been widened considerably and many new audio-visual aids have been pressed into service.

Now a days, there is so much more to be learnt, which cannot be taught to trainees effectively without audio-visual aids. It is an aid to learning rather than teaching. The application of audio-visual does not mean that it simplifies the work of a trainer, rather he needs more planning and preparation. These aids enable to acquire mental or physical skill in the least possible time.

Index